praise for gede parma

Ecstatic Witchcraft

"A smart, thought-provoking, and useful guide to the Wild-Wood Tradition of holy magick and a worthy contribution to the continuing growth and evolution of shamanic Wicca by a passionate and poetic member of the 'next generation.'"
—Phyllis W. Curott, priestess, attorney, author of *WitchCrafting*, and trustee of the Council for the Parliament of the World's Religions

"Gede Parma has written a book which is easy to read and follow while also looking at the subject in depth; a subject close to our personal hearts, the return of Dionysian Witchcraft."
—Janet Farrar and Gavin Bone, authors of *The Inner Mysteries*

"Intricate and engaging…a most impressive narrative of research, meditation, and intuitive insight that includes a prodigious number of spellcasting rituals for empowerment, liberation, and self-blessing."
—Michael York, author of *Pagan Theology: Paganism as a World Religion*

"This book should be required reading for anyone who wants to explore the deep mysteries which lie at the heart of all things magickal and mundane…This is the real thing. Read it and prepare to meet the gods."
—Kenaz Filan, author of *Drawing Down the Spirits*

"An accessible and deeply resourceful text for the modern Witch. Drawing from rich, anthropological history, Parma effortlessly presents magickal techniques, practices, and perspectives that are absolutely appropriate and timely to modern Witchcraft."
—Courtney Weber, priestess, writer, activist, and designer of *Tarot of the Boroughs*

"This guide is a portal that one can walk through to find something larger and more beautiful and never let it go."
—Ravyn Stanfield, Feri and Reclaiming priestess, activist, and acupuncturist

"Parma weaves together a dazzling tapestry of complex magickal philosophy, diverse shamanic ontologies, accessible practical tools, and a naked sharing of his own practices."
—Jarrah Staggard, WildWood priest

"An intimate window into one Witch's practices and philosophies. Gede Parma is a rising star in the Pagan multiverse, writing convincingly of his relationships with the gods and offering detailed instructions for others to join him on the path."
—Jane Meredith, author of *Journey to the Dark Goddess*

"This book will change the way you look at your own path and inspire you to new heights beyond the 101, and into the depth of Witchcraft as ecstatic spirituality."
—Devin Hunter, Witch, activist, and Dianic priest

By Land, Sky & Sea

"An innovative, comprehensive, essentially non-sectarian, pragmatic, and refreshing spiritual/magickal approach."
—Michael York, author of *Pagan Theology: Paganism as a World Religion*

"A fascinating buffet of ideas and practices from many cultures and traditions neatly packaged into a coherent system. Fresh and welcome material from the next generation of Pagan authors!"
—John J. Coughlin, author of *Ethics and the Craft*

"A positive, proactive approach to Paganism both traditional and modern. Lyrical, anecdotal, and practical by turns, Parma creates a syncretic Celtic knot of traditional shamanism and diverse spiritual techniques. This book will engage and refresh the seasoned practitioner of modern Witchcraft, and enlighten the novice equally. Recommended."
—Kala Trobe, author of *The Witch's Guide to Life*

"This book will be of use to anyone following the Pagan magickal path; not just Witches, but also druids and shamans. Destined to be a classic."
—Janet Farrar and Gavin Bone, authors of *The Inner Mysteries*

"Witches, magicians, and spiritual individuals of all varieties can learn from the sound, intelligent, and experiential advice found in *By Land, Sky & Sea*. The mystical techniques and honest advice given in this book will be a much-needed inspiration for those who wish to deepen and actualize their living spirituality!"
—Raven Digitalis, author of *Shadow Magick Compendium*

Spirited

"Woven through the writing is a treasure trove of visualizations, spells, and rituals that speaks to Parma's years of serious participation in the Pagan world."

—*New Age Retailer*

"Parma's book is knowledgeable, insightful, full of personal anecdotes, and laced with a passion and idealism that only comes with youth… this is a must-read for anyone who considers themselves a leader in the Pagan community or is working towards becoming a high priest or high priestess."

—TheMagicalBuffet.com

ecstatic
witchcraft

About the Author

Gede Parma is a Witch, Pagan mystic, initiated priest, and award-winning author. He is an initiate and teacher of the WildWood Tradition of Witchcraft, an Anderson Feri practitioner of the BlueRose Line, and a hereditary healer and seer with Balinese-Celtic ancestry. Gede is a proactive, dynamic teacher who is also the creator and facilitator of the two-year Shamanic Craft Apprenticeship, offered both in person and long distance. Gede teaches both within Australia and internationally and has spoken at such esteemed events as the Parliament of the World's Religions. He is the devoted priest-lover of the Blue God, Persephone, Hekate, Hermes, Aphrodite, and the Sacred Four of the WildWood. His spiritual path is highly syncretic and incorporates elements of traditional shamanisms, Balinese Hinduism, British-Celtic Witchcraft, Stregheria, Greek Paganism, Feri, Reclaiming, and WildWood Witchcraft.

Learn more about Gede at www.gedeparma.com.

GEDE PARMA

ecstatic
witchcraft

magick, philosophy & trance
in the shamanic craft

LLEWELLYN PUBLICATIONS
Woodbury, Minnesota

Ecstatic Witchcraft: Magick, Philosophy & Trance in the Shamanic Craft © 2012 by Gede Parma. All rights reserved. No part of this book may be used or reproduced in any manner whatsoever, including Internet usage, without written permission from Llewellyn Publications, except in the case of brief quotations embodied in critical articles and reviews.

FIRST EDITION
First Printing, 2012

Book design by Rebecca Zins
Cover design by Kevin R. Brown
Cover background image: iStockphoto.com/Kamil Krawczyk

Llewellyn is a registered trademark of Llewellyn Worldwide Ltd.

Library of Congress Cataloging-in-Publication Data
Parma, Gede, 1988–
  Ecstatic witchcraft : magick, philosophy & trance in the shamanic craft / Gede Parma.
—1st ed.
     p. cm.
  Includes bibliographical references (p.   ) and index.
  ISBN 978-0-7387-3299-2
  1. Shamanism. 2. Witchcraft. 3. Magic. 4. Trance. 5. Ecstasy. I. Title.
  BF1621.P37 2012
  299'.94—dc23
                                                              2012003886

Llewellyn Worldwide Ltd. does not participate in, endorse, or have any authority or responsibility concerning private business transactions between our authors and the public.
  All mail addressed to the author is forwarded, but the publisher cannot, unless specifically instructed by the author, give out an address or phone number.
  Any Internet references contained in this work are current at publication time, but the publisher cannot guarantee that a specific location will continue to be maintained. Please refer to the publisher's website for links to authors' websites and other sources.

Llewellyn Publications
A Division of Llewellyn Worldwide Ltd.
2143 Wooddale Drive
Woodbury, MN 55125-2989

www.llewellyn.com
Printed in the United States of America

contents

Acknowledgments xiii
Preface xv
Introduction 1
    This Book's Context and Orientation 4
    A Note on the Magickal Worldview
       of Infinite Possibility 7

Chapter One: The Meaning of Ecstasy 11
    Love as Divine Fire 13
    The Rite of Divine Fire 15
    Dionysos and Siwa 15
    A Note on the Conjoining
       of Siwa and Dionysos 23
    A Ritual of Reverence and Contemplation 25

Chapter Two: Cosmology and the Spiral Soul 29
    The Spiral or Triple Soul and the
       Three Worlds 31
    The Three Realms Alignment 35
    Between the Worlds…In All the Worlds 43
    The Elemental Pathways of
       Sacred Manifestation and Gnosis 44
    East of Where? 47
    A Shamanic Rite of Casting the Circle
       and Invoking the Elements 49

Chapter Three: Deity and Drawing Down 53

    The Gods Amongst Us 54
    Why Are the Gods Important? 56
    The Nature and Philosophy of the Hidden Potencies and Why to Honour Them If We Are Equal 58
    Deity versus Divine 61
    Working with the Gods as a Shamanic Witch 61
    A Note on Formalising an Allyship with Deity 65
    Drawing Down the Gods—Trance Possession 65
    The Spiritual and Shamanic Significance of Drawing Down 66
    Drawing Down as Holy Communion 70
    The Crescent-Crowned Goddess's "Three Times Three" Method of Drawing Down the Gods 72
    A Note on Gender 85
    A Concluding Point 86

Chapter Four: Spirit Allies 89

    Forging an Allyship with a Spirit Being 91
    Sharing Prayer 93
    The Beloved Dead 94
    The Waters of Reparation Ritual 97
    Animal Totems and Familiars 99
    Totem Pathworking (Animal, Plant, or Mineral) 104
    The Difference Between a Familiar and a Totem 107
    The Importance of Spirits of Place 109
    Ritual of Acknowledgement 113
    Walking with the Spirits 113

contents

Chapter Five: Moving Between the Worlds   115

    Trance as Foundation   120
    The Veil and How to Work With It   121
    The Veil's Ripple   122
    A Technique for Finding the Veil and
        Moving Through It   122
    What to Do When You Are on
        the Other Side   123
    Pathworkings   126
    The World Tree Pathworking   127
    The Power of the Directions   128
    Upon the Great Bird: The Mount of the Gods   132
    The Road to the Underworld   134
    The Well of Memory and the Sisters of Wyrd   135

Chapter Six: Ecstatic Spellcraft   141

    Spellcraft as Empowerment and Liberation   142
    Sorcery   144
    Spellcraft as Determination to Manifest
        Through the Elements   146
    Elemental Pathway of Manifestation: A Spell   148
    The Law of Three, Karma, and Spellcraft   150
    The Goddess Who Is All Guides Our Magick   153
    What Spells Reveal about the
        Nature of Things   154
    The Greater Good   157
    The Shamanic Spellcasting   160
    The Success of Spellcraft   166

Chapter Seven: Healing with the Power — 169

    The Laying-On of Hands — 170
    The Energetic Bodies and Centres — 171
    Working with the Spirits: Techniques for Deity or Ally Aid — 175
    The Restoration of Wholeness — 177
    Whole Self—Whole Earth — 179
    The Rite of Self-Blessing — 180
    A Shamanic Craft Healing — 181
    Shamanic Soul Retrieval — 188
    Self Soul-Retrieval — 194

Chapter Eight: Oracular Seership and Divination — 199

    Seeking the Vision — 200
    The Rite of Cleansing and Opening the Eye — 204
    The Mythic Reality — 207
    What Is Divination? — 209
    The Technique of Shamanic Divination — 210
    Just Knowing and the Deep Well — 215
    The Nature of Time — 216

Chapter Nine: The Soul Story/The Mythic Life — 219

    The Deep Well — 221
    My Soul Story — 224
    Living Myth/Mythic Life — 225

Appendix: Shamanic Craft Terminology — 229
    Shamanic Craft Principles — 231

Bibliography — 233

Index — 237

acknowledgments

Thank you to Elysia Gallo for putting up with my constantly shifting projects and for being so supportive of my work and me in general!

To OakSun Grove—Kate, Darren, Aaron, Jacqui, Chantelle, Kerry, and Danielle—beautiful Witches of the WildWood. You have all reminded me of why I love being involved in a coven!

To my first official shamanic Craft apprentices—Jae, Nika, Brendan, Laura, Rachael, Hope, and Rob—for obvious reasons.

To the priests and priestesses of WildWood, the wisdom keepers of the Wyrd, and especially to James, Molly, Hannah, Laura, and Jarrah, the trailblazers of our beloved tradition.

To Daphne (Eileen), Barbara Rose, Michelle, Adam, Christopher, Steve, Katrina, Don, Annette, Lole, Cahyani, Matthew, Sylvia, Angie, Drake, and Elysia—you all opened your arms and homes to me so tenderly during my first US tour.

To Courtney, Abel, Devin, Storm, Laurel, Diana, Shivian, Dylan, Matthew, Keith, River, Thorn, and Barbara—friends I made and met along the way.

acknowledgments

To my grandparents of beloved memory—for the gifts you have endowed me with in this current life and the yearning for the mysteries you have inspired within me.

To my mother, Ros; my father, John; and sister, Noni—the first family I knew and loved.

To Lucy—frolic free.

To Greg, the Hare—we loved, we lost, but we will remember.

To Phyllis Curott and Starhawk—your words and wisdom inspired me to become a writer.

To my gods and allies, and to Persephone, the Blue God, Hermes, Aphrodite, Hekate, and the Sacred Four of the WildWood, to whom I am priest and lover.

preface

This book is an accompaniment to my previous book *By Land, Sky & Sea: Three Realms of Shamanic Witchcraft* (which I will sometimes refer to as *BLSS* within this book). However, it is not a direct sequel—they are tied together through subject matter alone—and together these two books represent the basic material of my two-year Shamanic Craft Apprenticeship. Both books read independently of each other also. The book you now hold in your hands is a grounding and deepening in the current of Witchcraft I identify as shamanic[1] and will orient the seeker along the path to integrating fully the lessons of the spirit worlds and the wisdom of the old healers and priest/esses. This book, though presented as a grounding in a particular paradigm and philosophy of Craft, requires at least some contextual familiarity with Witchcraft as a spiritual tradition.

---

[1] There are various contemporary traditions of Witchcraft that readily identify as "shamanic" or "shamanistic," including the Circle Craft (which has been known as Circle Wicca and Wiccan Shamanism in the past), traditions deriving from Robert Cochrane's original group (Clan of Tubal Cain), the Feri Tradition (in its various forms), the Ara Tradition of Witchcraft spearheaded by Phyllis Curott, and the WildWood Tradition, of which I am an initiate.

preface

Many of the topics within these pages are deeply confrontative and can be dangerous. To read on is to acknowledge Witchcraft as a true wisdom tradition abiding only by the precept of *total freedom equals total responsibility*. I shall leave the ethics to the deeper selves of all of you.

I am an initiated priest of the WildWood Tradition of Witchcraft, which emphasises the shamanic foundation of the Craft and seeks to revive and celebrate it in the modern day. We consider Witchcraft a vital and ever-renewing tradition with deep, primordial roots. A tree may not grow towards the limitless heavens unless it is firmly entrenched within the earth; so it is with the spirituality of the Witch. Without our Mother we may not ascend the world tree to know of the delights of the heavens. If we do not first nourish ourselves and bear our grounding, we may never aspire to travel elsewhere or be strong and lucid enough to cultivate conscious experience. The lesson is to start where you are.

This book was written as an alternative for Witchcraft and Wicca books that introduce the seeker to a world of ritual and ceremony, correspondences and overtly Hermetic overtones, though there is nothing inherently wrong with this. I believe it is essential to first orient oneself to cosmological, philosophical, and spiritual understandings before entering the realm of ritual. Without knowing why we cast a circle (for example) and truly connecting with that implicit meaning, ritual merely becomes a series of empty gestures, words, and movements. Ritual should be alive with the innate magick that is its fuel; it should sing with emotion and effectively link us with our psyches, transforming us. This is the deep power of ritual.[2]

---

2 It is also important to understand that through years of conducting ritual and integrating the ways of Witchcraft into your life, you will soon come to realise that there is never an end to the depth and infinity of insight you will behold related to anything and everything. The circle may be one thing one day but take on an entirely different meaning the next. The path of the Witch who ignites his or her awareness is endless in this way.

preface

This book is the product of twenty-three years of mystical and magickal family enmeshment; eleven years of conscious spiritual growth and deepening; six years' involvement with what has become the WildWood Tradition of Witchcraft; intense, spontaneously derived, and consciously facilitated shadow work; and a triple-descent journey that punctuated the mythic influence of the Dark Ones in my life.

Within these pages you will find an outline for the shamanic Witchcraft apprenticeship. This course material is designed to ground and orient a Witch in the shamanic Craft and on the pathway towards shamanic apprenticeship, which in my mind can only be forged between self (the autonomous, independent individual) and the spirits and/or Self and All-Self. Each chapter provides theory, tools, and discourse on the various elements of shamanic Witchcraft. Those who follow my work will know that I define Witchcraft as an ecstasy-driven, earth-based Mystery Tradition, and I have gone into detail concerning these three aspects in my previous books and articles. However, I feel the need to explain what I mean by shamanic Witchcraft as being distinct from the broader concept of Witchcraft today, as this has been the direction my work has taken in the past five years.

The first book to truly open me to the reality that Witchcraft was and is at its core a European shamanic tradition was Kenneth Johnson's *Witchcraft and the Shamanic Journey*. The author goes into great depth and detail concerning the records of the Witch trials, and through an unbiased and comparative religious lens unearths a well-rounded theory that speaks of Witchcraft's origins in the shamanic traditions. Johnson refers to the night battles of Carlo Ginzburg fame (the Italian *Benandante*—the "good walkers"), Joan of Arc, the nature of "crisis cults" such as the development of American Voudoun and Native American Ghost Dance cults. Perhaps Witchcraft as it exists in scattered remnants even to this day was once a crisis cult, originating in the fourteenth century during social and political unrest. This certainly has parallels with the ideas raised by *Aradia, or the Gospel of the Witches* as received by Charles Leland in the nineteenth century from the Tuscan Witch Maddalena. I am not stating that Wicca as propounded by Gerald Gardner is a direct descendant of such shamanic practices; however, elements of the Gardnerian Craft certainly retain ecstatic and folk/peasant concepts and techniques. The shamanic Craft I am speaking of is a revisioning and a reclaiming of the older ways of seership, healing, travelling between the worlds, and spirit allies. In many ways, the historical and derivative conclusions drawn by Sorita d'Este and David Rankine in their wonderful book *Wicca: Magickal Beginnings*[3] may highlight the differences between a Witchcraft that is decidedly ceremonially oriented or based and shamanic Witchcraft, which can be summed up in my own words as "primal, ecstasy-driven, celebratory inclinations of nature-mystic Witchcraft."[4] In fact, as is discussed in the introduction to this book, Ceremonial Wicca and Shamanic Wicca are the two strands Raven Grimassi refers to when observing the trends of Craft practice and belief.

The ways and ideas of shamanic Witchcraft certainly draw their vitality from my definition of Witchcraft mentioned above; however, I feel the need to elaborate, if only to specify the exactness of the purposes of this book and its influences.

The shamanic Craft is a philosophy and a path that embraces the ecstatic, the wild, the gnostic, the transformative, and the visionary. A shamanic Witch is born to his or her fate and, through countless threshold moments (rites of passage/initiation), embraces the art of evolutionary consciousness so that a deepening of the spiral soul may

---

3   D'Este and Rankine offer five possible histories for the development of the British Wiccan tradition. Firstly, that "Wicca is a continuation of the grimoire tradition." Second, that Wicca descends from a Victorian ceremonial magick system. Thirdly, Wicca is the sole creation of Gerald Gardner and his co-conspirators. Fourthly, Wicca is the direct survival of a British folk magick. And fifth, that Wicca is the final form of a European Witchcraft tradition with roots in the Aegean and Mediterranean. Of these five hypotheses, d'Este and Rankine opt for the viability of the first complemented by the second.

4   Parma, *By Land, Sky & Sea*, xxii.

preface

take place. Essentially speaking, a shamanic Witch is a wild Witch—one who dwells by the precipice, on the edge, with one foot in this world and one in the next. We are given to magick, and magick is given to us. Nature is the foundation for spirit; the essence of nature is magick; and the magickal arts aid our reunion with spirit as a whole being. Nature is our sacred foundation; magick is our sacred charge.

There are several key concepts within the definition I have fleshed out above:

Ecstatic, wild, gnostic, transformative, and visionary: A shamanic Witch embraces ways and methods that dissolve the self as ego and societally imposed boundaries (ecstatic), evoke the untamed spirit within the human (wild), and bring true knowledge of self (gnostic), which are deepened through the cycle we call life, death, and rebirth (transformative) and affirmed by the Witch's gift to see and encounter the raw vividness of the world/s (visionary).

Born to his or her fate and through countless threshold moments (rites of passage/initiation): Most if not all Witches agree that a feeling of homecoming is a highlighting factor of returning to or arriving at the Craft. One traditional belief regards any true Witch as having been a Witch in a past life or lives. The Gardnerian saying (which may derive from the earlier New Forest Coven) declares "that we may meet, know, remember, and love again." Once a Witch, always a Witch. All of this points to the older belief of reincarnation through the tribal or family line.

On the topic of initiation: a shamanic Witch is brought into a tradition not necessarily made up of organised covens but a tradition of spirit allyship, land guardianship, and the gift of knowing the worlds and the roads between them. Self-initiation in the strictest sense of the term is absolutely viable, but in fact is the outcome of several other threshold moments in which the aiding and familiar (family) spirits work to empower, orient, and ground the shaman/Witch in the here and now. The circle is cast through this process, and upon reaching the point of origin, a true revolution of spirit has taken place, and there is a deepening—and the spiral begins.

The hereditary Craft and the Witches therein are not always genetically related to the family at large; individuals may be "adopted" into family traditions if there is significant interest either way regarding the individual's appropriateness within the family tradition. Largely we hear of the lines and magick being passed on from mother to daughter; however, I have also heard that though this may be preferable in some cultures (e.g., various Italian cultures), from parent (mother or father) to son is generally not considered any less desirable. In these contexts, if a soul has returned and has not been born into the ancestral line, the fate can still be intuitively or experientially read within the individual, and an adoption will take place. Ideally, at least in the older traditions of Craft, any initiatory ritual (threshold moment/transition) is seen to stand in for an adoption ceremony. An initiation in this context is a decision on the part of the existing coven/family to accept a new-old soul into the family/tradition. The initiation brings the individual into the current of the tradition, and energetically and spiritually connects them with the gods, totems, and spirits that guide and oversee the tradition.

The spiral soul: As mentioned above, initiatory experience naturally opens our awareness to the deeper reality of the spiral soul. The spiral soul is described in many traditions but not necessarily in the same manner; we often hear it called the triple soul of Huna and Faerie/Feri Traditions. As I am not an initiate of any of these aforementioned traditions, the names I give these aspects of the soul are my own but may be freely used. I model these three selves on the three worlds that, in truth, are the three souls of the macrocosm, or outer world. When the star self (sky), the talking self (land), and shadow self (sea) are aligned and in wholeness, evolutionary consciousness becomes the illumined pathway of Self, and thus, as before, we are self-initiated. Perhaps this is the reason why we are in the circle alone (no other human presence) at initiation in the WildWood Tradition.

Wild Witch: These two words together are the premise of the paradigms of the shamanic sacred realities. Perhaps I name it thus in honour of my heritage as a WildWood priest; however, my intuition, not my logic, is the determining factor here. "Wild" often equals primal to those who hear it; it signals raw and pure nature as it is rather than the romanticised version of nature as pleasant and lovely. When we consider again the teaching that there is no separation, and the mirror of nature is also the mirror of our internal divinities, one can then make the following assertion: that if we have undergone the elemental purification of walking life's path in honour and integrity, we partake of the holy mystery that says, "Here lies the way to ascension (the road to God), here lies the way to decadence (the road to oblivion), here lies the road to the Faerie country (the road to magick)." The Witch, honouring his or her spiral nature, will often simply walk in the direction of the middle way (the Faerie road), because he or she knows intrinsically that a road or path is never one-dimensional and will eventually turn and twist and bend—the crooked path. And here we find the element of risk that makes our journey worthwhile, for without it we have sacrificed nothing: the mystery. To be wild—and thus to be a wild or shamanic Witch—is to honour the pledge to the mysteries of the eternal question and to embrace it as the forever-way to God, oblivion, and Faerie… magick.

Thus the shamanic Witch, in my mind, consists of four definitive qualities:

> **One:** that our ways and lore are formed from ecstatic methodology, wild being, gnostic philosophy, transformative longings, and visionary impetus.
>
> **Two:** that we are born and made Witches, not necessarily through heredity but through the pacts we make with Self (and not the antiquated concept of Satan) to learn more deeply than is possible and to embrace the fate of homecoming, purpose, and the integrity of being made worthy through challenge to change via initiation.
>
> **Three:** that we embrace our soul's spiral nature (and thus the world's), the triplicity of self, which by its very numerological value speaks of breaking duality and reconciling the loathing of opposites by the melding of them.
>
> **Four:** that we proudly and with passion embrace the wilderness within and allow it free reign, not because it would be decadent or indulgent to do so, but because it is the way of nature, and the road to God, oblivion, and Faerie is one and the same.

I wrote this book to fill a void, which of late is smoothly disappearing. Authors and teachers such as Veronica Cummer, Janet Farrar and Gavin Bone, Raven Grimassi, Christopher Penczak, and R. J. Stewart have paved the way. I thank them, for I stand on the shoulders of giants, as do we all.

Therefore I dedicate this book to the giants, the titans, and the raw forces of nature that share so much with the shamans. And may it be so forever.

introduction

"There is the night-flight, the spirit journey, the ability to shapeshift, the power to heal and to harm, and congress with all sorts of spirits, Gods and Goddesses, the dead, and the powers of the Earth. There is the thin edge that needs to be walked between magick and madness, between life and death. There is the boundary that must be leaped or walked or stood upon, always a chancy business at best. There is the going-there and the coming-back-again with lost souls, healing knowledge, gifts for the community, new insights and ancient revelation."

Veronica Cummer, *To Fly By Night:*

The Craft of the Hedgewitch

What does it mean to be a shamanic Witch? In my previous book *By Land, Sky & Sea*, I outlined my personal definition of Witchcraft and how it parallels various traditional shamanisms globally. Anthropologically and culturally speaking, a shaman is an individual endowed with the seemingly supernatural gift to traverse the manifold worlds existing within and around each other simultaneously (as was the late Mircea Eliade's hypothesis). This foundational skill empowers the shaman to gather cosmic/spiritual information and knowledge and apply it by translating the abstract into the practical, forge relationships (allyships) with spirit beings (human and nonhuman), and further understand the mysteries of life (as embodied on earth by the tides and cycles of nature inherent within and without). Historically speaking, these shamanic skills are at the heart of all Witchcraft. The origins of the word *witch* lie in meanings as varied as wise one (*saga*, meaning Witch in Latin), bender or twister of power (*weik* in Proto-Indo-European), seer and knower (*weid* in Proto-Indo-European), singer of sacred songs (*varð-lokkur*, translating as warlock[5] in Old Norse), and a magickal priest/ess (*weik*, referring to one who consecrates with spirit (religio-magick in Proto-Indo-European).

The root of the word *shaman* lies in the Tungus *saman*, which means "one who is excited, moved, raised."[6] The derivative term now used by anthropologists to categorise a number of medicine wo/men, traditional healers, wizards/sorcerers, etc., is shaman. The root word *saman* may actually derive from a Tungus word meaning "to know."[7] In fact, traditionally the term has never been a noun; it is applied to the practice itself and thus all associated concepts. These age-old archetypes are akin to the traditional European roles of the village Witch, who held herbal healing knowledge and was the keeper of the wisdom of the earth currents and cosmic alignments. Like the myrk-rider and the hedgewitch, Witches by their very nature were and are fringe dwellers; by living on the edge, they were able to cross the nebulous

---

5 The term *warlock* has often been said to derive from the Old Scottish for "one who breaks oaths" and was applied to men accused of Witchcraft during persecution because it was thought that men were stronger in all ways than women and thus had much more to lose by signing a pact with Satan. However, according to Lady Abigail (as quoted by Storm Faerywolf in his article "A Conjuring of the Male Mysteries in Modern Witchcraft"), the original Old Scottish term *waerloga* means simply "male Witch" or "cunning man." The Old English term of the same spelling does translate as "oath-breaker."

6 According to Roger Walsh in *The World of Shamanism: New Views of an Ancient Tradition*.

7 Juniper, in her essay "What the Heck Is a Hedgwitch" in Veronica Cummer's *To Fly By Night: The Craft of the Hedgewitch*, speaks of the word *saman* translating as "one who knows."

introduction

boundaries separating the realms and return once more. Witches are true walkers between the worlds, with one foot in this world and one in the Other.

The Witch, like the shaman, had helpers—familiar spirits. During the Witch hysteria of Europe, the general folkloric belief was that Witches' familiar spirits were animal companions. This correlates with ancient shamanic, animistic, and totemic beliefs in many cultures. Shamans, like the medicine men of the Amazon, also work with the plant world, and spirit allies like peyote (*Lophophora williamsii*) and ayahuasca (*Banisteriopsis caapi*) are considered sacraments by indigenous shamans in the Americas. In European lore we, too, have our belladonna (*Atropa belladonna*), wormwood (*Artemisia absinthium*), and fly agaric mushroom (*Amanita muscaria*), all of which are known psychotropics (meaning "turning or altering of the soul") or entheogens (meaning "to generate the God within"). In fact, the majority of these plants are listed in old formulae for the infamous flying ointment. This ointment was one of the major factors in enabling Witches to "fly" to the sabbats, where, from spirit beings and a lord and lady of the sabbat, they would be instructed in magickal rites and achieve ecstatic states of consciousness through which mystic insights were obtained.[8]

In many forms of modern Witchcraft these older shamanic aspects still remain and are practised with vigour. Witchcraft is an ancient shamanic tradition with its roots firmly in Old European myth and lore. By virtue of this it is Pagan and borrows extensively from the indigenous and tribal cultures of Europe and through Indo-European migration from the East.

Raven Grimassi, a renowned and sometimes controversial historian of Neopaganism and Witchcraft, often divides modern Wicca into two distinct categories: Ceremonial Wicca and Shamanic Wicca. It is my belief—congruent with historical evolution—that ceremonial

---

[8] Johnson, *Witchcraft and the Shamanic Journey*.

aspects of Witchcraft and Wicca were developmental and grew out of shamanic foundations. Grimassi notes:

> As with much of Europe, ancient cave drawings and artifacts found in Italy reveal primitive ceremonial beliefs related to hunting and the animal kingdom in general. Over the course of many centuries, ancient shamanic-like beliefs evolved into tribal religion, eventually taking the form we now call *La Vecchia Religione*—The Old Religion.[9]

Essentially, the Craft of the shamanic Witch is a revivalist current that emphasises the underlying mythic and mystic components which give life to the ritual and ceremony we use to access these things in the first place. In fact, each is reliant on the other. In shamanic Witchcraft ritual and ceremony are understood as spiritual technology that enables us to connect and commune with the primal powers of the cosmos. It is important to comprehend this subtle truth, or else we become encumbered by pomp and order, and we lose touch with the eternal now. Spontaneous ecstatic communion is the heart of the Craft, not timed and ordered ceremony. Ultimately, the circle is life, and our invocations call forth the hidden potencies alive within the world/s. The shamanic Witch embraces the All-in-One and the One-in-All. Hail to the great mystery!

This Book's Context and Orientation

When held together with the contents of *BLSS*, the material in this book formulates the basic framework of the two-year Shamanic Craft Apprenticeship I offer to both in-person and long-distance students. The apprenticeship draws upon a somewhat eclectic (as a descriptive term rather than as a spiritual identifier) synthesis of ideas, customs, concepts, and traditions contextualised by my own personal discipline, deepening, and devotion. The material is influenced by the WildWood

---

9 Grimassi, *Hereditary Witchcraft*, 10.

introduction

Tradition, Feri understandings, Celtic lore and mythology, and Greek Mystery Traditions (specifically the Orphic and Eleusinian). As a WildWood initiate and priest, I am also actively and often engaging with the Sacred Four (the four WildWood divinities) and my other deities and allies and receiving new-old wisdom, lore, and technique directly. It may take me several months (or even years) to fully understand the implications of what I personally receive; however, the synchronicity inherent in life tends to weave the picture of wholeness beautifully. Due to this background in spiritual gnosis and revelation, I have found it a much simpler task to integrate the new material I am exposed to.

There are several instances within this book in which I refer to the Feri Tradition explicitly, and I have done so only if I have felt the insight is necessary. At the publication of this book I will have been formally training in the BlueRose Line of Feri for a year and a half; however, I have been observing and working with Feri concepts (not techniques) for several years now, and the stark parallels reflected in WildWood are immensely poignant. I also have a family background in animistic and polytheistic spirituality and religion, and I was exposed from infancy to a tradition that espoused ideas of spiritual technology as having magickal associations, as well as mystic pursuits of attainment to Divinity and the alignment thereof.

In this book there are nine chapters that speak on different elements of the shamanic Craft as I work with it. Firstly we will be examining the spiritual significance and meaning of ecstasy in a shamanic framework. In the second chapter we will delve into cosmology and the necessity of learning and attuning to the dynamic of the spiral or triple soul complex, and how this makeup reflects and embodies cosmic truths. I will share insights into the deeper realities behind casting the circle and directional emphasis and orientation; elemental philosophy will guide us. In chapter 3 I write of drawing down the gods and of possessory work in general—what it means, how it relates to a relationship of equality with our deities, and what exactly the deities may

introduction

be. I then continue waxing eloquent on our relationship (or allyships) with the spirit world/s and its denizens—how to observe, balance, celebrate, and honour our connections and exchanges. In chapter 5 I examine the quintessential shamanic trait of "moving between the worlds" and speak on the platform and springboard of trance—and how it propels us into accessing a broad range of skill sets integral to the shamanic Witch. In the sixth chapter I examine spellcraft in a shamanic context and offer several unique techniques and methods for successful and ecstatic spellcraft. Chapter 7 concerns healing and explores channelling "power," wholeness and renewal, soul retrieval, severing and cleansing of cords and attachments, and water blessing. In the eighth chapter the divinatory skills of the Witch are articulated through the shamanic lens, along with the associated harnessing of the Sight, channelling universal information, and the seeking and attainment of visions. The concluding chapter reviews the journey of the shamanic Witch and speaks of the soul story and the mythic life.

As we move through this book it will become obvious that there are certain guiding principles, which will be both implicit and explicit. The four guiding principles of the shamanic Craft as I teach it are:

1. The magickal worldview of infinite possibility
2. Nature is our sacred foundation—magick is the essence of nature—magick is our sacred charge
3. Sacred equality
4. Total freedom equals total responsibility

introduction

A Note on the Magickal Worldview of Infinite Possibility

"The internal logic of what Castaneda writes is totally real. I've done many of those things myself and seen other medicine people do them. People indeed walk up walls, walk through gateways; those things are not fiction for native peoples."

Arwyn Dreamwalker[10]

Stereotypically and historically, Witches and shamans both are conceived as being able to enact feats of supernatural strength. Physical flight; shapeshifting; commanding spirits, demons, and deities; oracular knowledge; casting spells and curses; and speaking with the animal and plant worlds are all among our traditional repertoire. Considering my own magickal career, I will personally review these apparent skills and seek to illustrate what I have come to call the magickal worldview of infinite possibility, or MWIP. I have witnessed physical levitation; worked with ancient forces to achieve significant tasks such as affecting the weather and linear time and space; shifted my energy-body into animal awareness; perceived future, past, and present events (from afar) in amazing clarity; cast spells to great success; and understood and communicated with both animals, plants, and other spirit beings. This is not supernatural; it is within my potential as a living and aware being, and thus it is within yours. Post-industrial society has divorced us from our innate and genetic ability to engage with the limitless realities that are ever-changing and always in flux. The MWIP is a paradigm-shattering paradigm—a paradox of paradoxes.

This experiential paradigm gives birth to the concept we call plurality and also to the idea that multiple realities absolutely may exist simultaneously at any given time. While I was staying in Berkeley during my 2010 American book tour for *BLSS*, I had the pleasure of

---

10 Dreamwalker is a shaman interviewed in Filan and Kaldera's *Drawing Down the Spirits*.

sharing dinner with several Pagans and one Christian whom I had met at the Parliament of the World's Religions in Melbourne. We were discussing atheism in Paganism, or rather the belief that there are certainly cosmic *forces*, though they may not be representative of embodied, discrete beings. Donald H. Frew, a Gardnerian high priest, spoke about putting the question to a worldwide mailing list of Gardnerian elders. The question was this: "Is it okay to be an atheist and a Gardnerian?" Don relayed that 50 percent stated absolutely not, and the other half were passionate defendants of the right to be atheistic; in fact, they themselves were. When pressured to explain what they meant, the overwhelming response was the view of Pagan atheism as stated above (a belief in or experience of cosmic and natural forces that may also be seen to be conceptualised as deities for the purposes of magick). Rachael Watcher (quite a well-known Wiccan in the Interfaith movement), who was sitting next to me, then stated that just as one could look at the circle as a theological pathway, one could also apply it strictly as a magickal tool. It is one's paradigm, or perspective, that decides the way in which a concept or experience will seem (or appear) to be.

Beyond all else, the shamanic Witch is concerned with pragmatism, however contextualised by the MWIP. Therefore, the shamanic Craft teaches us that first we must be concerned with experience and only after allow this to be belief[11]—and even then to always question.

If we are able to surrender to infinity and suspend disbelief even for a moment to directly know how far-reaching a possibility is, we begin to cultivate confidence within ourselves so that we may trust in the unfolding of the great mystery and become an active and integral part of the Allness that is.

Infinite possibility means that we truly understand Allness. Ultimate reality, which is considered synonymous with God, is never ultimate unless we are able to conceive of the concept of infinity and know

---

[11] Victor Anderson, the late Grandmaster of the Feri Tradition of Witchcraft, was often quoted as saying, "Perceive first; believe later."

introduction

that it is contained within the All; that the All is truly beyond itself and the seed of its realisation. A shamanic Witch honours these truths as primordial and preliminary; without them, how are we able to interact with the primal forces of reality to achieve our goals or further fulfil our ecstasy-driven destinies? It is essential to first consider that magickal spirituality isn't hypocritical—it is decidedly overt, sometimes subtle, and often pragmatic.

Magick is an art, a vital force, an integrated philosophy offering deepening and illumination; however, it is also a signal for the mind to question. When we are faced with the absolute answer, magick encourages us to revel in the parallel nature of that answer's preceding question; perhaps it has a different answer attached to it, providing an alternate reality and extending into a world not touched on by the "absolute" answer. Perhaps magick is the way in which we relate to our own conceptions of reality and truth? Perhaps magick allows us to rise above our own self-imposed dilemmas and see the bigger picture and the manifold traces of the artist/s? Magick reminds us of our own art and creativity and restores the brush to our waiting hands. Magick is the inspiring source for the question of infinite possibility; the answer is magick. Here is a technology—a dynamic, a paradigm, a metaphor—that escapes all absolutes and paradoxically opens us to the Absolute/Ultimate/Truth/Reality (as above).

The mystery in this is the eternal unknown and the spiralling journey that forever deepens our inherent connections while forging new ones. It is the grace of being that we can only intimate in the quiet spaces in between. The magickal worldview of infinite possibility is a way to translate the words written down before language ever was… to hear the music of the spheres though we are bound to silence…to drink of the deep well, though there is no depth…to perceive before perception and know before knowledge, and then to stand back and see that all is as it is and will be forever.

May the journey begin!

chapter one

the meaning of ecstasy

> *"I am consciousness, a thread connecting all living creatures on Earth. I am briar. I am rock, alive and vital. I am cloud, drifting on the high winds of consciousness. I am cattle dog, living on a farm in Tasmania, and I am Great Dane, loving my master. I am hare, running fleet of foot. I am bird, singing on a branch in a garden. Winter is ended, spring is here, and I sing with the joy of life."*
> Michael J. Roads, *Journey into Nature*

Mircea Eliade described shamanism as a technique of ecstasy. The Greeks understood ecstasy as *ek stasis*, which translates literally as "outside standing" or "to stand outside." When the word *ecstasy* is then contextualised as a magickal and spiritual technique (as it was considered to be a philosophical and spiritual ideal in the Greek Mysteries), it is clear that the shaman or Witch is experiencing ecstasy as standing outside of oneself (as ego) and, in achieving such a transcendent state, is enlightened to the Great Immanent Divine. That thing we call self is equivalent to that thing we call cosmos. The self is the All-Self.[12] In my previous books I spoke of this sacred truth often; it is

---

[12] See page 195 of my book *Spirited* for more details.

an innate reality in my life. As a priest of the Craft, I am devoted to the service and celebration of the All-Self in its varied and infinite expressions. Each self, each being, is holy and beloved of the great mystery, and thus attaining true ecstasy is our destiny. The concept of the pure will can be understood when we think upon this notion. If we are all enlightened, then attuning to and realising our own pure will helps us to remember the wholeness (holiness) that we are. It is our choice to forsake and dishonour our divine origins, but it is also our choice to embrace it.

The Mystery cults of ancient Europe, such as the Orphics, Pythagoreans, druids, and Witches, all have their own particular ways and methods of reinforcing and evoking this sacred reality. The famous Orphic initiatory declaration of "I am child of Earth and of Starry Heaven, but my race is of Heaven alone" urges us to embrace our stardom, leading to salvation. The symbol of the Pythagoreans was the pentagram, an archaic and cross-cultural occult symbol known to contain the phi ratio explicitly and thus to reflect the intelligence of nature and the godhood of human beings in its basic design. Witches and druids of the past and the present have many ways of acknowledging, accepting, and affirming our destiny of ecstasy; as Diana says in Doreen Valiente's *Charge of the Goddess*, "And ye shall be free from slavery; and as a sign that ye are really free, ye shall be naked in your rites; and ye shall dance, sing, feast, make music and love, all in my praise."

I translate the teaching of this stanza as "freedom and ecstasy." In embracing the naked body, Witches are making a huge philosophic statement: we declare the body to be divine and not abhorrent, godly and not sinful. In fact, the Goddess of the Wise is charging us to do so, and furthermore to "dance, sing, feast, make music and love" all in her praise. Even the simple blessing of "blessed be," which may have been absorbed into modern Wicca via Christianity, bears deep wisdom. The meaning is congruent with the philosophies and teachings of the Craft—blessed are all things by their very nature. It is our destiny to recognise this simple truth and, in embracing it, to transcend the ego and be freed.

Ecstasy is to be filled with the presence of bliss, but only through love. A vision I had of Lord Siwa (Shiva) indicated this to me quite obviously. Siwa is often depicted with a rose at his crown, from which is issuing forth a fountain of pure water or a beam of holy light. The water/light is bliss, ecstasy, and only through the rose (the gate of love) may we be made worthy to bathe in the presence of the Divine. To love is to know the mystery, for both are ineffable, and neither can be explained rationally—it is the intimation of the heart. In letting go of the ego's need to control and categorise (filter experiences), we surrender to the Pure Will, the natural flow of the life force, and we return to our destiny, ecstasy. Hence, Witchcraft is truly a world-*embracing* tradition rather than a world-rejecting one.

Love as Divine Fire

"Whether man or woman, conscious practitioner of the ancient Mysteries or one who simply lives with vitality, a life fully lived is one illuminated by the divine spark within oneself. And that God, who is also mortal, is within each of us. He was within me now; grateful and aroused. I was aware of communion in every part of myself—in body, mind and soul. I had found the God and he was love."
Phyllis Curott, The Love Spell

Love is often touted in New Age philosophies to be synonymous with the being/force/concept many call God. As a Witch I do not relate to the Divine as a plane of neutrality or as an overarching force of suspension/creation (not overtly, anyway); rather, the Divine is a shining, a depth within of intrinsic connection and the power of presence. All things are divine—all things are God. This is the great mystery. Love, then, is the feeling or experience of the Divine's fire (its will to be) in our lives. The Celts called an experience of channelling imbas/awen (poetic life force, or love) "fire in the head."

chapter one

Fire is an ascending element, with a desire to grow higher and higher. It burns up air as it does so and transforms all that passes through it. On a tamer note, a candle flame is often enough for one to realise the holiness of a moment. In fact, the lighting of candles in many spiritual traditions is a solemn method of acknowledging and petitioning divinity as deity, to draw forth a concentration of divine presence. Where the land meets the sky meets the sea, there a fire is lit.

Fire was stolen from the Olympians by Prometheos. A blue flame is considered to be the symbol of the Spirit of the Old Ways in Stregheria, a sign of the presence of the Fey Folk; as the well-known Pagan prison chaplain Patrick McCollum once told me, when earth is taken from a well (earth and water), breathed upon and lit (air and fire; the four elements as one), a blue flame is ignited. Many Eastern religions are called fire-worshipping cults because of an emphasis on fire in their rituals.[13]

Fire illumines; it transforms through destruction; it enlivens, warms, and impassions. Fire is love. Consider the images of the Christ and Mary baring their flaming hearts in Catholic iconography. The understanding is implicit in many faiths around the world: fire marks the presence of the Divine—love.

Love, by its very nature, is multifaceted, and from a spiritual perspective it is much more than the love depicted in the tear-jerking romantic comedy movies. Love is frightening, harsh, soul-wrenching, and destructive—and, quite simultaneously, it can be empowering, liberating, calming, soothing, and gracious. Love is as love does, and more often than not, love is a verb. When we think of love—as the Tungus Siberians think of their shamans as an action, as something done within the world—we come to realise that without our participation within the sacred reality, we may not feel the divine presence—the fire in the head or heart or belly. We must embrace the world and the world will embrace us in return. The gods help those who help themselves.

---

[13] The Parsees, modern-day descendants of the Zoroastrians, are an illustrating example.

the meaning of ecstasy

The Rite of Divine Fire

This simple rite will help open you to the all-pervasive, underlying omnipresence of the Divine. You will need the following:

- A white votive candle
- A rose (whatever colour you prefer)
- Lighter/matches

Breathe into stillness. Light the candle, and place the rose before it so that it sits between you and the candle. Gaze peacefully at the rose and candle, absorbing the sight holistically. Don't attempt to impose a vision or instigate a movement away from the here and now. Breathe in deeply, right down into your abdomen, filling your lungs, and sigh vocally. Do this three times. Sit and watch. Observe. Be in the moment. Receive. Breathe.

Dionysos and Siwa

Hymn to Dionysos[14]

Great Two-Faced Lord, Dancing One of the Green and the Black,
Of the Red and the White, leader of the Maenads,
Frenzied Lord of the Wild Things,
Dancer of Death and the Covenant of the Vine,
Rich in the blood, thrumming and drumming,
Inside of my heart and the heart of the people!
O Raving One—O Thrice-Born God!
Bull-horned and roaring,
And the hunter of souls,
We open this temple, this plain, unto your
Holy Presence and may the fire draw up!
May we sing the holy words unto you…
IO IO IO EVOHE!

IAKKHOS! DIONYSOS! ZAGREOS! IO!

---

[14] Written by Gede Parma.

chapter one

Hymn to Siwa/Shiva

Naagendra haaraaya thriloochanaaya bhasmaangadhaaraaya maheshwaraaya, nityaaya shudhdhaaya digambaraaya tasmai nakaaraaya namahshivaaya.[15]

Translation: Salutations to Shiva, who wears a serpent as a garland, who is three-eyed, whose bare body is covered with ashes, who is forever pure and the very embodiment of sacrifice.

Lords of Divine Ecstasy and Surrender to Bliss[16]

I am a devotee of Dionysos. I was born into a family that honours Lord Siwa, Mahadewa (meaning the Great God). I am not the first (and certainly not the last) example of these two deities being consciously linked.[17] Dionysos, who is most often associated in the popular mind with his aspect of Bakchos (the raving wine god), is also the spirit of wild ecstasy and abandon, the leader of the frenzied maenads (his staff-carrying followers) and an ancient deity of initiation (death and rebirth) revered by the Orphics. The following are some of his lesser-known attributes in the form of epithets (divine titles); however, they clearly demonstrate his shamanic nature:

- Agrios (the Wild One)
- Antheos (Blossoming)
- Bromios (He Who Roars)
- Bythios (the Deep)
- Dissotokos (Doubly Born)

---

15 This is Sanskrit, one of the oldest languages in the world, deriving from the Proto-Indo-European language.

16 Dionysos—Divine One of Nysa; Siwa—Auspicious One. In Bali we pronounce and spell Shiva as Siwa—*see-wah*.

17 Please refer to *Gods of Love and Ecstasy: The Traditions of Shiva and Dionysos* by Alain Danielou (Inner Traditions, 1992). Many historians and religious comparative researchers feel that Shiva and Dionysos are the same god or derive from a prototypical Lord of the Dance and Ecstasy.

the meaning of ecstasy

- Ekstatophoros (Bringer of Ecstasy)
- Eleuthereos (Emancipator)
- Iatros (Healer)
- Khoreutes (the Dancer)
- Lyseos (Liberator)
- Phanes (Illuminator)
- Teletarches (Lord of Initiation)

Dionysos has been called many things in his vast history. His myths of genesis vary greatly; however, in wholeness and review, the meaning of twice-born or even thrice-born can be understood. Dionysos is born as Zagreos (the Hunter; the Collector of Souls) from the union of Persephone and Zeus (who seizes her as a serpent/drake in the underworld). Persephone, Lady of the Underworld and Queen of the Dead, carries now the seed of the Potent Sky Father. The most high has come together with the most deep, and from this union of opposites comes the third—the promised child who will break the duality and dissolve the boundaries to bliss. Zagreos is then seen to be angrily pursued by Hera (Queen of Olympos, Lady of Winds, Old Goddess of Nature) as the Death-Waging Hag (from the Greek *hagnes*, "pure"), and she commands the Titans, the raw and primal forces of nature, to tear Zagreos into many pieces. They first trick the young Zagreos into replacing the sceptre and the apple (symbols of sovereignty and wisdom) with the thyrsos (pine cone–tipped wand), a spinning toy, and a mirror. As Zagreos becomes hypnotised by his own reflection, the Titans surround him and undertake the task of destruction with the wild ferocity only Titans can wield. They then stew him in a cauldron (symbol of regeneration), boil, roast, and devour the seven or fourteen pieces of his body (similar to the Osirian myth of dismemberment by his brother Set). However, of course, the allegory is punctuated most clearly by the symbols.

chapter one

The cauldron is the source of immortality in Pagan myths, and thus though Apollon, Athene, and/or the Muses (depending on the myth) are sent to gather the pieces of Zagreos and inter them at the centre of the world itself (the *omphalos,* or navel, at Delphi), the beating heart is entrusted to Semele. Semele is the mortal mother of Dionysos's (re)birth, and once again Hera's ire is aroused. Hera encourages Semele to implore Zeus, the king, to reveal himself in his divine splendour; though he refuses at first, she continues to yearn for it until Zeus cannot help but acquiesce to his delicate lover. Indeed, he appears as lightning, and Semele is reduced to ash.[18]

The newly formed Dionysos in the womb of the now-dead Semele (and this occurring at the time of the winter solstice) is now sewn into the thigh of Zeus himself, who will protect the child until his rebirth at the spring equinox. Much of the seasonal cycle now celebrated by Neopagans the world over can be found in this ancient Orphic/Olympian-variant myth. And thus can we attest to Dionysos's thrice-born nature—born first from the union of Persephone and Zeus; secondly at the winter solstice, when Semele is destroyed and he must be prematurely extracted; and thirdly when he comes forth from Zeus's thigh at the spring equinox. He is the Dark Lord of the Underworld as the first Zagreos, the saviour of spring (and the rebirth/resurrection of life) as he who is reborn at the equinox and also the strange eclipse moment in between (the winter solstice), which I have now come to embrace.

In my personal work with Zagreos, before I actually looked at the literary historical documents and references, he manifests to me as a terrifying sabbatic lord upon the plains of Thessaly, an area in modern-day Greece known for its Witches and magick. There he showed me symbols of three triangles intersecting as one—of a crooked triangle with the symbol of a solar eclipse in the centre: his raw, beating heart

---

18 Semele is reduced to ash just as the Titans were by Zeus's wrath after Zagreos's dismemberment. The human race was said to spring from these ashes and the blood of Zagreos.

the meaning of ecstasy

as it was occulted by darkness and then reborn, almost spontaneously, into the light once more. We have here a true bringer of initiation, a Lord of Ecstasy, for the mirror that entrances the young divine one becomes the catalyst for the entire unfolding of the life-death-rebirth of this God-King. The mirror—the self-reflection, the revelation of self as divine—is the threshold moment that instigates true initiation. Not only does it mirror (to use the pun) the many modern Craft rites of initiation, it also is the classic making of the shaman. It is for this reason and many others that Raven Grimassi claims Dionysos as the original prototype for the Witches' God:

> "We shall discover…that ancient writings reveal that Dionysos is born at the winter solstice, dies in the fall season as a harvest lord figure, dwells in the Underworld, is renewed, appears in seasonal rituals, has a female goddess consort with lunar and Underworld aspects, is a Green Man figure, and is a fertility god associated with horned animals such as the bull, goat, and stag."[19]

Shiva,[20] on the other hand, is not necessarily considered to be a horned god, though his Indus Valley (c. 3300–1700 BCE) representation on the Pashupati Seal (or apparent representation) is definitively a bull-horned figure, said to be seated in lotus position, surrounded by wild animals and triple-faced (the Trimurti?). The imagery bears stark resemblance to that of the Cernunnos figure on the famous Gundestrup Cauldron. Shiva is, however, a wild god, whose key role in tantric yoga and philosophy proves that he is also a deity of taboos and the breaking thereof—powerful techniques to drive one into ecstasy. Meditating or sleeping in a cemetery is a common magickal act for many involved in the tantric arts, and to do so would be absolutely impure in the conventional Hindu outlook.

---

19 Grimassi, *The Witches' Craft*, 58.
20 Great, solid information on Shiva in his manifold aspects and related symbols can be found at http://www.hinduwebsite.com/hinduism/siva.asp.

Although a great majority of the stories associated with the god Shiva concern the holy family composed of himself, Parvati, and Ganesha,[21] there are others that explain his divine nature.

Shiva is one of the Trimurti—the three divine, supreme powers of the Hindu godhead. Shiva traditionally represents the destroyer aspect, while Brahma is the creator and Vishnu, the preserver. One myth tells of Shiva's birth. The power of Creation (Brahma) and the power of Preservation (Vishnu) are debating which one is the most powerful. Suddenly, a great pillar of shining light appears before them. It extends into the highest height and the deepest depth. Brahma becomes a goose and flies to the top of the pillar or tree (as roots and branches are described), and Vishnu becomes a boar and digs into the earth, searching for the bottom. However, the two return without ever having discovered the limit to the great pillar, and at this moment Shiva simply walks out of the pillar. They witness this great power, and thus Shiva becomes destruction and balances the cosmos.

In this myth it is not hard to see the shamanic realities referred to. The three powers represent the three worlds and perhaps also the three selves/souls. The great pillar/tree is the world tree, the axis mundi, also sometimes represented as a mountain (e.g., Mount Meru, sacred to Buddhists, Hindus, and Jains; and Venusberg of German folklore, related to the Witches' sabbat).

Shiva is often depicted with four arms, four faces, and three eyes. One of his most beloved aspects is as Nataraja—the Lord of the

---

21 The elephant-headed deity whose merging of human and elephant occurred because Shiva accidentally cut off his newly created (from Parvati's dead skin scraped off during bathing) son's head, as Parvati had placed him at the doorway of the palace to deter any unwanted villains from trespassing. Ganesha did not know Shiva, and Shiva did not know Ganesha, and as the son would not stand aside for the father, he severed his head. When Shiva discovered his crime, he travelled north until he came upon an elephant, whose head he severed and replaced for Ganesha's lost head. Ganesha is the first god one prays to in a traditional Hindu puja (devotional ritual), as he opens doorways and lifts obstacles. In this way he is like the Voudoun Papa Legba and the Greek Hestia, Hermes, and Hekate.

the meaning of ecstasy

Dance—whose depictions are commonly found on altars of Shivaite Pagans and Hindus. Growing up with Siwa, it was much more common to behold images of Siwa in peaceful lotus pose, emanating silent wisdom. I have never really noticed my father hold any other deity above Siwa, although Saraswati is also important to him; he calls her the goddess of education.

The way in which Shiva is traditionally depicted is obviously symbolic of his innate powers, gifts, and areas of influence. Generally speaking, although Shiva is regarded as the deity of destruction, and some say a look of his third eye will utterly obliterate, my interactions with the Dancing Lord have been about surrender, freedom, letting go, and becoming at one with the cosmic flow. Destruction—of illusion, of attachment to ego, and of the paradigms of separation—facilitates such liberation and awakening, but just as Kali devotees think of Kali Ma as love and compassion overall, rather than as a deathly, avenging war goddess, so it is with the Shivaites. Depending on one's inclination, philosophy, or path, darker aspects of the god's nature might be explored, but this varies from individual to individual. Those involved in tantric pursuits uphold Shiva and Shakti as the two potent forces of the universe. Shakti is power, life force, and what is, and Shiva is the blossoming, the coming forth, and the penetration of this cosmic power so that it becomes sentient, intelligent, aware of itself, and thus affirmed (as parallel to the Feri tales of Creation). Tantric rites seek to affirm and celebrate the life force, and often this manifests as the human body's (and mind's and soul's) capacity for pleasure. Hence the immediate connection of tantric practice with sacred sexuality. I will leave it to others more versed to convey the finer points of tantra; however, a great starting point is Dr. Jonn Mumford's *Ecstasy Through Tantra*—not only an apt book but an apt title for the purposes of this chapter!

Historically and culturally speaking, both Shiva and Dioynsos are considered to be wayward deities, outside of the approved and conventional ways of thinking and acting, and therefore representing boundaries, barriers, limits, and the destruction and surpassing of these things. When I speak of ecstasy at workshops and seminars and amongst the aspirants and dedicants studying for priesthood in the WildWood, it has become my statement to speak of ecstasy as the Greek "to stand outside," qualified by "to stand outside the self as ego" and, in walking away from self, walking into the core of Self itself. This act, this magickal and mystical[22] pathway is innate within the human spiritual (and biochemical) framework. We are urged to move beyond and to move through and to deepen as a result. This is the pathway Witches have either consciously or unconsciously worked with for centuries, if not millennia, along with all mystics, seers, shamans, and medicine people. It is the reason for our spirit flight, our trance, and our ability to become vessels and mediums for the spirits and to speak with the spirits.

The identification of Dionysos with Shiva does not only make historical and cultural sense (although in practice these deities are two very distinct beings). Mythically speaking, Dionysos's journey to the East, initiated by Hera's curse to wander the world in madness, enlightens Dionysos to the process of fermentation—the divine liquid of intoxication we now call wine—but he also returns whole. He is no longer completely raving, if you will, and has passed through the barrier of what it means to be compartmentalised as anything by society. He has entered salvation, freedom—has become a saviour in being an example to all those who are lost and wandering and yearn for wholeness. In this way, the practice of ecstasy as a holy technique is a pathway to free us of the shackles that bind us, and open us instead to the marvels of the mystery. Shiva, too, urges us to let go of ego, to surrender to the All, and to be at one with the peace thus instilled. Shiva in his Nataraja aspect is depicted as standing on a demon or dwarf, representing ignorance and ego, and poised in a graceful warrior stance as

---

22 Coming from the Greek *mystes*, referring to an initiate.

a circle of flame surrounds his shining body. To stand on the demon is to prevail over ignorance and ego, and the circle of flame is the circle of transformation—it represents the liminal, the between, the world of the spirits, and our ability to coexist in a useful and hopefully benevolent way. His posture could indicate not only esoteric symbolism but also a yogic stance that could very well lead the mind to such liberation and ecstasy.[23]

One could wax eloquent on the intricacies of Shiva and Dionysos and their contrasts, comparisons, and connections for an eternity; instead, I wish to conclude this chapter with a ceremony of reverence and contemplation of the Lord Dionysos and the Mahadewa Siwa!

A Note on the Conjoining of Siwa and Dionysos

Cultural misappropriation is a sore spot for some in the contemporary Pagan community, perhaps more so relating to the tendency in broader New Age philosophies to view all of the world's wisdom as a piece of the monolithic box of spiritual treasure from which we can freely take. Initially I was not going to include this little section here, until my acquisitions editor pointed out to me that Hindus may not necessarily identify as Pagan, and therefore by working with deities of Indian/Hindu origin I might be blurring the boundaries a little too much.

Interestingly, I'm one of those rarer Pagan "converts." I was raised in Balinese Hinduism, which possesses a blend of animistic, polytheistic, and monistic theology. My family's tradition is very much steeped in magick and mysticism; spirit possession, divination, healing, ceremony, and prayer are all referred to and practised. However, the Pagan cultures, traditions, myths, and deities of Europe (especially the Aegean and Mediterranean world) called for me, and I answered; I

---

23 See Goodman, *Ecstatic Trance*.

was aroused by the archetype of the Witch and felt her essence within my being. I knew that Pagan Witchcraft was my path, and not Hinduism. In saying that, however, Hinduism obviously still permeates my spirituality. In fact, as I type, there is an altar behind me on which sit both Lakshmi and Ganesha. Kali and Siwa are both strong influences on me, and I employ Hindu mantras at times in my magickal work and prayer. For these reasons I did not think it odd or inappropriate to work with Siwa and Dionysos together—as long as there is consciousness of this and respect and reverence. I have also made sure to highlight that some academics, historians, and mythographers actually believe that Siwa and Dionysos are the same god.

Hinduism, like Paganism, is an umbrella term. It is not a monolithic, static religious tradition without diversification or unique expressions. In fact, it is not unheard of to refer to Pagans as the Hindus of the West, and Hindus as the Pagans of the East. This is not simply underpinned by the notion that Paganism is any spiritual or religious tradition that is not Abrahamic; this reference actually seems to derive from our common Indo-European ancestry. Hindu traditions actually have a great deal in common with the Celtic cultures and customs of Western Europe; the parallels are often startlingly clear. There is now a burgeoning movement within contemporary Paganism called "Indo-Paganism," which refers to the blending of Eastern and Western principles and practices with meaning, purpose, and passion. I do not identify as an Indo-Pagan; however, the recent mergence of the Hindu and Pagan religious and spiritual communities (especially in the United States) is an alliance and friendship that I have much hope for.

In saying all of the above, please keep in mind that there are underlying social, political, historical, and spiritual issues that may present possible predicaments or expanded perspectives. The key, as always, is to approach all things with profound humility and respect, with a desire to learn and grow with knowledge, and with a reverent mirth, which enlightens the gods.

the meaning of ecstasy

A Ritual of Reverence and Contemplation

This ritual is a melding of traditional (reconstructed and readapted) Greek blessing rites with an adapted Hindu puja to Shiva. The aim of this ritual of reverence and contemplation is to do just that—revere and contemplate—and to allow the movement of self into All-Self through devotion.

Materials Needed for the Dionysos Altar:

- Black cloth
- One small (ceramic) bowl containing water
- One white votive candle
- One stick of frankincense
- A bunch of purple grapes
- A personally preferred wine (in a wine glass)
- An image/statue of Dionysos
- A thyrsos (a pine cone–tipped wand—can be easily made by finding a suitable branch and either super-gluing a pine cone to one of the ends or tying it down with hardy twine)

For the Shiva Altar:

- White cloth
- Two statues/images—one of Shiva and one of Ganesha (to open the way)
- Mala prayer beads[24] (worn around the neck to honour Shiva)
- Two silver or stainless steel vessels—one for sandalwood paste and the other for the five liquids

---

[24] Mala prayer beads are a staple of Hindu worship. There are 108 beads, often with a counting bead to keep track. They are often made of sandalwood, which is considered a very holy plant and scent in the East, although the mala beads worn to honour Shiva are generally made of Rudraksha (Rudra-eyed) seeds, a tree native to the Himalayas.

- Five liquids—ghee, dairy milk, coconut oil, water, and rose water
- Fresh flowers, coconut fruit, and an assortment of fruit (tropical is best)
- Jasmine incense (stick or cone variety)
- Two white votive candles (one for Ganesha and one for Shiva)
- Sweets/cakes as offerings for Ganesha

Begin by clearing and cleaning the space to be used for the rite in whatever way you see fit, remembering to both clean (physically) and cleanse (energetically).

Create two altars in the East—one to Dionysos and one to Shiva. On Dionysos's altar, place his image towards the back, and set the white votive candle in front of it. In front of the candle place the bowl of water, and balance the stick of frankincense on the bowl. Place the thyrsos next to the image. Place the glass of wine on one side of the candle and the grapes on the other. On Shiva's altar, place the image/statue and arrange the mala beads around it towards the back; place the white votive in front of the image. Place the image of Ganesha on the right of Shiva, with the second votive in front of his image. Place the two silver vessels in front of Shiva's candle and the flowers, coconut, and fruits in front of the vessels. Place the sweets/cakes and the five liquids aside, ready to pour, and place the incense at the very front of the altar.

Ground and centre. Gaze at the altars and take in what is displayed, holding and conveying the essence of the two gods of ecstasy. Light the candle before Dionysos and call upon the primal fire:

> *Great Primal Fire, ascend to us with the dawn and rule the sky. Glory of the sun, with burning lustre, illumine even the silver goddess Selene. Ethereal Fire, radiant heat, light-bearer, power of stars, cause now the blooming of the iris and the rose, and to the grain be kind.*

the meaning of ecstasy

Hear now this prayer of supplication and be thou ever innocent, serene, and gentle to this land. Great Primal Fire, I invoke thee![25]

Light the votive before Ganesha's image, and chant the following several times over to invoke his blessings and to open the way for the rite: "*Om Shri Ganeshaya Namah.*"[26] Place the sweets/cakes before the image as an offering to Ganesha.

Gaze meditatively at the two flames upon the two altars and visualise the space encompassed by the joining of these two flames into a sphere of incandescent fire, which purifies the area. Incant the following with impassioned force: "*Hekas, O Hekas, este bebeloi!*"[27]

Now take the frankincense stick and light it from both flames. Then, with intent, plunge it into the bowl of water on Dionysos's altar, saying: "*Kherniptomai!*[28] May this water be purified by the sacred flame."

Carry the water around the space three times in a sunwise manner, sprinkling as you go, and chanting: "*O Theoi, genoisthe apotropoi kakon!*[29] O gods, turn away evils!"

Once you have completed the third circumambulation, place the bowl of water, now considered ritually impure (as it has absorbed the miasma/impurities of the mental state and the place), out of sight and away from the space. The space is now fit and ready to officially welcome the gods.

Welcome in the two gods of ecstasy in your own words.

Into one of the silver vessels on Shiva's altar pour the five holy liquids—ghee, dairy milk, coconut oil, water, and rose water—and declare this offering to him as you gesture in blessing to the flowers, coconut, and other fruits. Anoint yourself and the image of Shiva with

---

25 English translation of the Orphic Hymn to Primal Fire (I have adapted it slightly, although this is the version I use at my weekly devotions).

26 Meaning "Om and salutations to Lord Ganesha."

27 Translated literally, it means "Away, O away, you desecrators/profanities!" Pronounce as *heh-kas oh heh-kas es-tay bay-bay-loi.*

28 Meaning "Purify!" or "Be pure!" Pronounce as *kai-yr-neep-toh-may.*

29 Pronounced as *Oh thee-oy gen-oys-thee ah-poh-tra-poy kak-on.*

sandalwood paste to connect with his power and providence. Finally, light the jasmine incense and white votive in his name.

Pick up the glass of wine and recite the following in blessing over it with intention: "From sun to seed, from seed to vine, from vine to grape, from grape to wine. *Kherniptomai* in Dionysos's name! *Io Io Io Evohe!*"[30] Drink deep, and then sprinkle a little of the wine over the grapes and pour the rest to Dionysos.

Holding the thyrsos in hand, recite the Orphic Hymn to Dionysos given at the start of this section. Take the mala beads from Shiva's altar and use them to count while you chant 108 *Om Namah Shivaya* mantras. Allow the chanting of the mantra to arouse a soft trance state that will guide you to introspection. After the 108th repetition, close your eyes, bow your head in reverence, and sit in silence for as long as is natural.

When ready, open your eyes, and again gaze peacefully at the two altars. Repeat the following with intention:

> *To the two gods of ecstasy and revelation; to the great ones*
> *of death, decay, and rebirth into light from chaos; to the holy*
> *beings of mirth, reverence, and the balance between all things,*
> *let there be peace now within me and around me, and let it touch*
> *the hearts of all who come into my sphere. I have communed*
> *with you for purity, presence, and power. I am purified, present,*
> *and powerful. The peace of the lords of the world resides*
> *now within me. I am reborn in this moment. IO OM!*

Take a moment to return to equilibrium, and when ready, begin to unravel and deconstruct the space with respect for the deities and the spirits of place. Leave frankincense to honour them.

---

30 Pronouce as *ee-oh ee-oh ee-oh ee-voh-ay*.

chapter two

cosmology and the spiral soul

> *"But the shaman's worlds and levels are more than interconnected; they also interact with one another. Shamans believe that these interactions can be perceived and affected by one who knows how to do so and that the shaman, like a spider at the centre of a cosmic web, can feel and influence distant realms."*
> Roger Walsh, *The World of Shamanism*

As Witches we look to nature, the great teacher, for divine inspiration. Nature is the Spirit manifest—God's most perfect expression. Therefore, it is within nature that we will find the secrets, the hidden potencies (the gods and spirits), and the teachings of life apparent. Humans, too, are part of nature, and recognising and remembering this is essential for our spiritual sanity. As Phyllis Curott so eloquently put it, "Standing in the cleansing, empowering surf, I knew that evil is something that arises within human begins when they become disconnected from the natural world."[31]

Witches often weave poetic allegory and metaphor through natural elements in order to ignite consciousness and to receive gnosis.

---

31 Curott, *Book of Shadows*, 170.

chapter two

As an organic tradition, the Old Ways are self-perpetuating within the human dynamic, and their origins are within the ether and dreaming of their own being. Even after centuries without them, those returning to the Pagan traditions of their ancestors are struck with a universal feeling of coming home. Our traditions, lore, and customs are renewed and revitalised forms aiding those who practise them to attune with age-old forces. However, as Raven Grimassi demonstrates very successfully and clearly in his books, a great deal of modern Witchcraft and Wiccan theological and practical structures are derived from periods much earlier than the mid-1900s.[32]

Cosmology is the study of the world/s and the way it is—the framework of the cosmos and how it manifests organically, and how we perceive or interpret those manifestations. Each and every person possesses a cosmological, if not ontological (perspective of being), outlook, though not all are consciously derived or arrived at by way of personal gnosis, revelation, or communion. It is the nature of Witchcraft as a mystical tradition to ignite consciousness and to embrace the world in this ecstatic state—one that invites transcendence from a centre of immanence. Thus we are privy to the ways of cosmology, though ideally we understand these perspectives as useful maps and lenses to interact with a living universe/multiverse/whatever.

In *BLSS* we worked within the paradigm of the triple realms, as the classic shamanic representation of the cosmos has essentially manifested in sacred triplicities. It is not only the world as an external entity that is threefold, but also the spirit within the body. It is also useful to look at the human spirit as essentially a tripartite division. This concept, at least in the modern Craft traditions, is best conveyed by the various branches of Faerie/Feri[33] Witchcraft.

---

32 Refer to the bibliography for details of Grimassi's works.

33 The spelling of Faerie changes according to the line and sometimes the individual Witch. Obviously all spellings are valid; however, according to Storm Faerywolf (the progenitor of the BlueRose Feri Line), the spelling of Faerie became Feri sometime in the 1990s because Victor Anderson wanted to distinguish Feri Witchcraft from the Faery Tradition (taught by R. J. Stewart) and other forms of Faery Wicca.

Depending on whom you speak to and on what line of Feri you are training within, the triple soul is named variously. The three souls, or selves, are often identified in the following way:

- Talking self (ego, or I am that I am)
- Younger/lower self/fetch (shadow, or I am the guardian of the God)
- Deep/god self (higher self, if you will, or I am the Divine within)

Although I am now a student of the BlueRose Line of Feri (as of December 2010), my perceptions and experiences of the three selves are not entirely governed by Feri insight or lore, though in and of itself, Feri, like WildWood, is wild and ever-changing. My understanding of the three selves is informed by Feri conceptualisations and by personal gnosis and raw experience. Personally, I refer to talking self using the same term; younger self as shadow self; and deep self as star self; however, I am apt to change and shift how I speak of the three souls.

The Spiral or Triple Soul and the Three Worlds

I connect the three souls with the three worlds of the shamanic paradigm. Therefore, in my work, talking self is the agent or companion of land/middleworld; shadow self is representative of the sea/underworld; and star self is the emissary of the sky/upperworld. I also place these three selves within the body at what Christopher Penczak calls the "three cauldrons."[34] The concept of the three cauldrons is said to stem from an Irish teaching/tradition ("The Cauldron of Poesy"—see

---

34 See Penczak, *The Three Rays of Witchcraft*, 60–74. Penczak mentions that the teaching of the three cauldrons derives from a sixteenth-century Irish *fili* (mystic-poet) poem called "The Cauldron of Poesy." Another friend of mine also speaks of receiving brief training in the three cauldrons for his third degree, but different names were used. I have used the names Penczak refers to them as, as this was how I first heard of them and I find them to be apt descriptions.

footnote 34), and to me it sits right intuitively, so I have begun to refer to it when sharing my concept of the triple soul (which I prefer to refer to as the spiral soul).

The human body itself has often been portrayed as a symbol of universal intelligence—of God or the Divine; the impetus for life. The best-known historical example of this is Leonardo da Vinci's Vitruvian Man, which is a Renaissance image of a muscularly defined male figure spread-eagled over sacred geometry that follows the course and orientation of his body. The pentagram becomes manifest as the sacred star, the God nature within the body, the Immanent Consciousness that many of us in the postmodern Pagan culture call "Goddess." Looking at the body as a map for spiritual reality is an ancient concept and a purely Pagan or indigenous one.

The three cauldrons are as follows: the cauldron of the head, the cauldron of the heart, and the cauldron of the belly. In many cultures, the "soul" of the individual is said to reside within the head. For example, in my father's Balinese culture, the head of a newborn must not be touched so that the physical (grounding) touch will not interfere with the settling soul. Therefore I place the star self in the cauldron of the head.

The cauldron of the heart represents the interface between the star self (cauldron of the head) and the talking self (cauldron of the belly). The heart centre (also the centre of the seven-chakra system and therefore the transmuter of vital life force)[35] speaks to me of the shadow self because, as a character in one of Charles de Lint's extraordinary Newford books (*Spirits in the Wires*) puts it, "the shadow is the guardian of the soul." Some may debate why the shadow self (as dark

---

35 In my mind, this seems to express that all signs point to love and compassion being the seat of what is Divine. This is echoed by another sentiment of Phyllis Curott's—"Some say the energy we work with is neither good nor bad, but simply neutral…And yet the encounters I had with raising energy, witnessing a drawing down, working in trance and experiencing visions and epiphanies all convinced me that the energy we worked with was love" (*Book of Shadows*, 214).

as it sounds) should be placed in the cauldron of the heart, as the heart is of love and the shadow is our repressed negative nature in mutated form. I would argue that when we look at the shadow as it is and seek not to simply cast it as a psychological and mechanistic compartment for what we cannot bear to look at, we find that the shadow is, in fact, the primal template for the soul—the animal within; the pure, raw beating heart of life; the yearning to exist; desire. Of course, it is our yearnings and desires that are so often judged harshly by a Western society dripping in the morality of Abraham. However, the shadow is the guardian at the gate—he who protects the sanctity of the inner temple; the divine self embodied by star self. What else is the temple enfolded in and protected by but love? The shadow self demonstrates to us that our child self (to use another of its manifold names) is innocent—in the Feri tradition, this is expressed as the black heart of innocence. That very term encompasses with poetry the truth at the centre of the cauldron of the heart and the shadow that sits there.

This, of course, leaves the talking self (or ego) to the cauldron of the belly—the grounded rhythms of the manifest world; the daily cycles that inform the way we think, act, and respond. The belly is the place of fire, heat, transformation, gestation, growth, and fear. It is the centre from which we live and act, based on both internal and external stimuli. In the WildWood Tradition, when we acknowledge the presence and providence of the three realms, we gesture down to the earth for land, up to the heavens for sky, and, to seal this, we cup our hands together at our chest (heart) for sea. This aligns not only the self within the three worlds but also the three souls at the three cauldrons within the body.

It was with much consternation that I included these ideas in this book as, frankly, the idea was not a self-determined one. To be deeply honest, much of what I write and know comes right through me and then settles within me for a time to bubble and boil. When I drink from the brew, the potion changes me and my perspective. I cannot always attest to personally understanding the details, but I ensure that my personal discipline provides sacred time and space for gnosis to strike and for gradual understanding to evolve.

Originally when I looked at the standing, erect human body and intuitively began to link the three cauldrons with the three souls and the three realms, I questioned placing the shadow self at the heart, because if the body is considered to be the world tree, then shouldn't the shadow self of the underworld be placed at the lowest point to reflect the order of cosmology? Other questions of a similar vein began to crop up, and I began to reject the whole concept; however, it kept returning, and not with light and sonic booms (as sometimes does happen to me in my visions), but with a gentle surety that seemed to say, "look harder, there is wisdom here." The harder I looked, the more I pondered; the more I relaxed into knowing, the more the concept became an idea (an "indwelling Goddess," as Ly de Angeles would say) and the substance of knowledge became apparent. To study this substance and to apply it and understand its application is the road to obtaining true wisdom in the secret sciences and the mystical paths. More importantly, though, is the deeper truth that any idea, concept, map, or path should never be abided by in a hidebound or dogmatic manner. It should, in truth, guide and enlighten oneself to Self—that sacred centre held within the centre in all things (the holy centre). To walk a path of spirituality is to aim to find communion with the Divine/the Spirit/the Essence of What Is/the Mystery.

In studying the three souls of the one spirit (what I call "Own Holy Self") that dwell within the temple that is each of us, we can begin to garner the wisdom of being. Through metaphor, poetry, ritual, allegory, and symbol, we can look beyond the superficial and connect with the eternal. When we energetically align the three souls, as is a daily practice within Feri (and is something I encourage within my Shamanic Craft Apprenticeships), we are magically forging a renewed wholeness so that we may, to use a Church of All Worlds

cosmology and the spiral soul

term, "grok"[36] (understand in fullness) life, its mysteries, and therefore the essence within that makes us who we are—consciousness, which gives us the very drive to desire to know! A Witch with this ignited consciousness/awareness weaves with the mysteries and celebrates the sovereignty of Self that is found when we accept responsibility for our wyrd and karma and thereby charge ourselves to service and celebration. Our threads glow in the tapestry and thus we become wholly a part of the flow of fate; we become living agents of the life force and are able to communicate and interface within, between, and through. This is the power of the Witch and of the shaman.

The Three Realms Alignment

This technique is foundational in the shamanic Craft I teach, and when combined with the triple or spiral soul alignment (a version of this will be provided below), they allow for an external-internal equilibrium.

The three realms alignment draws upon the essence of each realm (land, sky, and sea) in broad expression and condenses and concentrates their potencies into the three cauldrons held in the body at head, heart, and belly. It is also a more powerful way of "grounding and centring" and becoming the world tree/tree of life. There are also methods of aligning the three realms without focussing on the three cauldrons; however, this method draws upon the concept of the Feri triple soul alignment.

The three realms alignment aids in bringing what is outside inside (invocation), and the triple soul alignment has almost the opposite effect, bringing what is inside to the outside (evocation). However, it is neither invocation nor evocation that forms the core of the magickal act of either of these techniques; it is alignment and equilibrium.

When we draw in the essences of each realm and condense and concentrate them within the natural energy receptacles (cauldrons)

---

36 *Grok* is used in the Church of All Worlds as the CAW derives its original inspiration from Robert Heinlein's *Stranger in a Strange Land*.

within our bodies, we come to a pure alignment and a reflection of the external into the internal (as without, so within). We draw upon what is broad, substantial, and conceptual, and we infuse our beings with the potencies of the cosmos, thereby empowering ourselves to reveal and behold the holy centre (which exists in all places due to the limitlessness of All) and become the world tree.

The three realms alignment can be undergone before or after the triple soul alignment—either way determines an interesting, vivid, and palpable outcome. To align the three realms within the three cauldrons before aligning the three souls creates a pulse-point (inward-outward distillation-expansion) that flows into a primal and ecstatic connection with the potency of Self. To align the three souls before aligning the three realms within the three cauldrons is to create a space whereby we establish connection to Self before we move out and effect change in the world by becoming the fabric of its being.

The Technique

Breathe using the whole breath technique.[37] Cup both hands together below the navel, at the belly. Take a deep breath in; visualise and feel a red-black cauldron in your belly—feel its weightiness, its presence, its receptivity. Breathe out. Take a deep breath in, and allow your attention to delve down deeply into the land—embrace the physical, the dense, and the immediately manifest. Breathe out. Take a deep breath in, and mentally and energetically draw in the essence of the land (this may appear as green in colour) into the cauldron of the belly and, holding on to this breath of power, say aloud, "Cauldron of belly, hold land!"

---

37 The whole breath technique forms the first chapter of *BLSS*. In brief, it involves breathing in through the nose and into the belly for the count of four (or desired length) whilst visualising light entering the body. This breath is held for the count of four. The exhalation for the count of four comes from the mouth as an audible "haaaa," and the light is perceived to flow out of the body. Four counts after the exhalation, the light returns through the crown of the head with the next inhalation. Overall, there are four groups of four counts in the whole breath.

cosmology and the spiral soul

Cup both hands at the crown of your head and breathe out. Take a deep breath in; visualise and feel a yellow-black cauldron in your head—feel its weightiness, its presence, its receptivity. Breathe out. Take a deep breath in, and allow your attention to expand outward to soar through sky, through the celestial spheres, to embrace the starlight of the deep, dark chasm of space. Breathe out. Take a deep breath in; mentally and energetically draw in the essence of the sky (this may appear as violet or purple in colour) into the cauldron of the head and, holding on to this breath of power, say aloud: "Cauldron of head, hold sky!"

Cup both hands at your chest, at your heart, and breathe out. Take a deep breath in; visualise and feel a blue-black cauldron in your heart—feel its weightiness, its presence, its receptivity. Breathe out. Take a deep breath in, and allow your attention to delve and expand outward simultaneously, embracing the sea that encircles you and is heaving and sighing within your being. Feel and see the waves; smell the sea-salt air. Breathe out. Take a deep breath in, and mentally and energetically draw in the essence of the sea (this may appear as silver-pink in colour) into the cauldron of the heart and, holding on to this breath of power, say aloud: "Cauldron of heart, hold sea!"

If your eyes are closed, open them. With your power hand, trace a shining triquetra of light before you, saying: "By land, by sky, by sea…"

Hold your hands out, as if channelling more light into the symbol, and chant: "By the ancient trinity…"

Open your arms to enfold and embrace the triquetra into your body and being, and, as you physically move your hands back to your heart and absorb the power of this conjured light, say: "All three realms aligned within me."

Hold your hands to the ground; visualise and feel that roots are delving deeply down into the soil, through layers of compacted stone and clods of earth, down through veins of mineral and gold, down through pockets of underworld gas and chthonic water, finally drinking in the earth-fire of the pulsing planet's molten core. Drinking that in, it rushes up through your body—which has become the trunk of an ancient tree—and you say aloud and with deep resonance: "I am a child of earth…"

Bring your arms up; your branches and boughs spiral and spin to paint the arc of the heavens as they journey higher, raised and aided by breezes and winds, through every layer of atmospheric pressure. Finally they break through the biosphere of Holy Mother Earth and drink in the silver-white light of the stars. This light races down swiftly, like quicksilver, like lightning—into your body and being. You intone: "…and of starry heaven…"

Bring your hands to cross over at your heart, and feel the meeting of the fire of earth and the fire of stars. As your heart pounds in your chest, feel as each wave of this cosmic sea pounds the shores of your soul; you feel enlivened and deeply centred. You feel that the opposites, the extremes, have been reconciled within the holy tween—within that force which derives from and is cradled by their love for one another. As the sky stretches down in infinity to hold and be embraced by the earth, the living land, so is the foaming, cresting sea the liquid alchemy of their fusion and love (between the two). You hold this, and you say: "…and the sea within me knows and remembers."

This three realms alignment with the three cauldrons and the becoming of the world tree is sealed by the chanting of the following: "I am the world tree for all eternity; so mote it be!"

The Spiral Soul Alignment

Breathe using the whole breath technique (see page 36).

Visualise and feel a yellow sphere of light at the crown of your head. This is talking self; feel the name vibrate throughout the yellow light, striking a deep reality. Talking self names, categorises, delineates, communicates in worded language, and provides direct interface between human beings. Without talking self one could not say "I am…" and differentiate from wholeness or unity and express uniqueness. Take in a deep breath of power and send it to talking self—it glows with vivid radiance and becomes brighter and cleaner. Do this twice more.

Visualise and feel a red sphere of light below your navel. This is shadow self; feel the name vibrate throughout the red light, striking a deep truth. Shadow self dreams, senses, feels, and communicates in symbolic language. Shadow self is the primal ally of the Witch and is our truly primal, animal self. Without shadow self one could not see, touch, taste, hear, or smell, or receive impulse, intuition, or instinct. Take in a deep breath of power and send it to shadow self—it glows with vivid radiance and becomes brighter and cleaner. Do this twice more.

Visualise and feel a blue sphere of light above your head—a blossoming star. This is star self; feel the name vibrate throughout the blue light, striking a deep power. Star self knows, is wise, sees beyond, and is directly connected to the limitless divine. Without star self we would not be connected to the divine source in all things—we would not be able to truly claim our sovereignty of Self and divine origin (though all parts of Self are equally holy and sacred). Take in a deep breath of power and send it up to star self—it glows with vivid radiance and becomes brighter and cleaner. On the third breath out, throw your head back and breathe "ha" up into star self.

Star self plummets down into the belly and shadow self; they rise to meet talking self at the heart centre (the place of mergence, harmony, and alignment). They become one—the three primary colours running to mix and meld together. When you feel their holy unity, say aloud and reflect on the following:

> *Who is this flower above me? (land and talking self)*
> *And what is the work of this god? (sky and star self)*
> *I would know myself in all my parts. (sea and shadow self)*

Seal this alignment by reciting the following with powerful intent:

My spiral soul is now aligned
Beyond all space, beyond all time;
Within me now the trinity
Of the land, the sky, and the sea.
I now invoke Own Holy Self,
Here and now—so mote it be!

A Note on Congruence and Contradictions

It may be noticed that there is not necessarily congruence in the correspondence between the three realms alignment and the triple/spiral soul alignment. The three realms alignment works with the three cauldrons as "anchor points" for land, sky, and sea. If talking self is companion to land, then it would make apparent sense to align the spiral soul from the following "physical" anchor points in order to retain both consistency and congruence:

- Talking self in the belly
- Shadow self in the heart
- Star self in the head

The linear order is also different. In the three realms alignment the order is land, sky, and sea (and this is the same ordering for my Shamanic Craft Apprenticeship and also for *BLSS*); however, in the spiral soul alignment the linear order (if you will) is talking self (land), shadow self (sea), and star self (sky), though star self first meets with shadow self (the bridge) and not necessarily talking self (which we would assume star self would meet first if coming "down") when initiating alignment.

In receiving,[38] formalising, and passing on these techniques, I have felt it necessary to retain some form of contradiction to challenge and

---

38 When I speak of "receiving" lore and techniques, for the most part it is directly from the spirits. I interact with the otherworlds on a daily basis and find the primary distinction between this "mundane" realm and the magickal realms as far too dichotomous for my liking. It certainly does not reflect my experience.

confront talking self, to excite shadow self, and to illumine star self. In doing so, we come to realise that the "inconsistencies" are not discrepancies and that there are many vital and valid pathways and paradigms. However, these techniques are not set in stone and are open to evolution and adaptation. If one feels drawn to create congruity between the three realms alignment and the spiral soul alignment in terms of the anchor points used, the techniques (or their effects) would not be compromised. The outcome may provide a different sensation, insight/gnosis, or energetic vibration; however, different is often admirable.

I encourage you all to explore, deepen, contradict, challenge, and walk the wild or crooked way with ignited awareness and deep integrity.

Casting the Circle

Most Witches in this day and age will first learn how to cast a circle before performing rites and casting spells. Though it is not always considered necessary to do so, especially by non-Wiccan traditions, a circle is a useful and psychically supportive method of ensuring the safety of the Witch and empowering and reinforcing the energy raised within. These are the factors in casting a circle that most people hear about. However, the circle's fundamental principle is largely one of orientation to eternal space and endless time—to here and now.

When we cast the circle, we are in fact tracing the boundaries of the boundless. We are enabling the human mind to comprehend the infinite and thereby gifting the Witch with the ability to create with the living universe. As we walk the perceived boundary of the circle, we visualise light forming a sphere above and below that directs the "magnetic" principles of the life force (magick) to do just that. As we weave together the beginning and the end of the circle (which, in truth, has neither), our conscious mind surrenders to the unconscious, and we penetrate the great mystery (though we must cross the dark abyss). We (the self) are saying to the world (the All-Self), "All that exists, all that was, and all that will be: here it is, now and forever!"

Beyond the High Magick aspects of casting a ritual circle there lies a mystery that effectively joins the participants with the limitless Divine—with Ain Soph Aur, Ceugant, Brahman, etc. We walk the circle, we become the circle—the circle that, in effect, draws forth the very essence of the sacred through to the holy ground we tread. All that is—it is here, in this moment. The ignited consciousness of the Witch actualises the eternal now and the truth of one-in-all, all-in-one. As Plotinus demonstrates, "Each being contains in itself the whole intelligible world. Therefore, All is everywhere…Man as he is now ceased to be the All. But when he ceases to be a mere ego, he raises himself again and penetrates the whole world." The circle as a symbol of an underlying sacred reality effectively communicates the interconnection of all things and thus the greater being—the bigger picture. We are able to transform our consciousness, transcend the ego as limited "I," and dissolve into the All-Self. Thus, we are oriented to the universe as a whole and not to a version or piece of it. We are able to, as the old philosopher states, "penetrate the whole world."

As we cast the circle we are also reinforcing our experience of the Divine as immanent. We are mentally/communally conveying that this circle is cast not to sacralise but to commune with the inherent sanctity of things. If we were attempting to imbue a place or time with a sacred quality, we would be casting squares or triangles (and in some High Magick orders this is done). As with all things in the magickal arts, the symbolism is potent and often universal. The circle (and the spiral) is the symbol of infinity, rebirth, the womb (from which we emerge), and the ever-renewing cycles of mighty nature.

cosmology and the spiral soul

Between the Worlds…In All the Worlds

"The circle is cast. I am between the worlds, in all the worlds. What happens between the worlds touches all the worlds. What touches all the worlds changes all the worlds. So mote it be."

Above are the words I use to seal and affirm my circle during my weekly devotional rituals. They are unique to my personal path, but I believe I absorbed the "between the worlds, in all the worlds" from Starhawk and/or Reclaiming. I use these words because they embody the attitude I seek to reinforce and manifest consciously day by day. As the circle empowers the Witch to touch the limitless and to enter into the time of no-time and the place of no-place, so does this extend to the idea of the liminal, or what I like to call "threshold consciousness."

In the WildWood Tradition we teach our aspirants that the tween and twixt places are magically potent and desirable for ritual. For instance, if you stand where the land meets the sea meets the sky (on the beach at the edge of the water), you will be standing in a holy (whole) place charged with the power of the three worlds meeting. For this reason also are the sabbats, the esbats, dawn, midday, dusk, and midnight (the stations of the sun) considered powerful occasions. In fact, *az zabat* in Arabic means "the powerful occasion" and is considered a possible origin for our word *sabbat*. Ultimately all places are liminal and between, especially if we consider that as humans we tend to be entrenched in dualistic paradigms. Knowing this, however, we can utilise this understanding quite powerfully—here is the mundane, here is the magickal, here is the circle in between; I am liberated and free to bathe in the numinous!

If we are between the worlds, then it only makes rational sense that we are touching them all, and thus we bring further depth and insight into the preceding section on casting the circle. I cast the circle to temporarily construct an affirmed sacred space in which I am between the realms and thus able to contact all simultaneously (or one or two in particular). Therefore, by entering the tween place, I enter the River of Life, which surges through the veins of the body of the Goddess, and I become not only one cell of the greater being, but I am empowered to move and exist as the greater being—I actualise the deep potential within myself to be a creator. It is not only possible to create in a linear point-A-to-point-B fashion when we are within the circle (and we are at all times; we must merely be conscious of the fact), it is also possible to divine the future, know the past, and understand the present (due to timelessness), traverse the manifold realms, and consciously interact with spirit beings. When these things are done for the benefit of something more than self as ego—self as necessity, community, and cosmos—this is contextualised as shamanic. This is the true Witch's way.

The Elemental Pathways of Sacred Manifestation and Gnosis

"Earth my body, water my blood, air my breath, and fire my spirit."
Author unknown

After the circle is cast, we generally acknowledge and formally invite or invoke the elemental powers. Depending on the tradition, this is done as separate to an invocation of the Mighty Ones, or the watchers who guard and witness the rite (i.e., in the Gardnerian tradition). However, I tend to view the elements and the associated elemental spirits as synonymous with the Mighty Ones; or rather I do not work actively with the spirits identified as such.[39] My allies are the elements themselves; without them I am nothing.

Though Spirit both precedes and is the product of the elements' fusion, as the well-known Pagan chant above illustrates, the elements are the building blocks of life and thus activate and orient my consciousness. As I teach it, the elements also form an alchemical for-

---

39 However, I do work with the WildWood totemic guardians of the elements—horned owl/air; cunning fox/fire; king stag/water; mother bear and cub/earth. I am also beginning to engage with the Feri guardians.

mula akin to ancient shamanic teachings. When we take the general outline of elemental invocation starting in the east with air, and then travelling deosil to fire, water, and then earth (this is the general way in both hemispheres), we discover a pathway of manifestation from least dense to most dense. When we consider the energetic dynamics behind spellcraft (determination and manifestation), it becomes clear that the elemental formula empowers such practices. By air we first conceive of our desire; by fire we impassion ourselves to dare to seize it; by water our will is channelled and thus directed; and by earth it is made manifest and grounded in tangible reality. By touching and triggering the highest vibrating of the elemental planes, we affect the natural process of manifestation, which is initiated by desire. This we know as Witches through the various creation stories we have received and envisioned concerning the Cosmic Goddess, who dreamed herself into being, looked upon her reflection, and desired it—thus all came into being.

If we trace the circle backwards and unravel it, we begin with earth and end at air, where we originally began. When I was travelling in the UK in late 2008, I had an insight through the WildWood symbol and how the two serpents were always drawn meeting four times with their coils and then meeting and kissing at a fifth point. It seemed to equate with the fivefold kiss in my mind, and suddenly the elemental associations of each point kissed in the rite became known intuitively to me. If we regard the human being as a geometric or symbolic representation of the Divine, and we hold the head to contain the divine numen as limitless potential (as Qabalah and countless pre-Abrahamic cultures do), then we are able to lift the veil of separation that seeks to brand us as "lowly" or "sinful" and awake to our primordial, innate godhood. Linking this insight back to the fivefold kiss[40] to illuminate the point:

---

40 The words here are from the version of the fivefold kiss I teach to my shamanic Craft apprentices, which is derived from personal gnosis through a WildWood symbol. They relate to the elemental pathway of gnosis—tracing back from most dense (earth) to least dense (air) the circle of spirit, which contains and comprises the alchemy of the elements.

- We kiss the feet and say: "Blessed be these feet that dance upon the earth." I associate this with earth, as the feet stand upon the temple of the Holy Spirit, earth, the flesh of the Divine.
- We kiss the knees and say: "Blessed be these knees that kneel in the River of Life." I link this point with water (tracing the circle backwards to unravel it), as when we kneel we surrender and flow with the natural rhythms and tides of the world around us.
- We kiss the sex (womb or phallus) and say: "Blessed be this sex that burns brightly with the fire of generation." I associate this point with fire, as this is the holy seat of the generative life force. This is the portal to passion and unbridled desire.
- We kiss the breasts and say: "Blessed be these breasts that draw in the breath of life." I link this point with air, as behind the breasts are the lungs, which take in and expel oxygen to sustain the vitality of the body. This is the place in the body in which the air is literally enshrined.
- We kiss the lips and say: "Blessed be these lips, which sing the songs of spirit." I associate this point with spirit, the fifth element, because it is through the lips that we correspond and communicate with each other in an enlivened and raw manner. Our language—our words—shape our perceptions and therefore our realities. Words are a powerful tool of shaping consciousness, and spirit is the substance of that consciousness.

Thus, by unravelling the elemental circle back to its point of origin—spirit—we are able to transcend the illusion that we are separate and without divinity and truly see and intimate that at the core of our selves lies the hidden potency some call the Holy Guardian Angel, the

Buddha, or the I'dea—the indwelling Goddess. Knowing this sacred truth liberates the soul to soar to heights unconceived by the mind, which believes itself to be determined by supernatural forces rather than the creativity that flows through all—that is within us as well as without. The most dense is the most spiritual; the Flesh is the Spirit, and the Spirit is the Flesh.

East of Where?

When we invoke the elemental powers we are telling a story; we are consciously weaving our own soul strands in with the native cosmology of the world/s. We are conveying a message of innate belief to those around us, but more importantly we are illustrating universal laws that, if celebrated, will allow us to partake in the sovereignty gifted to all living beings.

We have previously established that nothing in existence is without its elemental support. On a chemical level, air represents matter in a gaseous state; fire is the energetic interchange of heat, electricity, etc.; water is all matter in a liquid state; and earth represents the physical forms which spirit becomes. Behind all of this is the prime mover—the spirit that pervades, informs, and directs all things. This subtle fifth element embodies the active intelligence of a living cosmos. When we invite the elements into our circle, we are retelling the ancient story of creation—we are alluding to the hidden principles that make up life. But where do we call the elements *from*?

Needless to say, the elements live in all things; in fact, the elements *are* all things. However, it is traditional to invoke the elemental powers from the four cardinal directions, as has been illustrated. Depending on the tradition and the geographical region, the elemental directional allocations will be different; however, the general placement is air in east, fire in north/south, water in west, and earth in south/north (depending on the hemisphere). Why the directional emphasis?

chapter two

A while ago I listened to an episode of *Elemental Castings*, T. Thorn Coyle's podcast. In this particular episode Thorn conducted an interview with Wiccan prison chaplain Patrick McCollum. The interview is quite lengthy; however, the two talk about the concept of the immanent divine and how one of McCollum's early teachers in the Craft took him to a vacant parking lot and asked whether he could see the sacred in this place. At first he replied that he couldn't, but after thought and reflection (and a word or two of insight from his teacher) he realised that yes, despite the asphalt-covered earth, everything present had its origins in nature—was and is nature. This realisation is one many urban Pagans and Witches come to cherish. The necessary step after receiving this particular insight is then to consider that humans have a very powerful and often unconscious impact on the world. We are able to manipulate, through sheer devotion and stubborn will, the energetic patterns that imbue the world of form with paradigms by which to arrange itself. Thus, despite the raw elemental origin of all things (because it had to come from somewhere), we have twisted and degraded our raw materials and created a world which rests on the idea that we are separate from nature, that nature is godless, and thus we are able to abuse our resources and destroy and desecrate those things that are essential to our livelihoods.

When we cast the circle to embrace the All and then call upon the elements via the directions we, introspective Witches, are then encouraged to look outward to the world of form which we walk, eat, and fuck in, and *celebrate* it—restore its inherent sacred nature. We invest attention in the outward world as an extension of our own internal identity. Without acknowledging our powerful connections, we forget what it means to be alive. When we look to the east, the north, the west, and the south, and then return to the centre, we are saying—"To the east of *here* is air, to the north of *here* is fire, to the west of *here* is water, to the south of *here* is earth. Here. Now. Forever I am in the here and now!" We become enlightened to the fact that we are standing somewhere in place; we are alive and conscious in the very centre of all things, because the horizon reclines into the infinite, and we are able to look out around and be faced with boundlessness, with life, as embodied by the elemental agents of power.

A Shamanic Rite of Casting the Circle and Invoking the Elements

I have decided to include a shamanic rite of casting the circle and invoking the elements for interest's sake and also to provide any curious seekers with a potential template. You will need nothing other than yourself as director of the rite and offerings for the spirits of place (e.g., frankincense), unless of course you feel drawn to include symbolic representations of the elements or you feel incense and candles would help to arouse the primal senses and create an appropriate atmosphere. It is important to understand that the words mean nothing without emotional understanding, insight, and investment fueling their expression.

Align the spiral soul and the three realms.

Touch your hand to the earth/ground and declare the following with conviction: "Spirits of place, I lay this offering for thee. May you welcome me as I welcome you. Blessed be." Place your offerings.

Face the east as the direction of the rising sun, hold out your power hand to shoulder level (point with your index finger if you prefer), and begin to walk deosil (with the sun) whilst envisioning light gathering and concentrating around your sacred space. Intone the following three sentences; one for each of the three rounds: "I am here. Here is now. Now is forever."

Once you have completed the circumambulations, the sealing and affirming statement can be made:

> *The circle is cast as it was, as it is, and as it always shall be.*
> *I am between the worlds, in all the worlds. What happens*
> *between the worlds touches all the worlds. What touches*
> *all the worlds changes all the worlds. So mote it be.*

chapter two

Facing east, clap three times loudly. After the third clap, as your hands pull away from each other, vibrate the word *east* through that space. Call forth the spirit of air with your power hand outstretched to the direction (at shoulder height): "East of here is air! Hail and welcome, air and east! Blessed be."

When you speak the word *here*, bring your outward-stretching hand to your heart. Upon uttering "hail and welcome," open both arms outward, as if to embrace and bring both hands to cross over the heart when sealing the invocation with "blessed be." Continue this for north, west, south, and centre.

Facing north/south,[41] clap three times loudly. After the third clap, as your hands pull away from each other, vibrate the word *north* or *south* through that space. Call forth the spirit of fire with your power hand outstretched to the direction (pointing straight and upward): "North/south of here is fire! Hail and welcome, fire and north/south! Blessed be."

Facing west, clap three times loudly. After the third clap, as your hands pull away from each other, vibrate the word *west* through that space. Call forth the spirit of water with your power hand outstretched to the direction (at waist height): "West of here is water! Hail and welcome, water and west! Blessed be."

Facing south, clap three times loudly. After the third clap, as your hands pull away from each other, vibrate the word *south* or *north* through that space. Call forth the spirit of earth with your power hand outstretched to the direction (pointing straight and downward for earth or straight and upward for fire): "South/north of here is earth! Hail and welcome, earth and south/north! Blessed be."

Stand in the centre of the circle, facing inward, clap loudly once and declare the fusion of the four elements. Call forth spirit and open

---

41 If you are in the Northern Hemisphere, deosil refers to a clockwise direction (rather than anticlockwise for the Southern Hemisphere), and thus the east-north-west-south route becomes east-south-west-north.

both arms as if to embrace the centre: "In the centre of here is spirit! Hail and welcome, spirit and centre! Blessed be."[42]

To unravel the circle after the work or communion, give thanks and bow facing the east and standing in the centre—farewell spirit, then earth, water, fire, and air (turning to face each direction as you do). The following devocations may be used:

Centre: "Here was spirit. Here is spirit.
Now and forever, blessed be."

Earth: "Here was earth. Here is earth.
Now and forever, blessed be."

Water: "Here was water. Here is water.
Now and forever, blessed be."

Fire: "Here was fire. Here is fire.
Now and forever, blessed be."

Air: "Here was air. Here is air.
Now and forever, blessed be."

To open or uncast the circle, simply walk widdershins (against the sun) and draw in the power of the circle through your receptive hand as you make three circumambulations. At your third and final circle, draw in the last of the power and then let it pour out through you into the earth. Seal this by saying:

*Into the earth for healing. The circle is open but
unbroken. Merry have we met, merry have we been,
merry may we part, and merry meet again.*

---

[42] A further spoken blessing that will accommodate and give reverence to the above, below, and centre direction is a WildWood circle-casting seal, which states "As above, so below—to and from us all things flow."

chapter three

deity and drawing down

"We are far more used to seeing the spirit world as an all-powerful cornucopia from whence all things flow, but in many spirit-working traditions gods and man work together."
    Kenaz Filan and Raven Kaldera,
    Drawing Down the Spirits

In my first book, *Spirited: Taking Paganism Beyond the Circle*, I devote an entire chapter to exploring the many "isms" that exist in the modern world's Pagan paradigms. These include polytheism, animism, pantheism, monism, henotheism, ditheism (duotheism), and archetypal psychology. This chapter will discuss the shamanic understandings of Deity as what I have come to call the "hidden potencies" contained within and saturated by concentrated divine power. This chapter will also delve into the age-old Pagan practice of trance possession, also termed "drawing down" or "aspecting."[43]

---

43 Reclaiming priestess Ravyn Stanfield told me it is a general rule in the Reclaiming Tradition of Witchcraft that the vessel does not fill with the deity's presence/force more than 70 percent. In this sense there is still a degree of self-consciousness and determined engagement on the vessel's part. This, then, is what is meant by aspecting—a light form of facilitated drawing down and not full possession.

chapter three

The Gods Amongst Us

"In Neopaganism, most of our important spirits are what we refer to as a god. To us, that generally means an entity who is bigger, older, and wiser than we are (and perhaps more than we'll ever be). It is an entity who sees further down the threads of causality and possibility and may guide or protect or teach us."

Kenaz Filan and Raven Kaldera,
Drawing Down the Spirits

In a shamanic worldview, which possesses powerful animistic perspectives (a world populated by spirits), the gods are powerful beings of mythic stature who know their purposes explicitly and are bound to fulfil them. Indeed, these cosmic hidden potencies are so endowed with meaning and devotion that they have become, apparently, greater or transcendent to the lowly humans who serve them. Shamans and Witches (and other aware people) know better.

In *Fifty Years in the Feri Tradition*, Cora Anderson wrote of the gods:

> It must be understood that the spirits and the gods do not have physical bodies as we do. Although the gods are much lighter life forms than ourselves, we are all in the same family. We can create much more mana[44] than beings having only etheric bodies. The gods need us and we need them.

This echoes sentiments made by Gerald Gardner in his published nonfiction works on Witchcraft.

Traditionally, Witches related to the gods as powerful and potent spirit beings who are either allies or indifferent; rarely is a deity considered to be particularly ambivalent towards a human being or the

---

[44] *Mana* is a Hawaiian word referring to life force; to me, it's another word for magick.

human race.[45] Depending on the depth and sincerity of your personal relationship with your own deities, guides, totems, etc., you may feel the desire or need to dedicate yourself as priest/ess or devotee to them. More broadly, I have termed the conscious relationships we cultivate with spirit beings *allyships*, as this word reinforces the mentality that we are working together to achieve a goal and unravel the strands of fate, and it seems stronger than the word *alliance*, with its political overtones. The idea of allies cherishes the animistic and pantheistic experiences of the world as alive and intelligent rather than stagnant and inanimate. However, I will explore these concepts in more depth in the next chapter.

When working with the beings we name deities, it is simply enough to know that we are also divine and thus no different, except in contrast with the subtle allusion that somehow the gods perfectly and explicitly understand their purposes and endeavour to fulfil them to every end. This is part and parcel of flowing with the pure will of nature. The gods are hidden potencies because they have also been called the Mysterious Ones (Feri/Reclaiming) and the Mighty Ones (British Traditional), and thus in creating working relationships with them we become the hidden children, because we have released the restrictive and damaging idea that we are somehow less than. Many Witches consciously embrace their spiritual pathways as roads towards fully actualising their personal divinity—to become (a) god/dess. This philosophy is echoed in West African religions such as Voudoun, which teaches that the lwa (the venerated spirits/the messengers and mediators of the one god) are our beloved dead who have evolved into powerful spirits encapsulating both cosmic and terrestrial orders.

---

45 There are deities in the various world pantheons that are viewed by the general populace to be adverse to the harmonious order of the universe, including Set, Satan, etc. However, time and philosophical discernment have both proven that these "evil" gods are actually powerfully dynamic and an essential component of the organic wellspring we call life. Destruction, death, and decay are necessary processes of release and rebirth.

chapter three

Why Are the Gods Important?

I call the gods the hidden potencies because in reality they are themselves embodied concepts—paradigms and energetic spirit maps who guide us through specialised ability and inclination. The gods of fire are necessarily, by natural evolution, denizens of the creative arts (Brighid), smithcraft (Hephaestos), volcanoes (Pele), and transformation (Kali). The gods of healing are also the gods of solar influence and light (Apollon), hygiene and cleanliness (Hygiea), and the plant world (Airmid). All things are connected; however, specialised groupings and resonances also naturally occur.

The gods, if we consider the Yoruban and Celtic teachings, are also our ancestors—the beloved dead that we have crowned "deity." We have gifted the immortal lines of procreation and perpetuation with powerfully literal and symbolic leaders and sovereigns. Those spirits which have become our deities draw their power from the cosmos at large and the raw forces in nature, which are the driving catalysts for change and growth; however, it is also true that they have become deities because of potent skill in one form or another. Consider the Tuatha de Danaan and the mythological cycles that tell their stories. The people of the goddess Danu form the fifth invasion wave of Ireland and thus add to the historical overview of the legendary island. Those of Irish descent are said to be born of the children of Mil (the Milesians, the Gaels) who conquered Ireland and created a treaty with the Tuatha de Danaan to honour their spiritual sovereignty and memory.[46]

The stories which speak of Lugh Lamfhada and Cú Chulainn speak of ancestral memories we have absorbed and passed on in sacred lineage. In fact, there are beliefs amongst various Celts today that engender the idea that the Gaels may be descended from the Tuatha, if not also from the various pre-existing peoples of Ireland also, such as the

---

46 The name of Ireland itself—Eire—derives from Eriu, one of the three sisters of sovereignty connected to the Tuatha de Danaan and their tribes.

Firbolg. After all, there are many tales of intermarriage and love affairs between the invading Gaels and the Sidhe folk (the people of the hollow hills—to which the Tuatha de Danaan retreated and made their homes).

I mention all of this because it is within such myth that we begin to understand that there isn't all that much difference between the human characters and the deities. There is constant and seemingly mundane prattle and pretence that goes on between the two. The stories also help to align the audiences with the mythic associations of various characters. For instance, Lugh is the many-skilled god of light because he was able to impress a gathering of his people by announcing to a gatekeeper that he possessed all the skills in one man that the people within the walls attested to individually. Many of those skills were mortal tasks and endeavours, but they are treated within the story as absolutely vital and on equal footing with apparently supernatural ability. It also has to be understood that the "supernatural" isn't necessarily *super* or *beyond the natural*; in fact, in traditional societies, it would be ludicrous to suggest that the gods were beyond nature, because nature is all things, and the gods are contained within that blessed mystery.

This would seem to beg the question: why are the gods important? Why do we venerate and honour beings that are not beyond our own potential? Why do we sacrifice to forces that are not in any way superior to us? The first answer or insight to be given in regard to this question is that Pagan traditions and teachings tend not to view the world as compartmentalised; the dividing lines are often blurred and inconsistent (eternal paradox). Animistic and pantheistic worldviews embrace all things as sacred and consider all things as possessing a numinous force that connects it intimately to the unitive force, which engenders and inspires all things to begin with, though there isn't necessarily a definitive beginning. Thus, the gods would never be considered above or beyond our personal potential, and that is absolutely why we venerate and honour them. The gods are perfectly aligned with their divine destinies and ultimately know their explicit and implicit purposes within the web of life. Thus to consciously open to one's will and to live expressing it in every moment is to become god-like, and, eventually, to transcend the illusion of separation and claim sovereignty of Self—and thus sovereignty of purpose and destiny. The gods are models and metaphors for us to align and ally with to further work towards actualising our potential and fulfilling our karmic purposes.

In *Spirited* I speak of how I perceive the gods if using a polytheistic lens. I described the idea that the deities are energetic force forms built around or deriving from the raw catalytic powers in nature—fire, lightning, storms, earthquakes, rain, etc. This also extends into the conceptual or emotional—transformation, fear, love, anger, radiance, beauty, truth, etc. I tend to be of the opinion and experience that all beliefs, ideas, and opinions are true in the sense that if they are able to marry with and integrate others they are viable, because they expand and open our minds and souls, rather than closing or limiting us from experiencing the transcendent. I think of transcendent as immanence extending beyond (panentheism)—the indwelling consciousness eternally existing and thus changing. When we are able to transcend and still understand that we are within Self, we are well on our way to personal godhood.

The Nature and Philosophy of the Hidden Potencies and Why to Honour Them If We Are Equal

Paganism forms the context for most, if not all, Witchcraft. Paganism translates most simply as the reverence of What Is as divine providence—that the here and now (and thus the earth) is the sacred manifestation (or body, if you will) of the spirit. This principle can only be truly understood when experienced. We have been so conditioned by the paradigm of duality that if one chose to say body and spirit, an instant conceptual dichotomy is entered into, rather than a simple, functional difference between two capacities. One is unadulterated, uninterrupted essence (spirit/force), and one aids in housing (body/form) said force in order for us to know it and for it to express itself to be known—an art of yearning surrendered to in the beginning. All, however, is divine.

Our deities, the hidden potencies, are creative stimuli (and creative encompasses destructive by its own natural definition). To illustrate the point made here: Demeter is considered a Mother or Earth Goddess archetype, and thus she is empowered by a dynamic current beyond her own ego (or the self which says "I am"). She is also who she is—Demeter—which gives rise to the fact that I am speaking of her now, mythically derived or not; she *is* because I am speaking of her and have a knowledge of her beyond myself (or the self which says "I am"). The reason for this is because there is a spirit within the "I" of Demeter that animates her myth and lends to her presence in the worlds. The spirit is hidden; it is a potency because it has deepened and exists fully on many levels, conscious of the variety of manifestations it adopts to carry out such a function. This hidden potency is magically and spiritually adept, not necessarily through guile (although there are spirits who have taken that road to potency) but because of the origin, process, and continued perpetuation of the living myth of Demeter.

The spirit of Demeter exists unquestionably so; philosophically speaking, no one could ever deny that. It is irrelevant whether we say archetype, demon, illusion, fancy of folk-need, or heroine; Demeter exists because I am speaking of her now with an awareness of her sphere of influence. I know her because she allows herself to be known, in the same way that this computer before me allows itself to be known, as does the chair I am sitting on and the vase of faded roses before me. They, too, are potent, because they exist and I know of their presence, and thus enters the Principle of Sacred Equality. Truly, the term god/dess or deity is a functional and experiential term we give unto spirits and things that reveal themselves to us from a "hidden" capacity as having influence and thus providence, and having direct relevance and thus relationship with our own living souls—potencies. In this way it can also be ascertained what is meant by the concept of lwa and orisha amongst the traditions that originate from the West African diaspora. That the spirits the Yoruban cultures honour are evolved ("transcended") spirits of ancestral lineage that have potentised through natural processes reflects this. They have embraced or flowed into or come from a mythic heritage and differentiated and self-actualised to the point where the ego is not the boundary, it is the origin supremely surpassed. It is the seed of a force field or form that lends itself to presence, providence, and influence on a scale not always personal, often universal, but definitely communal. Thus are the deities creative stimuli for the ongoing organic processes of what we call the universe.

This begs the question: why uphold a deity or honour a deity if I am quintessentially equal to them? The answer is clear: why not? If we are all divinely equal, the honouring of each part of that divinity may be attributed to a yearning for the wholeness of those parts and a reconciliation of difference by the nature of inherent interconnection. You are equal to your mother, though not in every function. However, if you did not honour your mother as a mother and love her for her care and compassion, the relationship would soon become severely imbalanced and negatively affect both of you until honour and respect entered the exchange of the relationship. Thus, we are all defined by what we are in relationship with. Our qualities evolve and adapt to what and who enters our sphere of potency—living myth. The fact that Aphrodite, Hermes, Hekate, and Persephone (amongst others) enter my sphere of potency, as I enter theirs in the name of honour and reverence, is because I identify an indwelling identity who is upheld and enlivened by their presence and relationship. I am who I am, beyond my ego, because of them, and they are uniquely who they are with me *through* me. Aphrodite, to and with anyone else, would not be *my* Aphrodite, but it would still be Aphrodite. Thus is the nature of spirits and of potency, hidden or not.

Deity versus Divine

Many religionists would equate Deity with the Divine as a "be-all, end-all" ultimate definition. This limits the spiritualist (as opposed to the religionist) from accepting that they are also divine, or of God. In the Craft we learn the art of drawing down, or voluntarily facilitating trance possession, which will be explored later. I want to emphasise here that what we call Deity is in fact simply a small part of the overarching "allness" that is the Divine. Divinity is simply another word for the radiance of all life, for the eternal blessing that is innately connected to being. Deity or deities (the gods, the hidden potencies) are within us and without us; they are archetypal, autonomous beings with their own agendas and accords. The force that many would call God[47] is not so much "Deity" as another synonym for the unitive force pervading consciousness. This is why we call it a mystery. Approach the gods as you would approach another human being, with invested interest in experiencing their unique truths and realities, and the response may astonish but definitely empower you.

Working with the Gods as a Shamanic Witch

The shamanic Witch perceives all things and beings as possessing personalised intelligence and awareness. Thus, as described above, the gods are worth our time and attention because they represent eternal potencies that we either aspire towards, honour as great and worthy, or would wish to temporarily borrow to enrich and empower a particular

---

47 Victor Anderson was quoted as saying that originally the word *God* meant "that which is to be reverenced," and that is all.

aspect of our own or someone else's life. Here I will describe the various allyships a shamanic Witch may have with a deity:

Soul God/dess

A deity to whom we are irrevocably and undeniably devoted simply *because*. These are the hardest allyships to explain or rationalise, and I would go so far as to suggest that they are akin to the concept or notion of soul mates within human interrelation. Without this particular term, many people would identify this kind of relationship as one with their patron or matron deity; however, I believe a soul god/dess extends far beyond the often utilitarian nature of divine patronage. A soul god/dess cannot be sought out, it merely happens—and when you know, you know.

Patron or Matron Deity

This is a deity to whom we are allied because of our own unique skills and predispositions. For instance, a poet may be allied with Brighid, a healer with Asklepios, and a dancer with Lord Siwa. A patron or matron deity may become a soul deity if the particular alignment is strong and karmic enough to enhance the connection. For instance, if you are absolutely defined by your poetry (as a metaphorical creative wellspring of all life experience) or by your healing (as an eternal pursuit to aid in the enhancing of the vitality of wholeness), then chances are the allyship will deepen into something much more intimate. Patron deities are either extremely obvious or elusive, and as with any kind of spirit being, there may be more than one (and often is), especially if you are devoted to a few sciences, arts, crafts, professions, etc.

Working Deity

This is a deity to whom we are allied on purpose. This allyship is often noted as Neopaganism's spiritual downfall, or proof of the rampant cultural misappropriation perpetrated by eclectic practitioners or styles. Cultural misappropriation does happen (in many traditions and situations), and my advice is to always approach external or foreign cultures, customs, deities, spirits, etc., with an attitude of humility, respect, and no expectations. It isn't a crime to pray to or work with a deity that is not of your people or culture; in many eras in the past, this happened often when Paganism was still the spirituality and religious attitude of the majority of Europeans. However, it is essential to first have reason and resonance if such work with a deity is to be embarked on.

My friends often joke that I must have a giant, blazing neon light blinking above my head attracting denizens of the spirit beings, as many a god and goddess have knocked on my door. I am allied with so many deities that my devotional weekly invocation to them has become a spiritual litany of sorts through which I become entranced and open energetically to their presence and influence. Each of these deities is either of my blood (related ancestrally through people and culture) or of my breath/spirit (unapparent connections—most likely karmic/past-life service). However, despite these subtle categorisations, it takes a while after initial contact is made for me to agree to the allyship, simply because I do not wish to impinge or misappropriate culturally or misinterpret the communications. Generally, nine times out of ten, the contact is for a reason, and an allyship based either on devotion, skill, alignment, or a circumstantial working arrangement will begin.

Again, with any deity (or any being, for that matter), it is important to first familiarise oneself with the associative correspondences (on all levels) and myths pertaining specifically to the deity. It pays to approach any deity with careful time and consideration so as to honour the exchange and empower it.

Power Deity

This is a deity to whom we are allied for self-empowerment. Sekhmet is a great example; she stalked into my circle in early 2007 after a rather horrendous breakup and, taking over my body, she slashed and tore away at the residual negativity, guilt, and remorse. She renewed my life force and vigour, and gave me strong claim over myself. I now count Sekhmet as one of my gods of breath, and ever since our first encounter I have discovered a strong feeling of past-life connection with her and Ubasti. A power deity is akin to the concept of a power animal.

Familial Deity

This is a deity to whom we are allied because of strong familial bonds, and this also goes for "chosen" family, i.e., strongly connected circles of friends and spiritual families. A familial deity may not necessarily translate as one in which you invest any particular emotional relationship; however, because of underlying and enduring connections with particular people, these deities begin to notice and greet us on equal terms. For instance, I would identify Siwa, Ganesha, and Saraswati as familial deities because they are my father's main gods, and he actively prays to them for my and my family's health and well-being. Energetically they have become working deities through concerted effort. Other familial deities may simply respect you from afar but never engender other contact.

It is important to understand that these categorisations of deity allyships are never so cut and dried, and that tends to go for all things in life, especially when related to the esoteric. For instance, it is quite possible for a familial deity to become a working deity and then a patron or matron and perhaps eventually a soul deity. In every situation and with every deity, it is important to regard all as individuals with their own unique worth and mythos. Retaining and cultivating an open mind and explorative attitude will ensure a perpetually fertile spirit.

A Note on Formalising an Allyship with Deity

I will not include any particular rituals here, as I have found in my own personal experience that when it comes to affirming the allyship (however it is defined, whether working deity or soul deity), the experience is absolutely relative to the deity, the feeling, and the situation. For instance, when it came time for me to acknowledge my priesthood to Hekate, I simply walked outside, sat down, grounded and centred, lit a silver candle, and spoke casually with her. I recall her responding in a very similar, laid-back manner. I did not create or affirm space, I did not utter a delicate prayer or invocation; I simply sat down with her and connected and communed, because that is what felt right. On the other hand, when I first chose to dedicate myself to Persephone's priesthood, I did devise a ritual for the winter solstice that would formally bring us together in such a union. It was the first time I employed traditional Greek ritual and language, and I did so to honour Persephone's legacy and origins. Ultimately, my advice here is to honour the deity and the burgeoning or affirming allyship by researching, communing, and intuiting.

Drawing Down the Gods— Trance Possession

The ability to become a vessel for the spirits—to draw down the gods into physical incarnation and to provide the deities a way to viscerally express themselves in forthright presence—is known as trance possession. Many contemporary Pagans use the term *drawing down* or *aspecting* (as in the Reclaiming Tradition) to mean the same thing. Drawing down the gods is not necessarily something that is included in the everyday Witchcraft handbook. Allusions to the Drawing Down of the Moon ceremony that occurs in British Traditional Witchcraft is often outlined, but the internal process undergone by the vessel (the Witch or priest/ess who will become the deity) is rarely, if ever, explained in any detail. In this section, I will provide a technique provided to my mother coven in early 2007 by our crescent-crowned goddess, who, while inhabiting my body, spoke a three-times-three (nine steps) method of effectively drawing down the gods. I am able to share it with any and all, but if you do pass on the method, please honour its origins and transmission by referencing the WildWood Tradition and our beloved lady of the moon.

The Spiritual and Shamanic Significance of Drawing Down

The practice of drawing down and trance possession links us with and reinforces our philosophies of immanence and deity versus/within divinity. We are able to perceive and interact with the hidden potencies and acquire secret wisdom whilst activating psychic wellsprings of power within. When we draw down the gods, we are effectively conveying a powerful message to not only Pagans, but the world: "The gods are within our reach, and we are able to know and bless them, and they are able to know and bless us."

One of my closest friends, Awen, has wisely observed that being able to witness the wonder and reality of the gods viscerally and vividly allows us to transcend the barriers which inhibit us from understanding the holy truth of interconnection.

In the introduction to this book, we discussed the magickal worldview of infinite possibility and how opening the door to the hidden worlds inspires initiatory awakenings of magnanimous proportion. We are able to access and be privy to wonders we would never have dreamed of previously. Infinite possibility becomes a concrete and overt reality rather than a metaphorical subtlety. The difference is this: Witches enact their innate ability to reach for the stars and become them rather than be limited to star gazing. Life teaches us that awareness of is awareness with, and thus even knowing and seeing the stars is enough for many; perhaps this is the distinction between Witches and "muggles." Witches embrace infinite possibility as personal destiny rather than a guiding metaphor. Either way, this relates absolutely to the issues of confidence and trust that allow us to welcome in the deities completely and surrender to their will.

In shamanic cultures, the fact that spirits are inclined to express themselves physically through our bodies and its varied functions is accepted cosmologically. Animism opens the door to perceiving the spirits, and engaging with them is a matter of consciousness, preparedness, and integrity. The spirits respect the same things humans do, as we are all of each other, and thus the Golden Rule applies here—do unto others as you would have them do unto you. Trance possession or mediumship of any kind is a gift granted by humility, ecstasy, and sacred contract. As devotees and practitioners of a wisdom path, we are concerned with the accumulation of knowledge for practical and poetic application in any dimension. It should also be noted that though ecstatic bliss is a product of successful trance possession, to correctly effect a drawing-down experience, ecstasy is a vital component.

If we consider the West African diasporic traditions once more, we discover that the lwa and orisha are prone to "riding" their devotees like horses. Most rituals within these religions are concerned with such outcomes, and great offerings and sacrifices are made before, during, and after trance possessions to secure the benevolence of the various spirits. I coined the term *allyship* to embody such interrelations between humanity and venerated spirit beings such as the gods and the lwa. Cultivating an allyship is akin to sustaining a celebrated friendship. Time and effort must be paid, as well as attention to detail, not to mention open honesty. We are then able to encounter the spirits on both their and our terms and create equal partnerships in which all parties benefit. In fact, it has been my experience that the act of ritual itself is an offering that pleases both the spirits and the human participants, as the energy is raised and shared communally, bringing us all to ecstasy.

Anyone who has drawn down will tell you that there are various states of consciousness relating to the depth of the trance and dependent upon the psychic predisposition, preparedness, and experience of the individual undertaking the ceremony. For instance, those who are natural seers are already open to the spirits; similarly, it is a shared opinion that Witches are very easy to hypnotise (if we are willing), as we voluntarily open ourselves to such mental and emotional suggestion regularly. Proper preparation in its many facets is a necessity as well. I encourage all of my students to either eat very lightly (meaning no meat and no refined carbohydrates or sugars) or to fast for the day of the drawing down (which generally happens after sunset), and perhaps also for half of the previous day. I touched on the sacred nature and magickal usage of fasting in *BLSS*; however, I encourage anyone interested in the details and dynamics of fasting to read *Shadow Magick Compendium* by Raven Digitalis.

Willow Polson references four levels of drawing down in her book *The Veil's Edge* in terms of personal consciousness and how it is gradually deepened until full, or authentic, possession is reached. These derive from an essay presented at an annual conference of the Covenant of the Goddess in the United States. However, many people, due to a multiplicity of reasons, will never reach (or let themselves reach) full possession; therefore, these "grades," if you will, do not so much form a hierarchy as much as varying layers of trance states as related to the act of drawing down deities. These four layers are as follows:

> **Enhancement:** The state in which the vessel feels imbued with the energy and mythos of the deity, but not necessarily its visceral energetic presence. The vessel is still very much conscious of ego.
>
> **Inspiration:** The state in which the vessel has deepened consciousness so that the presence of the deity may be received. The deity is connected on an energetic level at this time to the vessel and may direct the body with unique expression and offer wisdom

and advice through the vessel. The vessel's understanding of ego begins to blur.

Integration: The deity has merged into the vessel, and all acts and words are of a different nature—almost ephemeral or else very unlike the usual character of the vessel. In this state, some would say the vessel is half full with the deity's presence. The vessel begins to lose comprehension of self as ego and Self as deity.

Possession: The deity is fully within the body/vessel and acts and speaks of its own will and accord. Feats of great strength or other "supernatural" acts may occur, such as the raising of winds, the touching of hot coals or incense without harm or physical response, acrobatic movements, etc. The vessel may have no or little memory of the experience once the deity has departed.

I find this model a very useful one when explaining how trance aids in the facilitation of drawing down a deity. I tend to use a car-driving metaphor when explaining the contrasting states of consciousness. *Enhancement* I would refer to as "You are behind the wheel, and yet the deity is sitting and talking with you from the back seat." *Inspiration* is "You are still behind the wheel, but now the deity is directing you." *Integration* translates as "You are now sitting in the passenger seat, and the deity has taken the wheel." And *possession* would be "You are either in the back seat or the boot/trunk of the car!" Interestingly, when I first read *Drawing Down the Spirits* by Kenaz Filan and Raven Kaldera, they used a very similar analogy. Filan and Kaldera, both very experienced vessels/horses (a Voudoun term for the devotee who is "ridden" by a lwa), speak of more states than just the four described above, and so there is always more terrain to cover. Again, however, these models and metaphors are simply guides to establish some sense of clarity and orientation as we make our way through the mystery.

chapter three

Drawing Down as Holy Communion

"Well, you see, you don't really believe in the Goddess so much as you experience her."
    Phyllis Curott, *Book of Shadows* (Jeanette's words)

Many would consider the Great Rite (athame to chalice; phallus to womb; other to other) as the Holy Communion of modern Witchcraft; I believe the act of drawing down is similar. When we bring together the lovers of life[48] as underlying, eternal unity, we experience clarity within, and the revelation of One-in-All and All-in-One becomes living fact rather than guiding principle. In the same way is drawing down a coming together of apparently polar opposites, human and divine, to achieve epiphany through ecstasy—to see self in all things and embrace life as one's fate, karma, or wyrd is to acknowledge one's own sovereignty. Knowing this, it is hard to mistrust the deities as they share sacred space and time with us to communicate wisdom and inspiration to the world. It mustn't be forgotten that the deities also revel in being incarnate discretely in the flesh—of having potential potentiated and being able to actively express in the world of form the power and potency of the force that informs it.

The Holy Communion of drawing down concerns the liberation of the deep star self into accepting its primal origins—that we are each stars born of the dust "in whose feet are the hosts of heaven" (*Charge of the Goddess*). We re-member the disparate and lost pieces of our true shining glory and restore it to Origin—to peace and wholeness—ever minding that wholeness is the eternal journey to fulfilment led by primal desire. Holy Communion within any tradition essentially is the founding principle of what religion[49] means to be. Thus, when Catholics receive the Host, each devotee is truly eating and drinking

---

[48] I have used the name "lovers of life" to avoid the heteronormativity implied by usual perspectives on the Great Rite.

[49] If we consider *religio* (the Latin) as referring to a "relinking" rather than a "binding to or back."

the body and blood of Christ—the Anointed One—who will redeem and enlighten his believers to the kingdom of God. On this, Christ declares in the (gnostic) Gospel of Thomas: "Split a piece of wood, and I am there. Lift up the stone, and you will find me there."[50] Similarly, when Wiccans consecrate cakes and wine, the emphasis is on the eternal cycle or continuum of divine ordination, and so each Wiccan absorbs into him- or herself the power and potency of the powers that be, which shape and shift the worlds and are within and surrounding us all. Thus, drawing down the gods relinks us with our divine selves; the all-consuming truth illumines the rich darkness, and we come to the great mystery; there is nothing more and nothing less.

Drawing down a deity necessitates the coming forth or blossoming of our own inner divinity, or self-deity; the God/dess which dances within the soul and is the ancient, forever spirit flowing with the pure will. This is why it is never too late to reawaken to the world, because despite the terror we may inflict, the hatred we may sow, or the disaster we may intentionally wreak, it is always possible to claim sovereignty and total freedom from our past.[51] As the wise say, "Total freedom is total responsibility." Thus, in re-empowering ourselves and rejecting acts of evil, we are choosing to be virtuous—as Kresphontes says, "No dualism of 'good and evil' exists in the Immortal Cosmos. We become virtuous only because we choose to be such." The gods rejoice in this, because the difference between forgetting and forgiveness (of and through self) is that we are sorry and seek to make amends, to clean and purify the wounds, and to reawaken what was once perhaps a wasteland of our own making into a blissful paradise of limitless light. All of this is mere allegory in the face of the experience of Holy Communion, in whatever way it manifests. This verifies to me the claim most Witches make about our wild spirituality. Ours is

---

50 http://www.gnosis.org/naghamm/gthlamb.html

51 This is not to say that we can escape the consequences of our actions or somehow void our karma or absolve "sin" in the way of the doctrine of the confessional leading to forgiveness, as in the Roman Catholic Church.

an experiential spirituality in which we dive deeply into the mysteries, and only after returning do we formulate our beliefs (not expectations) on primordial patterns that are woven into our very being.

The Crescent-Crowned Goddess's "Three Times Three" Method of Drawing Down the Gods

In this section, I will outline the nine steps and describe in detail the practical significance of each as effective steps towards fully surrendering to Deity and also the autonomous internal processes that help to facilitate this transformation of consciousness. As mentioned above, this method is sacred to the WildWood Tradition; however, we are not barred from sharing it with others interested in experiencing trance possession. It is with humility that I share it, and I ask only the same if it is passed on. In all circumstances I ask that you please respect the origins of this technique.

Cautionary Notes

When I have taught this method in workshop or public settings, I have always stipulated that, apart from one volunteer who will become a vessel and draw down deity, all in attendance should only go as far as step 6. The reasoning behind this in a workshop scenario is a practical one: when dealing with the possibility of working with more than one deity, the beings could conflict in a disastrous way. We often hear accounts of Witches and Pagans calling in several deities at once to ritual who all derive from different cultures, people, and pantheons. Often, simply because of energetic unfamiliarity, the spirits clash and the ritual deflates or implodes. However, there is also the chance that the aspect of the deity who has entered the space at that particular moment bears a severe personal dislike to another participating spirit. For instance, it is often joked that calling Kali and the Morrigan into the same space would result in some form of epic explosion. When I reflect on that particular possibility, it does not necessarily feel to me

deity and drawing down

that the oft-anticipated outcome would be the reality, considering the deities are in many ways energetically alike. Also, when we consider the deities beyond their "superficialities" (Kali is also the Compassionate Mother, and the Morrigan is Sovereignty), we can begin to see that perhaps the combination might be a potentially beautiful one. I would qualify this by also saying that the individual calling in these deities should have a well-established relationship with both and be able to interface with their presences equally (or close to it). I feel that this is the reason I can acknowledge the whole litany of my deities in my devotional ritual each week and feel only uplifted and deepened by the divine presences as a whole. Indeed, I speak the names of Kali, Hera, Hekate, Aphrodite, Persephone, Zeus, Hermes, and Pan (et al.) all in under two minutes. Other Pagan friends of mine have noted, however, that when certain deities are present in ritual space with them, they personally feel repelled, or perhaps the deity even vacates the space because of some personal antagonism. Personally, I acknowledge these experiences, as reality is hugely subjective, and I respect people's preferences when conducting communal or public ceremonies; alone, in circle, I act in the way that is right and contextual according to my personal path and the allyships that I hold sacred.

Another reason is that certain individuals are not yet prepared for the experience, both psychically and physically. To draw down a deity and to ensure absolute safety is nearly impossible. After I have returned to consciousness after drawing down, I am told that I have plunged my hands into fire, touched burning coals, and pushed burning sticks of incense into my palms and wrists; generally, when the deity leaves my body, it is suddenly, and my body falls to the ground. Over time, my body has conditioned itself to recover almost instantly from these happenings. However, there have been a few occasions where I have been sick for days after or in pain because of a knocked head. Generally speaking, when the deity brings fire or anything hot or burning near my body, either I do not register the pain (during or after) or there are no wounds or markings afterward (unless the deity wishes me to remember; I have two small markings on my left wrist from Epona that did not hurt). I believe the reasoning for this to be that when the body is elated or deepened in a heavy trance state, which authentic possession or full drawing down beholds, pain is not a necessary factor; just like the yogis of India, we transcend the body's registration of pain. However, there are some who, in their desire to succeed and prove their worthiness before their community and the gods, fool themselves into believing that they are indeed possessed or have drawn down and go about committing acts that verify this and then end up severely harmed because of it. Not only should the physical level be considered, but also the psychic and energetic aspects. To short-circuit oneself energetically engenders a dangerous situation in which, if the space is not properly prepared or the invocation is not specific, any manner of undesirable spirit could take advantage of the opening and possess the vessel. I have seen this happen on more than one occasion.

Dealing with the spirits is an ancient shamanic charge, and as Witches of this vein we need to excel in this art, because to do so is to respect the risk. There is nothing in life worthwhile unless it includes the element of risk. Through skirting the boundaries of risk and sometimes completely surpassing them, we empower ourselves through a dynamic tension that expands, concentrates, and enlivens consciousness to such a point that our potency increases. This should not be embraced because it is wonderful to be potent, but because potency—when flanked by love and wisdom—allows us to better serve and celebrate the life force and therefore to commit to change that will have effect, deepening the consciousness of Self.

Psychically speaking, damage can occur if one has not committed oneself to the actualization of self-sovereignty through the celebration of personal freedom and thus the cultivation of self-responsibility. The onus is on the individual to determine the pathway of one's

deity and drawing down

life. Therefore, if one is not grounded and centred, balanced within the energy bodies (chakra/triple soul alignments), anchored, autonomous, and able to correctly discern and judge[52] the shifts, changes, and fluxes of energy, then to draw down and effectively surrender is not only impractical, it could potentially be devastating. One needs to be grounded and centred so that psychic sustenance is available at all times, and the energy spent on holding the deity can be instantly replaced by connection with the infinite wellsprings of life force.[53] To be balanced within the "energy bodies" is to create and effect a wholeness that speaks of autonomy, self-respect, and personal attunement to pure will as manifest cosmically (thus we are able to meet with the higher vibrations of a discarnate spirit being, if you will). To be anchored and autonomous is to be held by one's natural inclination to thrive and continue to perpetuate existence. One's ability to discern and judge the patterns of energy allows the individual a degree of technical relationship with the magickal charge and thus the ability to enter into the communion on equal footing. Remember, we are of the gods and equal to the potential of potency expressed via their presence and action in the worlds.

Trance possession is generally only undertaken in the presence of others in a ritualistic framework. It can happen spontaneously outside of ceremony; however, to actively and consciously facilitate it autonomously in an inappropriate context is foolhardy. Ensure that there are experienced Witches and/or mystics (even if it is only one other) who understand the dynamics of drawing down and are able to actively support you in such an altered state and catch you if you fall or faint! If you are intending to practise the technique alone, please only proceed to step 6, and create a conducive space (e.g., a cast and consecrated circle) in which to cultivate the experience.

---

52 This brings to mind the Lady of Avalon's statement to Morgaine in Marion Z. Bradley's *The Mists of Avalon*—"A priestess is tempered by her own judgement."

53 Sometimes this is not the case and the deity fills you with a presence beyond the need for sustenance.

chapter three

The final note of caution I will speak on is one that T. Thorn Coyle and I spoke about when I visited her during my 2010 US tour. We were on the topic of trance possession and how it was integral to our personal traditions and paths. Thorn mentioned that for those who stem from Abrahamic backgrounds (or from post-Christ Western ideologies in general) in which deity is considered absolute, drawing down can become a troublesome pattern leading to unhealthy codependency and irrational addictions. For instance, there are some who, on the "omniscient" word of a deity, may commit self-harm or another act of "if I say jump…" In essence, the cultivation of self-sovereignty as gone through above (and in more detail later) should establish a relationship based on the principle of sacred equality. When forming allyships with a deity or other spirit being, it should never be based on subservience; surrender[54] at times, yes, but subservience, never.

This then brings to mind the question: why sacrifice to the gods or give offerings? My answer to this is that when I am giving sacrifice or making offerings, I am doing so in the heartfelt spirit of gratitude for the manifold gifts deriving from my relationships with the deities and spirits. Also, the majority of the time the offerings I give to gods are pledged so that a particular task may be carried out on my behalf by the deity. Give and receive. Ultimately, if an allyship with a deity becomes unhealthy and imbalanced because of a need to feel that the "absolute" nature of the divinity is comforting, then the sovereign ability to commune viscerally with deity and become a vessel for it should not be considered. It would be foolish and dangerous to court the interests of a spirit in such a way, when respect of self is the determining factor for all respect in any given situation.

---

54 I believe the true point of communion between oneself and one's deity is when *all* surrender to mystery that is shared between.

Step One—Centre: *To Become Aligned with Self*

As in all Neopagan[55] rituals, before "work" is performed, it is wise to centre oneself and be rid of extraneous thought and distraction. Allow the cycles of breath to instil deep peace within and open to the connectedness of life.

To centre is to be still within. It is an essential prelude to all magickal work and, indeed, a fundamental skill for life in general. Centring merely requires a rhythmic cycle of breath and the ability to surrender to the eternal now held within the chaos. I call this the cosmos within chaos, the harmony within disharmony, the jewel within the lotus (om mani padme hum[56]); my friend Jarrah (Awen) might call it Harmonia and Eris. At the core of it, this practice aims to bring alignment with self, so that we start where we are and are able to bring forth the potential lying within, collected and concentrated as it is within the "I am because I am." The attitude of self as own divinity, rather than simply "I am," creating a finite restriction to the enigma of ego, is paramount to true centring. This is the most important step, and hence it is the first.

Step Two—Become the Truth: *The self Is the Self (the Microcosm to the Macrocosm)*

All is one, and thus you are as the Divine is—there is no difference but what the mundane consciousness seeks to impose. Become innately aware of this sacred truth: that you are of the same essence as the gods. You are holy.

We have spoken of ecstasy and its pathways and products; in and of itself, it is as a river flowing to the sea, which mirrors the moon, which reflects the sun, which is a shining star within the cradle of the

---

55 I refer to the term *Neopagan* in this context because it cannot be verified or necessarily assumed that the ancient Pagans internally grounded and centred in the way that is familiar to us now.

56 A Tibetan Buddhist mantra roughly translating as "hail the jewel in the lotus."

cosmos born of desire… Allow the truth to resound within, and let go—dissolve into the oneness, and reverberate it within your being as boundaries blur and restrictions fade.

If we are able to truly "transcend" and recognise and attune with the immanent Divine, then we are consciously capable of taking within and becoming a vessel for anything that is a part of the dynamic creativity. Those beings that are birthed of perfect self-knowledge and who move with pure will as testimony to the great mystery are attracted to others who would do the same (namely the individual undertaking such work). Becoming the truth and surrendering to it in Allness allows this transfer of consciousness, and it ensures and enhances the faculty of reflection between "I am because I am" and All-Self as it is. Being that, in truth, there is no distinction, and that we are all submerged in the mythic reality, we are able to emerge from unconsciousness as Divine Truth.

Step Three—Know Thy Way: *Prepare Your Temple (Your Body), Ready Yourself Mentally, Emotionally, Etc.*

Before embarking on a journey such as this, it is wise to be skilfully and properly prepared in mind, body, and soul. Make sure that you approach this communion with the Divine physically clean, mentally and emotionally aligned and centred, and spiritually receptive. If you feel the need, cense/smudge and asperge your body with the aid of an assistant (or in solitude).

We have spoken about fasting, and here I will reiterate it as an effective way to achieve spiritual clarity by physical means. Acknowledging and being conscious of the body as temple is integral to successful trance possession. Quite literally, the deity will be enshrining itself within the vessel (the body as a whole), and thus the vessel should be as mentally, emotionally, physically, and spiritually clean as possible. Centring and opening to Divine Truth helps to initiate the cleaning of self through energetic and wilful alignment. By further extending preparation and purification of the body/vessel through smudging and asperging (air and fire, water and earth) or anointing the various power centres, the energy is brought into excitement and higher vibration. It is at this point that the trance truly begins.

Another point to consider is group dynamics. When someone new is drawing down for the first time in a large, open ritual situation, he or she will often express nervousness. I tell everyone that nerves are a great thing to be experiencing before embarking on such an experience or journey. My advice is, as any self-respecting Witch would attest, to attune to the overall group energy (the hype and the excitement gathering as the ritual commences) and use it to "electrify," or raise, the energy within the energy bodies, or auric fields. This not only ensures a raising of consciousness and thus a swifter transition from mundane restriction to magickal infinity, but it creates a powerful charge of confidence within the vessel, enabling him or her to overcome the barriers of the mind, and accept and embrace the experience of drawing down as Holy Communion. A note for conducting drawing down in a group situation is that the other participants should be psychically supporting the vessel also—projecting energy to aid in the transition or entrancement. There should also be guardians, watchers, or handmaidens in place to care for the deity manifest and the vessel's body.

Step Four—Tread Over the Threshold:
Take the Risk and Trust

For there to be a threshold, there first must be a door. Now is the time to envision your door to the realm of pure divinity. See it as you will, in clear and vivid detail. Take the risk and trust implicitly in the gods as you take the great leap into the unknown. Do not merely tread over—fly!

The symbol of the door arouses a sense of "moving through." In *BLSS* I speak of "moving through" as an analogy for expansion of consciousness and accepting Divine Truth (self as Self). Thus, the power of the door and treading over the threshold (those liminal "tween" planes of consciousness) equate to raw being; "Moving through the centre is the perpetual, never-ending course and journey through the continuum of life. In fact, moving through is dancing the continuum."[57]

This is a vital step, because without learning how to properly surrender or the true meaning of perfect love and perfect trust, we are lost in a sea of confusion. However, because this is a vitally empowering, tried-and-true technique (with morphic resonance), each step effectively lays down a foundational and necessary stone on the path. We are centred, we have become the Divine Truth, we are properly prepared in every way, and thus we are opened to trust in the truest sense of the word. We are ready and willing to take the risk and fly.

Step Five—Release All Judgement: *Forget Your Binding; Know Only Truth Without Illusion*

Allow all preconceptions, cynicisms, and judgements to disappear in the face of the bright light that now saturates your very being. Let all illusion of the separation between self and Self dissolve and disperse. You are now in the present moment, which unfolds perfectly in the sea of eternity.

Once on the other side of the door, there is only pure light—the raw energy that enlivens all things and that is underlying and all-pervasive. You are faced with formlessness, and the only reflection is vital force. Now is the time to release all bindings to ego and relax into the infinite. Once again, the preceding step has allowed us to prepare for the necessities of this stage of the process; we have learnt the lesson of trust.

Forgetting our "worldly" selves and surrendering to the fullness of the Divine is not something we are taught to allow in this society. Trust is not cultivated as a living aspect of human interaction in this

---

[57] *By Land, Sky, and Sea*, 56.

day and age. I must admit there are pressing reasons for this, especially when considering children and their safety. However, this is a method for drawing down the gods and will obviously be undertaken in a facilitated manner, with others present.

During this step, it is important to understand that Witchcraft emphasises the importance of experience over and preceding the formulation of doctrine or beliefs, personal or otherwise. In fact, this is one of the reasons I do not class Witchcraft as a religion, even though my understandings of religion as a concept have evolved. Currently I define religion as an externalised expression of spiritual impulse felt and contextualised in community. With this comes agreed-upon terms, ways of conduct, rites and ceremonies, and common cosmologies. In contrasting this with the historical and current trends of Witchcraft in its many facets, only a few Witch traditions would fall into the category of religion; Wicca is one of these. Witchcraft, in my personal view and experience, is a mystically oriented tradition affirmed by the individual's own connection (and therefore experience) with the cosmos in its fullness. Therefore, like all other tried-and-true methods carried out by Witches to achieve altered states of consciousness or to create change, the idea is to let go of any need or impulse to analyse, judge, or evaluate during the process. After grounding and disengaging from the energetic conduct (the process itself—both internal and ceremonial), then it is, of course, appropriate and absolutely encouraged that we seek to interpret the experience, and the analytical mind is welcomed back in.

Step Six—Become the Light: *Dissolve into the Light*

The light that illumines your being in this moment now wishes to invite you to be at peace with it. Let go of your humanity, let go of ego, forget your name and everything that comes with being "you"—release. Become one with the light.

In many ways, this step echoes its preceding one. We must surrender to the One-in-All and, in letting go, dissolve into this powerful unity. In doing so, we become one with the light that is seeking communion with us. Our own humanity is laid aside in the face of universal bliss found in the rapture of the light in this other place.

The word *release* is very important here. The ability to truly release, surrender, let go and let God (or gods) in is vital to a successful trance possession. The ego is to be honoured only insofar as it is able to discern, on the mundane level, individuality from one another. Without this groundedness we might never be able to recognise personal communion, experience, expression, etc., and this contrast of self from Self is the essential differentiation that induces ecstatic epiphanies of consciousness becoming at one with universal awareness.

Step Seven—Ascend: *Grow into the Light*

Pure unity inspires diversity, and thus you feel a vague sense of "I am" and a space is created for the you-light to grow into. Fill this space entirely, yet do not become antagonistic or dualistic towards the "other" light. Keep the peace and oneness.

The short explanation above is quite ambiguous; this is because we are courting paradox, as Witches are apt to do and thrive on! The best illustrating analogy I could relate to the mystic core of this step is the celebrated Goddess Creation Myth made popular through Starhawk's writings and heavily influenced by the Anderson Feri Tradition.[58]

In essence, this step concerns itself with a sense of "I am" and individuality held and nourished within a unitive ocean. The "you-light" is the carved and vibrating vessel that your entire self has become at this point in the process. The key in continuing successfully to the next step, in which the deity will be actually invoked (the preceding steps have all been preparation), is peace. Allow the identification of "I" and "other" to be loose and natural, and let it be an organic impulse

---

58 Refer to Starhawk's *The Spiral Dance*.

or recognition rather than a psychological or emotional reaction. At this stage, all feelings of boundary and limits are vague, as if in truth everything is in a perpetual state of "could be." The light that is you and the light that surrounds the quality of "you/I" share a common and primal heartbeat; listen and open to the song swimming through the veins.

Step Eight—Draw Down: *Open Yourself to the Deity's Force*
Perceive the deity from crown to base. See this being in all its glory and further open yourself to its divine current. Feel the you-light fold back to invite the deity with clarity and purpose.

Now is the time to excite beyond measure the body in its manifold guises and expressions. The energetic vibration within the vessel is at such a high frequency that an overwhelming raising of consciousness to the point of absolute one-mindedness, or thoughtlessness, will occur. Signs of elevated consciousness include physical shaking, rapid eye movement (REM), sweating (or any extreme of temperature), weightlessness, trembling of the lips/arms/hands/head, and (felt only by the vessel) waves of intense power whirling across and through the body. Others may begin to sense or see a kind of growth or expansion (as will the vessel)—the eyes may change (sometimes the colour will also) and the voice will alter, as will the stance, gait, and generally everything else too.

The internal visualisation or instigation should be focused on perceiving the deity in its fullness, pressed up against your own body with a quietly ferocious intensity. I explain this concept as "toe to crown"; the visualisation should be absolutely specific. The feet/base of the deity up to the crown of the being should be parallel and resting against your own; this is felt as almost erotic. In most cases, you won't have to try overly hard to picture the deity; she/he/it will generally appear quite instantly the moment you inwardly call. This can be helped or triggered by an assistant who will make a verbal invocation.

As with every step, surrendering is key. By this time it should be a known reality and response within your consciousness, and thus when the deity's magnetic presence suddenly sweeps from directly in front of you to behind and within you, the mental "click" of absorption and acceptance is only allowed if you surrender.

Step Nine—Thou Art Divine: *You Have Become the Deity*

Let it be so.

Thou art Divine. The mirror that is raised by this recognition will reflect now, if all has correctly come to pass, the image of the deity residing within. As explained above, the degree, or depth, of the trance will depend on several factors; however, don't be surprised if the "I" suddenly descends into an abyss of sweet nothingness, though at first you may experience a keen clarity of lucidity. This often happens to me when I am drawing down. By the time I come to, I have lost memory of the entirety of the communion, and I must ask others to retell the details. I tend to at least recall the initial feelings and goings-on and sometimes the "last" sensations as well.

At this point also, as I mentioned above, we may experience a startling sense of lucidity and almost come fully back to an "ordinary" state of consciousness; this is a natural response, and the ninth step is simply a reaffirmation of the truth that we are all divine. This knowledge will vibrate through your being and carry you over this potential pitfall into the state of ecstasy required for true vessel work.

To reiterate the teaching of drawing down as Holy Communion, the ninth step is paramount to an initiation into mystery. I can do it no more justice than to simply say that this is not something truly known until it happens; and then, and only then, will the shine in the eyes truly change.

A Note on Gender

"Remember that in the ecstatic state it is very common for male gods to possess females and for female gods to possess males. As a matter of fact, the reversal of male and female roles in a body has long been considered a typical sign of the true ecstatic state."
Margot Adler, *Drawing Down the Moon*
(Sharon Devlin's words)

The idea that only a woman may invoke a goddess and a man a god is ludicrous to me. First of all, this opinion tends to be (at least in my experience) espoused by Gardnerian and Alexandrian Witches of the hard-gard predisposition. This seems either contradictory or hypocritical, considering the concept and dynamic of polarity expressed as sacrosanct in these traditions of the Craft. Although neither is overtly particularly shamanic, the ideas and liturgy celebrated within these groups have filtered out into the general Pagan populace. I therefore feel the need to state my argument as to why I call it contradictory.

Within the BTW (British Traditional Witchcraft) traditions, polarity is high order. There is a God (Horned One) and a Goddess (Triple Goddess), a high priest and a high priestess, an equal number of male coveners and female coveners (ideally), an athame and a chalice; the list goes on. However, the most powerful magickal experiences occur when the polarity is activated—or rather when the male and female elements come into contact with each other and commune, i.e., the relationship between the God and the Goddess, the Great Rite/Sacred Marriage of the priest and priestess (and in token with athame and chalice), and the cross-gender initiation (the high priest initiates all females and the high priestess all men). Therefore, it only makes sense that if this cross-gender polarity creates deeply resonating magickal experiences, a man should invoke the Goddess into himself and a woman the God.[59] Of course, I am not of the BTW strain and in fact have no animosities against it or its Witches (and have many wonderful friends belonging to such groups). I do, however, express concern when others exclaim to me that my drawing down a goddess is sacrilege or not true Witchcraft. Surely, if this was true, the many goddesses who have expressed themselves through me in the past and who will in the future are missing something.

As a queer individual, I have never found it difficult to banish gender boundaries, and I simply accept everyone for who they are, not merely as someone is defined by the respective sexual organs which may exist (or not) between their legs. This includes the deities. Being who they are, the gods tend to be able to blur the perceived boundaries more often than not. In fact, according to the concept of polarity (and the ideal of balancing these forces of masculine and feminine within), men should be drawing down goddesses more often, as should women with gods. However, you will never find me pushing this on anyone, privately or publicly. What I am attempting to bring to the surface is the inconsistency of various claims within the Pagan community and why it is more liberating and empowering to do as we are called to rather than be constrained by hidebound beliefs that owe more to political and sexual agenda rather than spiritual exploration or truth.

A Concluding Point

The above method is just that—a method. It is designed to act as a springboard and provide a prototypical example, which, if approached

---

59 In Gardnerian Craft, if a male is not present to represent the Horned God, the high priestess may strap on the sword and do so; however, a man must never represent the Goddess. I know of one Wiccan coven in New Mexico that requires its students to go on "gender benders" as they work through the degree system, so that true understanding of masculine and feminine is integrated, and the polarity has been activated within. As the elder of this group told me, "We are not concerned with outside genitalia so much as the energies within."

and adapted personally, will work effectively. For any technique to work it must be personalised and adjusted to meet the measure (so to speak) of the individual working with it. Also, this method is taught only as an introduction to the practice of drawing down or trance possession. Many WildWood Witches learn and teach the method and never use it personally when they are entering into the trance state for direct communion and interface with the gods. Energetically speaking, the same stages are experiences in a deepening progression; however, the steps aren't relied on explicitly—rather, they form a default if the possession does not strike spontaneously or right away.

For those who are natural vessels, there are no methods (although they may help to facilitate "gentler" possessions), and possessions can occur quite rapidly and without any conscious effort. This is the case for me. My work has actually been to ensure that I am confident and potent enough to cultivate my sovereignty of Self so that I may be aware of when and where I am entering into a contract with a spirit to serve as vessel. It is not healthy or desirable to be "used" by a deity or spirit at any given time; in fact, this can be very dangerous, and it has happened to me on several occasions, though the deities and spirits were by no means malevolent. I had not yet become accustomed to my own disciplines and had not truly integrated the wisdom I sought. I actually feel the spirit or deity's presence as a "knock" against my aura, and I then decide based on the context and my own personal circumstance (emotional/mental state) whether to surrender and fuse or not. This may happen while I am in public and surrounded by people; I obviously make it known to the spirit/deity when the context is not appropriate. On other occasions a deity of a close friend would like to directly speak with the devotee, and so I will let my friend know and, depending on the answer, may enter into possession for the communion and interchange to take place. I am humbled in this work as a vessel.

We must remember and appreciate that the spirits are not necessarily human, and therefore they do not share our conventions or feelings for what is and is not appropriate according to any given context. We are dealing with raw, potent forces and beings who constitute the living cosmos. The lesson is the middle road—balance.

For further information, please refer to the already mentioned *Drawing Down the Spirits* by Kenaz Filan and Raven Kaldera. It is a must-read for anyone exploring this terrain.

chapter four

spirit allies

> *"Moreover the follower of the Faerie Way does not seek to command such beings, magical sword in one hand, spellbook in the other, like a medieval magician. Cooperation, not compulsion, is the watchword."*
> Hugh Mynne, *The Faerie Way:*
> *A Healing Journey to Other Worlds*

I have already used the term *allyship* within this book; however, I will go into explicit detail about it in this chapter.

The idea behind an allyship with a spirit being is rooted in the concept of sacred equality—that all things/beings that exist are inherently equal and empowered to express that fact. If we accept sacred equality as truth, we are then inspired to approach all beings within the All as "of worth." The important distinction is that all beings are born self-caused, self-knowing, and open to change and evolution in the forever-journey of experiencing, enhancing, and emulating implicit wholeness. Therefore, each and every being is unique and possesses particular stories and skills. I do not call a carpenter for medical advice, unless, of course, that carpenter is also somehow a naturopath or doctor, which, though not impossible, is unlikely. However, individuals are not bound by their professions or what they do for work; there is infinite depth and potential in each and every one of us. To embrace this reality is to open to a plethora of opportunities in rediscovering hidden treasures within each other or forging new connections entirely, perhaps with others or through the ancient art of evolution (people do and can change or transform).

Why am I spending time waxing eloquent on human nature rather than discussing the spirits and their ways? It is because humans are spirit beings too! We are as spiritual and powerful as any other being; knowing and working towards this is what activates our innate ability or nature. I always say, why fear the spirits when we have both a spirit and a physical body? After all, according to the alchemical formula contained within the elemental sequence of casting the circle (discussed previously), the most dense things are the most potently and directly spiritual. This would tend to inspire the thought that because spirits are discarnate, they are above our own physical laws! This is absolutely true, and so are we, if we would wish it. Spirit flight, the Sight, spellcraft, drawing down, and the very ability to communicate with discarnate entities and share power between us are all evidence of this shamanic skill. Perhaps this is why historically and culturally Witches were/are feared and linked with the faerie folk and other spirits. I won't lie and say there are no reasons to fear a spirit, or a Witch for that matter, but unless you assault, attack, or offend one, you will have no reason at all.

Witches of all kinds work with spirits; it is a distinguishing factor of our spirituality. Firstly, if a Witch is not deity focused (and so many are these days), he or she will be focused on working with magickal allies of some description. This is the very reason I coined the term *allyship* (over and rather than *alliance*)—to emphasise that we are ourselves, as Witches, part of a circle of allies working together in harmony to achieve goals, fulfil desires and needs, share knowledge, and nourish wisdom. We serve one another.

"Reverence and honour cannot be given when one has no understanding of the relationship between the recipient of the gift and the one

who offers it. In a true and meaningful exchange, neither one does exclusively the giving or receiving—both mutually participate in the sacred moment. Balance is maintained."[60]

The image I use is of a circle of friends holding hands without a break in the chain, as opposed to the concept of a circle of spirits or forces congregating around a central figure commanding and directing an army. This is not to say that on various occasions one spirit (this includes you) may be more to the forefront or centre of the work than the others, but for success—and having a circle of allies of many skills secures this—all agree to work in unison/synchrony towards achievement and fulfilment. An example of when the Witch would be in the centre of the circle would be during a spellcasting, when it is the particular desires or needs of the Witch that are being worked towards. An example of when a deity would be in the centre is during a devotional rite. However, all are sharing in the experience and therefore being affected by it. The central position is taken only for utilitarian or practical reasons of focus, potency, and general energy dynamics.

Forging an Allyship with a Spirit Being

Whereas the word *alliance* tends towards the political, the concept or feeling behind the term *allyship* is one of deepening connection and celebration. Honour, integrity, truth, balance, dedication, friendship, and perfect love and perfect trust are all key elements in the maintenance of an allyship.

Forging an allyship with another spirit being can often mean perseverance. Initially, however, there must be adequate cause for the initiation, and this can mean unknown attraction or endearment towards one another; this is enough for great loves. Whatever the conjoining reason is, and once it has been established that there is certainly a connection (for the moment, at least), an allyship can be entered into.

---

[60] *Spirited*, 132.

chapter four

As with working with the gods, there are various levels of relationships that will be shared with the various spirit beings. Some allyships will be circumstantial and related to locale (for instance, my allyship with various traffic lights); others will be more permanent and based on profession, inclination, or personality. An example of this would be my relationship with the elementals and particularly the sylphs and the gnomes. I like to sing and do so when I am alone quite often; therefore, I gained the attention of the sylphs from childhood onward. The gnomes I attracted into my life through the many prosperity spells and charms I have woven for myself and others; they have always been of aid in finding lost objects and also in helping to ground and relax me after high-tension situations.

These allyships, while not expressly initiated at any particular time or for any conscious reason, are truly within the realms of the "power-with" attitude or dynamic that Starhawk speaks of as shared power in communal context. All allyships are found within the idea of community, which means "shared unity," and thus we are all encouraged to look beyond the anthropocentric and to consider what and who else supports us in our continued celebration of existence. This is precisely the reason I do not believe it is accurate to call any Witch a solitary, for we are anything but. We are constantly and consistently joined to the whole of the vibrating web of Wyrd, and our awareness is on enhancing and deepening these connections at all times. In the WildWood Tradition we use the term *wanderer* for those of our fellowship who do not work within the coven structure.

After a certain period of time working and celebrating with a particular spirit being (or beings), a conscious allyship may be entered into. The communion to establish such an allyship does not necessarily have to occur within a ceremonial context—unless, of course, you feel that would enhance the experience. The simplest thing one could do is to align the spiral soul, open to the spirit being (call), and await arrival. Once the spirit being has arrived, speak openly and honestly with each other, and an allyship will either naturally eventuate or the idea may appear repugnant to the spirit and perhaps even to you. The latter is highly unlikely, especially if you have been sharing sacred time and space for some time prior. Again, if the allyship has been forged, to affirm its concrete reality, an offering may be shared. These offerings, as discussed above, are to reflect the inner divine nature shining within and in the moment becoming one and merging.

Sharing Prayer

When I pray to the spirits of the sky realms and the gods and goddesses of weather for either rain or clear skies, I begin by grounding and centring and then opening a channel of communication between land and sky. I vibrate the essential, direct meaning of my prayer into the ether and await affirmation of reception, which may come as an intuitive understanding or feeling, a strong response within my body, or a clairaudient or clairvoyant response (yes, no, "we'll see what we can do"). Of course, the spirits I pray to (though I am general about who they may be in my wording) are specific spirits of skill (weather and sky wisdom); however, I am also working with genii loci (spirits of place). Thus, depending on where I would like the effect to directly manifest, the spiritual entities (in particular) may vary; however, they are within the same family. This is all essential knowledge if one is to make prayer.

Prayer is meaningful communication, communion, and collaboration between beings within the cosmos. An allyship exists necessarily, despite the fact that it may be temporary or completely situational; either way it naturally occurs due to the shared prayer. A prayer can be a petition in the simplest sense; however, the way I experience prayer in a Pagan context—and especially as a Witch with ignited consciousness—is as a form of pooling resources to potentiate something specific. For instance, when I pray for clear, azure-blue skies (with few white, wispy clouds) and star-sprinkled indigo night-skies, I visualise this outcome as I would when casting a spell, but I offer the visualisation as a communication of intent and meaning with a spirit being (or group of beings) whom I consider to hold sway or skill in manifesting such a situation (sky and weather). Depending on how I am feeling about the situation, I might also spirit-fly into the sky realm and share counsel with the corresponding spirits. In *The Earth Path*, Starhawk speaks of one of her early Craft teachers saying to make friends with the clouds if she wanted to work with the weather. Friends are inclined to help one another, thus the connection is a mutually beneficial one of exchange and balance. Again, a successful prayer is not necessarily about the outcome, but it definitely concerns the communication.

A shamanic Witch may take a leaf out of the prayer book of the ancient Greeks. In ancient Greece, traditional prayer was often simply performed outside or directly in front of a house shrine or altar. It was generally done standing and with arms opened as if to embrace the deity or to offer up/out/down the prayer.[61] I will generally pray in this way, although at times I will also pray in the Balinese way—kneeling with both palms pressed together and placed to sit against the crown of the head and pointing to the heavens.

The Beloved Dead

"Ancestors, we call to/Light the flame remember you/through the veil, across the tides/we will remember your lives./All those who are a part/of our families and our hearts/sail across the sunless sea/wheel turning eternally."
Gede Parma and Hannah van der Es of WildWood

How can one begin to speak of the beloved dead—the ancestors who are the very reason we now walk the earth? During my weekly devotional ritual, after energetic alignments and space preparation and

---

61 This depended on to whom one was praying, e.g., if the deity is a chthonic, or underworld, spirit, then the hands and arms are directed downwards.

affirmation, I open my hands to either side as if holding the hands of someone on my left and my right—and indeed I am, for on the left is my mother and the people before her and the people to come, and on the right is my father and the people before him and the people to come. I then chant the following: "I stand in the centre—I am the seed, I am the outcome, I am the holy *immrama*, soul-journey of life!"[62]

If we truly reflect upon it, we are the entire sum of our ancestral line and then some. We are who we are, unique and therefore potent, but also the result of the blood, sweat, and tears (quite literally) of our ancestors and the stories they wove. We might not necessarily like our stock, and various members of our family tree may have committed unjust atrocities that we do not agree with or endorse; however, we must remember them. Re-membering in the true sense is reconciling the disparate pieces and fragments of memory and creating a new wholeness from their coming together. Therefore, in remembering there is forgiveness, rest, and revelation. We understand that through the tests and trials of time there is hope. Hope, the last to leave Pandora's box, is the stuff of life. We can only hope, because we cannot always know or be completely certain. To hope and trust and love—these are the blessings of the revelations of the ancestors.

When honouring the beloved dead, we work a timeless and powerful magick. We are ensuring their immortality in one way by honouring their names and telling their stories, and we are blessing memory and therefore the wholeness of reality by reflecting upon death and the hereafter. At the annual Spiral Dance ritual held by the Bay Area Reclaiming Collective in San Francisco, I experienced a potent honouring of the beloved dead.

Around ten Witches, whom I will name "death walkers" for the purposes of this book, walked a constant circle for nearly two hours speaking aloud the names of the beloved dead that had been contributed by

---

62 The term *immrama* refers to an Old Irish classification of mythic stories relating to the voyage of heroes to the otherworld. In the context above, immrama refers to the voyage of the soul through the deepening of the ancestral legacy.

the community. They were all of those who had passed through the veil since the Samhain before. I sat entranced with my friend Abel and heeded silently the private calls of desperation, of solidarity, of hope and peace. I felt true redemption in that meditation of sonic soothing—even restoration. At the culmination of perhaps twenty or thirty names, all of the death walkers chanted "what is remembered lives," and the earth folk gathered around them reverberated it back. I have a saying—"The song of our ancestors is the laughter of our children." To honour and acknowledge the beloved dead, the ancestors, is to take a spark from that firebrand of hope and kindle the fires of warmth and illumination that will hold and keep us through the darkness and death.

In the Legend of the Descent of the Goddess given by Raven Grimassi, the words "and in death we are shown the way to her communion" are given. In *BLSS,* I speak at length about the importance of embracing death as a threshold to renewed consciousness—to a reawakening of the amazing depth of potential we hold inside. The beloved dead are the spiritual allies who are willing and able to aid us in reclaiming these gifts. In fact, studying and reflecting on ancestral heritage will lend many clues as to why, how, and what this potential is.

Here is a ritual of reparation and reconciliation inspired by a part I contributed to a ritual at the inaugural Australian Reclaiming WitchCamp in Victoria. The sacred intention of that particular night's ritual was "we open our ears to the dreams alive in the land and step through the healing door." It was essentially a ritual in which we created a spell by holding our ancestors' dreams in one hand and the dreams of the land in the other. We then stepped through the healing door into balance and truth by crossing those dreams over our hearts. Before we embarked on sealing this spell, I wove together a spell of my own to charge the four bowls of water in the centre surrounding the altar. As each of us spoke aloud the names of our ancestors and their dreams, I drew these threads into one tapestry. As I moved to the centre of the circle with a pulsing, throbbing core of magick between my hands, I sung a variant of the chant that opens this section. The circle answered and joined the song. I sprinkled sacred ochre collected from a stream that travelled directly to the sea into each of the bowls, and as I did, the charge, the spell, became a part of the vibration of that water. Four graces carried those bowls out to the circle, and each person had the opportunity to wash their hands—not to clean themselves of any perceived past sins of the family, but for healing and wholeness, which only come with re-membering. We firmly wished to root ourselves in the eternal now and be cleansed within that undying moment. The following ritual takes its inspiration from that experience, which was a communally shared one, at Australia's first WitchCamp.

The Waters of Reparation Ritual

You will need:

- A ceramic or glass bowl filled with rain or spring water and large enough for you to dip your hands in
- Red thread
- Soil from the land you live on

Perform the three realms alignment (page 35) and the rite of divine fire (page 15).

The bowl of water should be placed directly in front of you as you kneel, sit, or stand; place the red thread to the left of it and the soil from the land to the right. You may choose to cast the circle for this rite, but it is not necessary.

As you breathe into the holy centre, begin to become distinctly aware of the water sitting before you—the water of rain or spring. Give reverence to the origin of this water, and invest sacred presence in the here and now.

Taking the red thread into your left hand, focus inwardly and honour your ancestors. Perform the following blessing as you hold out both of your hands to either side as if you are holding hands with invisible loved ones (which you are). Say aloud:

> *My mother on my left hand and the people*
> *before her and the people to come.*
> *My father on my right hand and the people*
> *before him and the people to come.*

Cross your hands over your heart, still holding the red thread, and say:

> *I stand in the centre—I am the seed; I am the outcome;*
> *I am the holy immrama, soul-journey of life.*
> *And thus do I call upon my ancestors.*

Visualise and feel the ancient and ever-renewing legacy flowing through you now from both lines that meet to merge in you—the third principle. As you focus on this pulsing power, charge the red thread in the name of your ancestors. Ask yourself, what were the dreams of my ancestors?

Place the red thread in the bowl, take the soil in your right hand, and focus outward to the land and to all that is a part of it (even you). If you are not already outside, walk outside now and sit upon the earth or at the base of a tree or where the land meets the sky meets the sea. Breathe into the holy centre and listen; open your ears to truly listen to what the land is whispering. What does the land dream of? Try not to ask any questions of and for your own ends—simply yearn and seek to merge with the land and its presence. When you have received the land, move back to your bowl of water and recite the following:

> *The land is dreaming*
> *The land is dreaming*
> *The land is dreaming*
> *And I have heard.*

Pour the soil into the water and cross your hands over your heart. Rock back and forward as you chant the following until you feel the natural crescendo and release the power into the water:

> *By the blessings of my ancestors*
> *I am made to be here now.*
> *By the sovereignty of land*
> *I am given this holy hour.*
> *By the dreams of long ago*
> *And the dreams that linger on*
> *I pray that I will reconcile*
> *What has been and gone.*

Throw your hands out to the water, and direct the raised power into the bowl. When you are ready, dip your hands into the charged and blessed liquid and wash your hands. As you do this, feel any blockages clear and any negative attachments swiftly dissolve; you are free of anything that would bind you.

Lastly, as you breathe deeply and rhythmically, listen to your Own Holy Self. What are your dreams? Have they been realised, are they unfolding? How do your dreams transform and renew themselves? What is your dreaming—your living myth? Meditate on this more deeply until you feel that you are able to make a personal pledge of reconciliation of self to Self. State and affirm this aloud as you pour the water directly onto the earth. The rite is complete.

Animal Totems and Familiars

In the introduction I listed several parallel factors that link traditional folkloric beliefs concerning European Witchcraft with shamanisms the world over, and one of the key underlying commonalities is a strong relationship (allyship) with the plant, animal, and mineral worlds. All three worlds can be considered familiars or totems in the true sense of the word. A familiar spirit does not always directly connote animal companionship, as is the popular opinion of a Witch's familiar; however, familiar spirits (the apparently demonic spirit helpers of Witches) often disguised or presented themselves as animals. The animals I present here are strongly associated with European Witches and have age-old shamanic links.

The Cat

The concept that black cats are an evil omen is not necessarily a native European belief. Originally it was a Celtic belief that having a black cat cross one's path was a sign of good luck; the blessings of the old religions become the curses of the new. Cats have long been considered extremely psychic, in-tune creatures and are known for their independence, secrecy, and elusiveness. The cat's medicine[63] is considered to concern independence, psychic insight, wisdom of the night (and otherworlds), and deftness in grace.

The Dog

"Man's best friend," the dog is the domesticated descendent of ancestral wolves (emissaries of the ancient god of death, dark, and decline). Hounds accompany the Witches' goddess Diana on her hunt and are therefore directly associated with the Lady of the Moon and with the mysteries of life and rebirth. In his many works on historical Witchcraft in Europe, Raven Grimassi comments that the presence of hounds (or a stag) depicted with Diana is a symbol of the God in animal form accompanying her on the hunt that is for and of him. In various traditions of Stregheria, the wolf and the stag are the archaic forms of the Holly and Oak Kings, respectively. Dog medicine is composed of loyalty, protection, guardianship, entry to the underworld (as in Kerberos and the wolf of Stregheria), and strength of conviction.

---

63 Here this word is used in the Native American sense—the indwelling magickal charge, potency, legacy, and wisdom of the being.

spirit allies

The Hare and the Rabbit

Both the hare and the rabbit have long been considered manifestations of Witches' familiar spirits in common folklore. The famous self-confessed Scottish Witch Isobel Gowdie openly spoke of her Witchcraft to the Scottish authorities and commented that she often changed into the form of a hare when travelling to the sabbat. Another strong association with Witchcraft comes from the lunar connection of hares and rabbits as seen in the moon. The wisdom of the hare and rabbit concerns fertility, the moon mysteries, secrecy, swiftness, trickster magick, and humility.

The Owl

Raven Grimassi mentions that the root for the Italian word *strega* (meaning "Witch") is *strix,* which refers to a screech owl. Marija Gimbutas associates most birds of prey with a bird goddess cult that, according to conjecture and several thousand unearthed bird goddess artworks, was popular in Old Europe. The owl is a largely nocturnal bird and is thus associated with the moon and her influence. In the Aegean/Mediterranean regions, the moon is largely associated with a feminine divinity (whereas in Northern Europe it is the sun that is associated with the feminine), and therefore the owl is again directly associated with the Goddess of the Witches. She is a totem of the Greek goddesses Athene and Hekate, the latter being the Titan queen connected to all things magickal and mystical—definitely a Queen of the Witches in the true sense of the term. The owl's medicine is of wisdom, second sight, the skill of the hunter (acquisition), and the world of shades and ghosts.

The Raven and the Crow

Almost cross-culturally, the raven is considered to be one of the first spirits (if not the first). In various Native American mythologies, the raven is the creator of this world. Similarly, Raven Grimassi records a hereditary Italian folktale in *Hereditary Witchcraft* in which the raven is the creator of the earth and of humanity. Consider also the plethora of well-known Pagan authors and elders today with the title "raven" in their names. The raven and the crow are associated with the mighty Morrighan, the Irish battle queen of death, sorcery, and sovereignty. Raven or crow is a messenger of the otherworld and acts as a psychopomp, or even as a harbinger of death, and therefore represents transformation and renewal.

The Snake and the Serpent

The snake and the serpent have an unfortunate associated stigma. Colloquially, the idea that someone is a serpent or a "snake in the grass" translates as ruthless, insidious, and decidedly malevolent behaviour. However, the long history of the snake as a symbol of the old religions is well established. The snake sheds its skin and thus is associated with regeneration, rebirth (life from death), and health. The serpents on Hermes's famed *kerykeion* (Latin caduceus) and the single snake entwining around the rod of Asklepios (blessed son of Apollon, the deified physician) are still seen on the sides of ambulances in Australia and decorating many an international logo concerned with health and healing (including the World Health Organisation). The mighty Celtic goddess Brighid is also associated with the snake, as on her holy day of Imbolc (the quickening) the serpent is said to rise again from the land (also a euphemism for the waxing strength of the masculine fertility principle). Brighid too is a deity of the healing arts. The serpent's medicine is strong and old—wisdom, fertility, renewal, waterways (that lead to the "world-encircling stream," the ocean), magick and sorcery, healing and balance.

The Goat

The goat is another dark emblem of Witchcraft in ignorant minds. The trial records during the Witch hysteria often link the goat with the devil; apparently it was a popular form for Satan to adopt. The goat is a horned animal and thus is linked with the Horned God and especially with the Greek Pan. The goat is also half of the infamous Baphomet as depicted by the French magician Eliphas Lévi. Raven Grimassi speaks of several Roman and Italian myths that link the goat with the fertility principle (again connecting with the Horned God). During Lupercalia, which is celebrated around the same time as Imbolc in the Northern Hemisphere, women and men would run naked through the streets as the men whipped them with straps of goat hide (at an earlier time it may have been deer or stag hide). In an Etruscan tale, Juno orders the infertile Sabine women to copulate with goats in order to restore their fecundity; however, a priest interprets this as being flagellated with goat hide. Therefore the magick of the goat speaks of unbridled fertility and sexuality, the mysteries of the Horned One, dark wisdom, and the strength of earth.

The Stag

In the WildWood Tradition we honour the Stag-Horned God as sovereign of the light tide (from Yule to Litha); however, the stag is the promised one who brings and blesses the harvest during the onset of the dark tide (from Litha to Yule). The Stag King (crowned at Ostara in our mythos) represents the powers of light, growth, and gain, and thus, of course, the concept of fertility. The stag is a symbol of kingship and the hunt, and again is associated with the goddess Diana in her various forms. He is Kern, the Horned One of the Streghe, and is thus one aspect of the two-faced god (also known as Janus or Dianus). The stag is carrier of the souls to the underworld, the lord of death and resurrection; he is potency and life force overflowing and the awful truth of raw nature.

The Frog and the Toad

Another familiar spirit commonly seen accompanying Witches in folkloric depictions is the frog or the toad. Though two completely different subsets, the frog and toad are popularly linked when associated with Witchcraft and magick. In many cultures, the frog represents the dew of the heavens and the rising of the sweet waters of the earth to nourish and sate the parched land. The toad is a healer, a wise one—perhaps a representation of the Old Crone Goddess. Though she may be "ugly," she is fearsome and revered. She is the tide of life contained and gathered in. Frog's medicine is the effervescence and creative fertility of youth; toad's medicine is the hard-to-come-by wisdom of rotting, wet things.

Totem Pathworking (Animal, Plant, or Mineral)

There are a multitude of totem-finding and totem-meeting pathworkings out there in the world, and the one that follows is neither better nor worse—it is simply another pathworking, with one difference. This pathworking emphasises the connection and communion aspect of the totem-human relationship. It does not assume that you have never met your totem or totems; however, it provides for those who have yet to do so.

It is recommended, as with most of the exercises and techniques in this book, that you perform the spiral soul alignment (page 38), three realms alignment (page 35), and the rite of divine fire (page 15) beforehand. You may either have someone else read the pathworking aloud to you as you trance, or you may wish to record it ahead of time and play it back as you follow.

> *Breathe deeply and rhythmically. Breathe into your centre. As you come closer and closer to your centre, every piece of you—every cell—begins to glow with the radiance of the Divine, and you flow into the limitless light. You become one with it, as you always have been and will continue to be. You realise that the centre is in all places—you have found the holy centre.*

spirit allies

There are flickering shadows amassing around you. Before you is a campfire, made for you by the one you have come to meet. You wonder at your surroundings. You notice you are in a wild place…how does it appear to you? What plant beings are present? What of the stones, the earth upon which you sit or stand? Can you smell or hear water near you? What is the colour of the sky? What are the scents moving through the shifting currents of air? How do you feel being present in this place—this wild place, far from the ordinary here and there of the mundane world?

As you ponder all of these things and more, you come to again realise that behind all of the thoughts and their attachments there is something strong, pervasive, and consistent thrumming within and around you. The heartbeat of nature is your heartbeat too, and gradually the beat becomes definitively audible, and the shadows seem to shake at each pulse.

As the shadows shake and writhe, the veil that seems to separate the worlds ripples, and from the other side of the fire you see a glimmer of light, which just as soon disappears. A silhouette draws itself together, coalesces from the shadows and the rippling air; a distinct form begins to emerge from that space directly opposite from you. As the form manifests, you suddenly see, in powerful clarity, your totem shining in the illumination of flame and ember!

Your totem draws ever closer to the flickering red-yellow flames, and it becomes apparent that you are both here for connection, communion, and counsel. This is the sacred time and space for you to share power, knowledge, wisdom, and insight together. Do this now, and indulge in the exchange. (Pause as needed)

When you feel that you have completed the exchange, an erratic and heavy drum beat begins to play, and your totem begins to dance and move to the primal rhythm. You find yourself mirroring this movement, and as you do, you feel your two essences merging in union. You find that you are becoming more and more akin to your totem, fused and flowing, until quite suddenly you find yourself looking through the eyes of your totem and staring across the dancing fire into what seems to be a mirror—for the reflection is exact, distinct, and nonhuman! You embrace this transformation, this sharing of skin and shape, of form and frame. You have not become your totem, you have simply drawn so close that you are sharing the same time and space and are able to borrow its faculties and experience. If you have feel the inclination, allow yourself time to explore the fruitful possibilities of this new mode of meaning and expression of existence. (Pause as needed)

As the dark dome of night begins to lighten at a distant edge and unearthly hues of wandering light seem to creep over the horizon, you find yourself in your human form once more, on the same side of the fire that you first approached. You acknowledge, thank, and honour your totem and your sacred allyship, and you recall your breathing, deep and rhythmic, until that focus saturates every piece of your being.

You are breathing…in…and out…in…and out. You are breathing long…and deep…long…and deep. You remember your physicality in the here and now, of the place that you are, that surrounds you and fixes you by laws of time and space. And yet as you open your eyes and become aware of this world once more, you know that if you wish or yearn to move through the veil once more to explore infinity, you simply need to find the ripple and slip through it.

Breathe. Centre. Ground. Be here and now.

The Difference Between a Familiar and a Totem

The word *totem* derives from the Ojibwe root *oode,* referring to anything related to kinship. *Totem* tends to refer to an overarching spiritually (animal, plant, or mineral) protecting and blessing a particular group of people (tribe, clan, family, etc.). This particular ally may actually embody or exist as the mythic ancestor of the group (a kind of egregore in the modern magickal sense). A familiar, on the other hand, is a personalised spirit helper who, according to the trend in Paganism today, tends to appear in animal form most of the time and may actually derive its magickal potency from being a living, sentient, incarnate animal rather than a mythic predecessor. Since the New Age movement, the word *totem* has come to mean, for those exploring newer variants of age-old spiritual philosophy or tradition, a spirit ally directly invested in aiding, inspiring, and guiding a particular individual. While acknowledging the word's history and its cultural context, I have also come to use the word *totem* in the New Age way. As with the deities, there may be varying degrees of intensity when it comes to the allyship; however, the two main distinctions I have experienced are "totem" and "power."

A power animal, plant, or stone is akin to a power deity in that they enter our lives to directly empower us and lend their vital strength and skill as needed. The Witch's familiar seems to encompass the idea of totem and power animal, as well as playing the part of a general guide, a friend on equal footing who shares interest, time, and space with the Witch. As discussed above, currently a familiar tends to be a living, breathing animal companion with a decisive and invested attraction to magick. Many pets become familiars if or when the Witch begins to notice their continued presence at or attraction to magickal rites. At an inner court meeting with OakSun Grove in which vision journeying was taking place, one dedicant's cat, Zoe, began to purr and prod rather overtly the moment everyone had sunk into meditative states. This happened each time we began to go into meditation, when previously Zoe had been extremely disinterested in our presence.

While totems may represent a clan guide or ancestral inspiration and wisdom passed on through oral teachings and celebrations (and stand as an embodiment of the mythic strength of a people), in the contemporary sense a totem may also act as an individual's spiritual ally in the energetic pattern of animal, plant, or mineral. A familiar is a personal guardian, guide, and friend with invested interest in an individual (and vice versa), and in many ways this can be synonymous with a totem. If the familiar is physically manifest as an animal companion, then a distinction begins to emerge. However, and ultimately, the origins of the word *familiar* lies with *familial* or *family*; therefore, the words *totem* and *familiar* are, in fact, synonymous and simply developed in different cultures, across an ocean.

I can attest to familiar spirits relating to the ancestors, as often after a particularly arduous or intense power raising, I will find that as I am grounding and equalising my energy with that of my surroundings, a multitude of etheric hands (which I sometimes see and sometimes feel), appearing like the white-handed cave images of some Aboriginal artworks, flutter around me, stroking my aura. I have always identified these spirit hands with my family's familiar spirits, and this has especial meaning to me now, considering an auric-cleansing technique Ravyn Stanfield (a Reclaiming and Feri priestess) performed on me had immediate parallels.

Ultimately, it seems, as with the casual usage of a variety of terms within the greater Pagan or even magickal community, the words *totem* and *familiar* may occasionally appear to mean the same thing and at other times represent variant concepts. For the purposes of this book, *totem* will mean a nonhuman spirit ally who is intrinsically a part of your living myth (there may be more than one), and a familiar spirit may or may not be human and may be ancestral. Again, a fine line.

The Importance of Spirits of Place

It is quite natural for a person to enter a new house, building, park, or region in general, and to receive a general or specific reading on the feeling, or energy, of the site. This is generally considered to constitute the "vibes" of the place, and the reading maps out the overall energetic blueprint or imprint of the location. However, my experience with reading vibes tends to fall into a different category of interpretation, and more and more Witches are beginning to or do feel this way.

Spirits of place come by many cultural names in both Pagan and non-Pagan traditions. The Roman term was *genius loci*, while the Irish might simply say "faerie" or "tuatha" (depending on their mythological frame); the Greeks might point to nymphs, or the English of the eighteenth and nineteenth centuries might simply reference "sprites." Either way, in this particular usage as spirits of place, these entities are embodied potencies—energetic constituents or residents that compose the raw physical expression of that land or area and are implicitly tied to it.

Spirits of place carry the vital charge of the land, and the term is indeed an umbrella term that may apply to a host of unique and specific spirits; but just as the natives of Manhattan's West Village retain and vibrate a specific charge (though each person is an individual), so do the spirits of place.

I feel that an illustrating example is needed here to truly flesh out the concept and reality of spirits of place. From late August 2010 to early January 2011, I travelled through England's West Country, Ireland, and the United States and Canada. For some of this time I was the guest guide for a sacred sites tour—Dragon's Eye Tours, created and facilitated by Wiccan priestess Christine Casey. I travelled through the States promoting the new release of my book *By Land, Sky & Sea*. I have spoken of grounding and centring as an appropriate and effective technique of grounding one's energies in new land and introducing oneself and communing with the spirits of place. By the same token, the giving of offerings is a highly sacrosanct practice and traditionally expresses the principle of sacred exchange (balance). Thus, as I travelled through the Northern Hemisphere and came to new lands, new places, and new spirits and guardians, I would spend sacred time connecting and communing. I would breathe deeply in, deeply out, send out roots and branches, become the mighty world tree, and then speak aloud my greetings and benedictions to the spirits of place. I would then bless offerings in their names and leave them by a tree, stone, river, or windowsill—any place that called me.

On my last night in NYC, my friend Dylan and I decided to explore Inwood Forest Park. I had previously walked the various forest trails and spoken with the very awake and very active spirits. It was only after circling and meditating in the place for a week that I came upon a boulder bearing a plaque that explained how the site I stood upon was the legendary meeting place of the Dutch colonialists and the Lenape Indians—the site of the infamous exchange of Manhattan Island for beads. I was also told that the surrounding forest was virgin—this, to me, explained the intensity of the presences I felt there. That night Dylan and I decided to walk into the forest. As we entered the shadows, I noticed a figure wearing white step aside from the path only metres in front of us and stand still in the line of trees, unmoving, waiting. I felt a strange intensity and asked Dylan if he could see the figure. Dylan at first replied that he couldn't, but then he began to make out a man he described as wearing white warrior garb. We both agreed that to walk forward might invite hostility, so we backtracked and walked away, and while neither of us felt in danger, we did feel a deep and penetrating stare upon our backs. I had intended to

spirit allies

leave offerings in thanks to the spirits of New York City for welcoming me to their land at the famous boulder, so before walking away completely from the forest, we paused by the boulder, lit incense, and made prayers of thanksgiving to the spirits of place. As we walked farther away I could make out several silhouettes of white-clothed, tall figures pacing back and forth at the very edge of the dark forest. These I took to be the warrior spirits of the Lenape, or perhaps something even older, woven into the very fabric of that untouched forest.

This example illustrates several important points concerning encounters and relationships with the spirits of any given place (though all will be significantly different). The first point is that spirits of place will not always necessarily be gentle, welcoming, or caring for human concerns. In fact, when I first ventured into the Inwood Forest to hold my devotional circle for the week, I ended up being absolutely drenched by a spontaneous downpour. It was the fastest circle I ever cast and ever opened. Once I emerged from the woods, the rain stopped, and I could only laugh. Despite the fact that I always acknowledge the spirits of place in all of my rituals and devotional circles, I felt that I was "chased out" because I had not given enough time or care to the offerings given. The next day I returned to give more offerings of frankincense and myrrh, which were definitely well received. This case in point proves that even the most spirit-aware and respectful Witches may unintentionally cause offence to the spirits.

The second point is to listen to your instincts and intuition regarding how to act and behave when the spirits of place make contact with you. I can't be absolutely sure, but I definitely feel that if Dylan and I had proceeded into the forest along that path that night, we would have been barred and perhaps even forcefully pushed out. I know of this happening to several Witches in Australia when experiencing the sacred sites of indigenous heritage. Conversely, if you feel genuinely welcomed and elated by the spiritual communication, then by all means proceed or linger.

Point number three: the importance of making, blessing, and giving offerings. The offerings must be of worth. Either the money spent on them must be reasonable or the appropriate thought and intent must have been imbued into the offerings themselves (will this offering serve or please the spirits and why or how?). For instance, it is not enough to simply pick up a rock on one's way to a ritual, gathering, or devotional and hand it over as divine offering—unless, of course, that rock struck you there and then as the correct item to offer. This may be because it resembles a symbol connected with the deity or spirit (e.g., an inverted triangle for Persephone or Demeter) or bears a colour connected with the deity or spirit; or perhaps there is no particular external sign of correspondence but it may simply feel right. The key is simply that the offering itself should represent the spark of divinity (to you) related to the deity or spirit, and therefore it will be of the essence of the spirit, and the offering of the gift is like a returning of essence to essence—filling out the wholeness and sustaining the vital charge of the spirit. In this way, Gerald Gardner was speaking the truth when he spoke of the Old Gods needing our help and attention, just as much as we require theirs.

Spirits of place retain and facilitate the flow of the vital charge of a locale; they are the emissaries of the living land and embody the divinities of tree, stone, leaf, stream, river, log, hill, and flower. They are also the potencies of skyscrapers, ships, skate parks, and alleys. As mentioned previously, this is perhaps why the genii loci are said to be synonymous with faeries, nymphs, and sprites, depending on the mythological context and the etymological usage of the word. However, popular and cultural uses of words do not always follow the linear path of word-meaning derivation. Often a people or group will create their own meanings for words, even if those words have ancient lineages. The spirits of any given place do not necessarily require what we think of as placation, not in the sense that the *buta kala* do (the chaotic demon spirits of Bali, which are sated with blood offerings

spirit allies

prior to Balinese ceremonies). Spirits of place do require one's respect, attention, and favour. The following ritual acknowledgement can be used as a template for any spirits of place offering.

Ritual of Acknowledgement

Stand where you feel the power of the place is naturally pooling. This site may be marked by an overt or thoroughly symbolic embodiment (e.g., a tree or stone). Ground and centre in the way that is familiar and potent to you (or use the three realms alignment on page 37). Hold the offering and charge and bless it in the name of the spirits of place. When you feel that the offering is full and overflowing with vitality, lay it down and gesture physically to it while stating aloud the following declaration or blessing:

> *Spirits of place, I lay this offering for you.*
> *May you welcome me as I welcome you.*
> *Blessed be.*

Now either carry out the work or ritual you came to do or turn and leave the site. It is traditional advice to not turn and look back; simply walk away with a silent understanding in your heart that you have perpetuated the balance of the cosmos and as such have sustained and celebrated the life force we Witches call magick.

Walking with the Spirits

I have defined Witchcraft as an ecstasy-driven, earth-based Mystery Tradition, and I have called it a sacred discipline, where discipline translates as intent, purpose, and rhythm and the conscious cultivation of these things in one's life. Discipline can also translate as my dear friend Laura's definition: "the pattern that arises from the soul when reflecting on the Divinity in the world."

chapter four

I have also declared my belief that one cannot be a Witch alone, for that would be anathema to all of our philosophies and our sacred truths. Nothing and no one is alone. A Witch is empowered not through or by external agency but by the innate connections we share with the multiplicity of spirit's expressions that exist in the cosmos we call the great mystery. We share and celebrate the vitality that flows through and animates each of us as alive and thus sacred. We are each a potency that is not only hidden but seeks expression.

The gods are hidden potencies because their expression is not won by self-actualisation alone, but the sheer and overwhelming desire to enmesh influence in the fabric of being and be of use and of relevance. Often the gods are born of myriad meeting roads along which the light, wind, rain, and warmth is carried so that the original seed may be nurtured and brought forth from darkness into light. The birth of the gods is a timeless act that precedes thought. Each of us must find that same origin within and bring forth the divine seed that our chosen or fated spiritual disciplines will nurture, nourish, and provide sustenance to grow and thrive. When we walk with the spirits, we sing to each other the song of here and now: *the circle is cast, I am ready, I am living, breathing, and death will only renew me…I choose to walk with you that we may help and heal each other in celebration of the life force we share.*

chapter five

moving between the worlds

> "Those shamans who did travel to them [other worlds] often had to reckon with an elaborate geography in each. Sometimes their spirit flight involved moving up or down onto these other cosmic levels, and sometimes sideways into alternative worlds upon the terrestrial plane."
> Ronald Hutton, *Shamans*

As I breathed in the land and opened my mind to the sky above, I felt a ripple to my right and a strong, ancient, yet vital presence over my left shoulder. I felt that the veil had lifted in response to my communion with the spirits of place, and so I shifted my consciousness and slipped through the veil to the tween, where I made a sacrifice to the old wood spirit and ibis of the Brisbane City Botanic Gardens.

Mircea Eliade called the ability to move between the worlds the "pre-eminently shamanic technique," and he postulated that this was achieved through ecstatic trance states. As ecstasy may be translated as dissolving the egoic barrier and liberating one's consciousness from separation to interconnection, the skill behind moving between the worlds is, of course, dependent upon both mental discipline and a strong acceptance of the magickal worldview of infinite possibility.

chapter five

Consider for a moment the generic, cross-cultural perception of the shamanic three worlds. The upperworld, middleworld, and underworld are all connected by the world tree, world mountain, or cosmic pillar—axis mundi. As I tend to resonate best with the world tree symbolism, I will refer to the axis mundi by that title throughout. To effectively travel and move between the worlds is to know the world tree as the centre, not only of the cosmos but of self-as-cosmos. If one can embrace the centre within and see the divine reality that declares the boundlessness of the mysterious reality, then we are able to affirm the world tree within and accept personal destiny (and biological wiring) as shamanic—to access the manifold realms and to attain wisdom and gnosis. As the Voudoun saying goes, "all are born of magic"—and thus it is destined that we should directly intimate the methods through which to make best use of that primal and undying connection.

Here is a glimpse of how I personally interact with and view the shamanic cosmology:

The sun (the capacity for the emanation of light or existence-knowing-itself) represents enlightened cosmic consciousness—the Weaver/God Herself[64]/Chaos birthing differentiation and thus dynamic contrast, causing reflection of "other" and therefore potential to be and thrive in being. Nature (at least from the perspective of this planet and this solar system) has shown us that our own sun alludes to the circular motion causing the interplay of day and night, which just so happens to emphasise the four cardinal directions. The sun rises in the east, is at its zenith in the north/south, sets in the west, and passes through our midnight south/north only to commit once more to the dawn and renew its familiar cycle. We know, of course, that this is because of

---

64 God Herself is quite a well-understood term in the Witchcraft community these days, especially as Feri/Faery Tradition becomes more public. God Herself is what Victor Anderson called the Star Goddess; it is an amazing thing to say aloud. Try it now: GOD HERSELF. It is more revolutionary even than saying Goddess, because people immediately associate Goddess with a gender-essentialist view of the Divine Female/Feminine embodied in a deity perhaps or even as an overarching force/being; but to say GOD HERSELF is to blow away all assumptions.

the planet's gradual twenty-four-hourly revolution (or thereabouts) and the 365.25 days of orbit around the sun annually (and our axis tilt). However, the metaphor strengthens the underlying message that cycles and seasons illumine and inspire our being.

Cosmologically speaking, the four corners of the world are illustrated by the sun and grounded in the middleworld of land, as it is only possible to conceive of directions if we are standing in one place and looking out from that "unmoving" centre. Only then can we adequately and poetically say *from here is east, from here is north, from here is west, and from here is south* and stand in the centre where they meet. Alchemically speaking, the four basic elements of life are placed respectively in these directions. The fact that there is a world tree joining the three realms and that there is a sun, a source of light to illumine, means that a shadow will be cast if the light is obstructed by the world tree. This "shadow" is what is known as the veil, and it allows us to understand, for all intents and purposes, that there is a nebulous "separation" between the realms, which only exists to tell us that we are passing between the realms.

The underworld exists beneath and within the roots of the mighty world tree. Coiled within the roots is a dark serpent of the earth, and this serpent is guarded by the three sisters of Wyrd, who are the keepers of the Well of Memory, which they grant access to only if those who approach are of noble heart. These three sisters are known by many titles, including the Norns (Norse), the Moreae (Greek), the Fates (Roman), and the Wyrd sisters (Anglo-Saxon). There are always three, or at least numbers divisible by three (like the nine priestesses of Avalon), and they represent the cycle of life embodied by humanity, or in this case the primordial feminine—the young maiden, the mother, and the ancient crone. The sacred triplicity of the Fate Goddess as honoured by Witches is undoubtedly ancient, and this is attested by myth and lore. The Well of Memory is often coupled with a Well or River of Forgetfulness. We are said to lose memory of past existences (as our souls are recycled) by drinking from this well. However, the Orphics of ancient Greece avoided the River Lethe (Forgetfulness) in the underworld and went instead to drink from the Lake of Memory so that their consciousness remained eternal and gnosis of the divine self would carry on. I believe that we are able to make that choice personally, and that in truth there is no difference between either of the rivers or wells, as they derive from the same primal waters. Thus, within this cosmology, it is only if we accept that our essences end upon physical death that we would inevitably drown ourselves in the River of Forgetfulness. Again, it is through the ways of nature that we can even fathom eternal life, and all things in nature are recycled, reborn, renewed, and restored. Newton's laws of physics also remark that energy can never be destroyed, it can only transform, and that all things are composed of energy.

The upperworld is reached by ascending the world tree and opening to the glory of the star-lit realms of light. Those who scale the tree to bathe in the sweetness of celestial light increase in vibration, and because of this the gods and spirits are able to be met with on equal footing, and visions unfold. It is also true that the vibration within the underworld is of necessary contrast to that of the middleworld (and those within), so "other" experiences are more able to occur in the realm below also. The upperworld reminds us of the limitlessness of light, and thus we are able to conceive of the beyond and are opened—split open, in fact—to the eternity of things. It is in the upperworld that we can truly claim the sovereignty of Self as divine and everlasting, but only by returning to the middleworld do we ground this simple truth and enact Being, which instigates the power to move between the worlds and attain to wisdom in the first place. The underworld helps us to understand this forever truth.

The tree's branches and roots mirror each other, as if to say there is neither up nor down, only what is. The tree's mystery, and thus the mystery of all, is whispered in the mutability of things and the constant reflection, one to the next, of the powerful truths underlying the potencies that allow us to open and embrace the Divine Spirit. The conduit in between the above and the below is the determining and qualifying factor related to the mergence of the worlds—their interconnectivity. The role of the shaman is to enact within him- or herself the reality and providence of the world tree so that the power of the gods is gifted and we deepen to the point of boundlessness. Only from the perspective of infinity can we truly understand and cherish the Allness that we require within the circle to be able to access the potencies that enact the creativity of the worlds.

In *BLSS* I write about the technique I find most effective for spirit flight. I also write about trance, vision-journeys, and oracular seership, which are all relative to one fundamental principle: that the self is All-Self; atman and Brahman; microcosm and macrocosm; as above, so below. What is contained within the greater being is in essence synonymous with the substance that is "I" or my Own Holy Self. The "I" dwells within us all and is not necessarily related to the ego. The "I" is simply the product of reflection, of sentience and awareness. The "I" factor allows us independent and therefore contrasting consciousness, so that we may effectively experience and create evolving memory. The paradox is that while we don't exist fundamentally, essentially we do. We are identifiable as the wholeness of immanence but separated out and distinct to allow for the realisation in the first place that even pondering "God," the Divine, Spirit, directly infers that these concepts are naturally ingrained in our deep selves. We are of the earth and the starry heavens, but our race is of heaven, as the Orphics knew.

In this chapter I will speak about techniques of trance as portals to the otherworld. I will also speak about the veil and on how to find and work with it, and on the multiple "roads" we may walk to explore the cosmic geography.

chapter five

Trance as Foundation

I have often said that the foundation of all magickal work is breath. If one can breathe properly, then one can weave with magickal power (life force) and indeed enter into and become it wholly and truly. This enacts the ability to cast spells; to draw down the spirits; to divine the past, present, and future; and yes, to move between the worlds.

In *BLSS* I briefly touched on the dynamics and principles behind trance and its significance to shamanic Witchcraft. However, this significance must not be underrated. I spoke of trance as self becoming intoxicated with the All-Self—the essential truth, as detailed above. However, trance in its basic utilitarian sense can also simply refer to an altered state of consciousness.

When discussing the definition of Witchcraft and qualifying the "ecstasy-driven" component, there are some who have suggested that forms of Wiccan Witchcraft do not rest heavily on trance. However, these positions may derive from the same paradigm that informs the belief that one does not necessarily have to practise magick to be a Wiccan. I sincerely believe and experience the casting of the circle, which is both a construct and concept of Wiccan technique, as an inherently magickal one. Also, to cast the circle (in whatever way and with whatever focus) is a gradual deepening of a state of consciousness that is highly conducive to magickal ritual. It is also a traditional Wiccan hallmark to raise power in the circle, to divine and cast spells, and to draw down the God or the Goddess; these are all magickal acts. I state this because at the heart of all of our "work" lies trance—it is indeed our foundation, and it begins with breath. If one can breathe, then one can trance.

In chapter 3 I mentioned the personal predisposition to certain states of consciousness when approaching trance possession. To highlight this, I wish to make it clear that there are some human beings who are naturally designed for deeper trance states and others who would not or could not handle the depth or intensity. However, neither is better nor more sacred than the other, and I make it a point to reiterate this. Another thought to consider is something that Ravyn Stanfield articulated to the teaching team at the inaugural Reclaiming WitchCamp in Australia. In response to concerns expressed relating to aspecting or drawing down and levels of trance, Ravyn said, "Our bodies are made for this." While I still maintain that there is such a thing as dangerous territory (not necessarily to be avoided) in our spirituality, Ravyn is correct in this assertion. We are incarnate; body is spirit—all is spiritual; we are infinitely designed for the capacity of magickal undertaking. Trance is part and parcel of a well-trained human being. Again—if you can breathe, you can trance.

The Veil and How to Work With It

The veil is another one of those amorphous or easily brushed-over concepts within the magickal and shamanic crafts. However, when speaking on trance, it is a necessity to consider the veil and the implications thereof.

As I illustrated above within my personal perspective of shamanic cosmology, the veil is the shadow caused by the tree obstructing the light of the sun (the "coming forth" of Divinity). Therefore, the shadow forms the edges of the periphery—it is as the subconscious. The veil is the glimmer, or what I like to call the "ripple," that we feel when we are close to the otherworld. This is not a geographically situated location specifically but a state of consciousness that invites such transition. There are sacred sites in this world that have been specially designed and engineered to evoke certain states of mind within visitors. These sites are often astronomically aligned and draw upon magnetic currents within the earth, e.g., Stonehenge or Avebury. Some of these sites are also naturally occurring within the landscape and are often known as power places in which two or more ley lines (dragon lines or song lines) cross and converge, i.e., Glastonbury Tor. It is at these geographical locations that the veil is constantly rippling.

However, the veil's ripple is only a breath away, no matter your geographical location.

The Veil's Ripple

The anecdote that I used to open this chapter was set a month before my handfasting in the botanic gardens in which it was held. I spoke with the spirits of place in that area to arrange for a rain-free occasion, and beautifully this was the case. As I breathed into my centre and began to merge with the land, I did in fact feel the ripple I speak of, and I knew instinctively that this was an indication of the shifting of the edges of realms. Mentally and energetically I grasped the edges of the wandering threads and swiftly slipped through the veil and through the worlds. I found this exercise to not require a great deal of effort, but it did require a concerted and conscious effort on my behalf.

Much of the dynamics of our energetic magickal work relies upon the confidence and skill of the Witch or magician. This is different than arrogance, where one believes they possess absolute capability and can do no wrong.

A Technique for Finding the Veil and Moving Through It

Breathe to your centre. Breathe to the holy centre (one and the same). Align with this forever truth.

Concentrate on your auric field, and when you are aware of its boundaries, mentally and energetically fill the aura with your presence and then expand it until it will go no further. Your energetic vibration should now be heightened.

Breathe and wait in patience and alertness.

You may feel the ripple without having to call the veil, but if that is not the case, mentally call out to the veil, the shadow, and fill yourself with concerted expectation. Soon you will feel the ripple, and when you do, mentally and energetically take hold of the veil and swiftly and surely slip through into the other. It is quite difficult to adequately describe how this will feel. However, it is one of those "take the risk and leap" scenarios. Even if you do not feel certain that you have "taken hold" of the veil, intuit your way through the process. Do this several times until you can feel the shift, even if it is fleeting. Slipping through the veil is like cupping water in your hands; there is a trick to doing it.

What to Do When You Are on the Other Side

The Other is considered the nonordinary reality of Michael Harner's "core shamanism."[65] I find the term *nonordinary* descriptive in the sense that it implies what is not included within accepted consensual reality. The overculture decrees through apparent consensus that certain aspects of what Witches might call the great mystery are deemed appropriate to the context and therefore substantially and objectively "real." However, when we truly study this attitude, it can be seen to be hugely subjective and less objective than originally thought (though, again, neither is testimony to what is true, authentic, or real). For all intents and purposes, the Other is just as real, if not intensely more so, than consensual reality.

When one has achieved the transition from "this" side to the other (the veil creates the illusion of separation, though of course it is simply a shadow), we are able to draw upon the depth of the wellspring of our potentiality. We are free and open because we have essentially allowed our minds to embrace more-than and what is beyond, as a transition has been seen to have occurred. This altering or deepening of consciousness is associated with trance, and thus we have attained the prime shamanic skill of moving between the worlds. What are we

---

65 I have never studied core shamanism as put forward by Michael Harner. In fact, what I know of Harner and core shamanism only comes from secondary sources.

chapter five

to accomplish with this act, however? What is the significance of this ability?

I have often said that the shamanic skill is less about moving between the worlds (or shifting paradigms, as the case may be) and more about the absorption of abstract information and the transformation and distillation of such knowledge into practical remedy or advice. Instead of referring to the ambiguous shaman-and-hunt scenario, I'd like to offer examples from my own shamanic services and cunning charges.[66]

This first example will speak about the apparent movement of my consciousness from one realm to another and then back again with renewed or newly acquired understanding.

Five months into my Feri training, I was directed by my teacher to travel into the air realm, or what he called the air temple. We did this by walking down the golden road that is also part of becoming one with the crossroads (a technique of opening to the tween and coming to the holy centre) and moving through a portal inscribed with the alchemical sigil for air. Since that first induction (as I had never overtly worked with "inner temples" of the elements), I independently explored at my own pace the power and providence of air. I connected and communed with the air guardian, and alongside me was Mr. Blue (otherwise known as the Blue God or Dian y Glas), as I had discovered he enjoyed the psychopomp role. On one particular visit to the air temple, the guardian of the realm took my hand and flew me up to a crevice within a cliff-face. There he passed on an incantation that seemed to come from both Latin and Hebrew. The incantation aided me in riding the wind with great ease! I was also shown a particular symbol, again resembling Hebrew characters, and it seemed to

---

66 I use the term *cunning charge* to refer to the fact that I am a working Witch. People come to me seeking help with love, finance, protection, property (selling and buying), finding lost objects, healing, and divination, and some (usually Witches and Pagans) request me as a vessel for a deity or spirit. I charge for the majority of these services.

moving between the worlds

resonate with the power of air. I brought back from this Other realm pieces of abstract information, knowledge, and symbology that nonetheless had practical uses.

This second anecdote will refer to the notion that, in fact, the Other saturates this side and that, indeed, there is no difference between the two. Many contemporary fantasy stories commenting on the Faerie realms often speak about the idea that the Faerie world and the realms of humanity move farther and farther apart; however, this has nothing to do with any energetic placement or movement of these planes or worlds, but of the overwhelming paradigm in Western cultures that declares Faerie to be fake. Faerie is still very much here and now; we simply have to accept that fact and shift our perception. When we have attained a confidence (different from belief) in this assertion, we are able to truly embrace our own innate capacity to move between the realms.

I am often called upon by friends and family (and this includes coven brothers and sisters) to identify spirits or energies within homes (and to commune with or banish them). In this case, Alex, one of my best friends, invited me over to check on a perceived spirit residing within her house (both Alex and two other WildWood Witches lived there). I had been told that running could be heard at night from room to room when all were in bed, and that the spirit had directly blown air in Alex's ears. I sat in the centre of the house and breathed into silence and centre. I then simply called out to the potential resident spirit and he appeared—cycling on an old pennyfarthing bicycle. He had intense green eyes; long, choppy blond hair; and a blue tailcoat with a red undergarment. He was a Faerie. He told me his name was Jack and that he had been attracted to the house because of the Faerie altar that had been built in the backyard by the Witches and also by the primal energy raised during a recent Dionysian ceremony held in that same backyard.

After this initial meeting, I moved downstairs to sit and talk with my friends. In the empty chair directly opposite me appeared Jack, smiling broadly, eyes gleaming. I told Alex Jack was present, and she began to ask questions through me but directed at Jack. Jack found this most hilarious and decided to give what I thought were sardonic answers in return. For instance, Alex wanted to know if her offerings of chocolate and wine were satisfying. In response, Jack requested three drops of no-pulp orange juice in white wine. I couldn't help but laugh. As with many of the Fey, Jack could not be said to abide by any human sense of "morality." He conveyed to me that he worked on an equal-opportunity give-receive basis and that he would bless the house if offerings were constant and consistent. This is congruent with Faerie lore and with my interactions with a variety of spirits. All of this information was simple for me to access, and the only key to acquiring it was the confidence in my skill to do just that—and, of course, breath and trance.

Pathworkings

Here you will find pathworkings that aid in the exploration of the major realms and regions of the shamanic cosmos. The style of pathworking is open and will hopefully provide an effective springboard from which to delve more deeply into the mythos and teachings of each realm or feature. I encourage the personalisation of experience and also the invitation to reception, or rather the idea that these encounters and interactions are profoundly authentic, and thus elements of surprise and unfolding will unravel without self-determined volition. When we close our eyes (or not) and journey inward, we must remember the lesson of the spiral soul and that, in fact, when we feel we are drawing inward, we are simultaneously moving outward, and conversely, when we journey out, we are moving into the holy centre.

With this in mind, journey well!

The World Tree Pathworking

The world tree, or the tree of life, is the axis that represents the wholeness of the three worlds. It is the centre and the circumference—the matrix and the keeper. The world tree is our ladder of ascent, our spiral staircase into shadow, and our doorway to the four directions. The world tree is where we come to meet at the crossroads and celebrate our ancient and ever-renewing Craft.

> *Breathe deeply and rhythmically. Come to the holy centre. Embrace the forever truth—that self is All-Self. You dissolve into the boundless, the limitless infinity of the living cosmos. Breathe deeply and rhythmically.*
>
> *Awaken to yourself standing before a titanic tree spiralling and spinning into eternity. You cannot perceive the beginning or the end of this tree—this giant. As you look upwards, you see the boughs and branches pierce the veil of the heavens, and the light of sun and moon moves like an endless wheel in a continuous arc above. You look downward through the entangled mass of roots and glimpse secret streams of glistening water that seem to travel in undulating patterns until they disappear at the lips of what looks like an ancient well. You hear the hissing of serpents and the breath of dragons. You hear the distant call of an eagle, and you crane your head to perceive the limitless, coalescing light of the arc of the sky. An eagle, a majestic bird of prey, traces the symbol for infinity directly above you. You become gradually aware that you are now standing right next to the tree, and its girth is imperceptible. Under the shade of the tree, the veil of night falls upon you, and you sense rippling in every corner. Corner of what?—this thought echoes through your clear yet alert mind. The four corners of the world—this*

answer ripples back through the ether shimmering at the edge of darkness. Suddenly four roads appear, creating a convergence at the tree—a mighty crossroads.

Prayer

World tree, tree of life, I am born of your holy centre, I stand at your mighty crossroads, and I am enlivened by the here and now. World tree, tree of life, I am your own holy child. I am the world tree; for all eternity, so mote it be.

The Power of the Directions

The four cardinal directions represent the spatial awareness of the land—of the manifest, the incarnate, and the corporeal. To be able to conceive of the directions means that we have a point of reference anchored in space and time, and this of course helps to reinforce that we are indeed in some place and by honouring the directions we potentise that place to become the convergence of the four directions and thus the mighty crossroads—that world tween the worlds. This is further heightened by the fact that the three other directions are present also. The great above and the great below—because here we are, standing at the world tree, branches spiralling upward into radiance and roots delving downward into the well. The centre, the seventh direction that each of us brings and activates within—the true reference point of the unfolding of the directions—is the gift of being and the ignited awareness that comes with acknowledging and celebrating this earnest fact. Everywhere we are is a centre—or, in fact, the holy centre.

By walking into each direction, along each of the roads, we open to the pathways of manifestation and gnosis, depending on which way we walk and with which intention. To walk the motion of the sun, to mimic the light's arc and movement, is to ally oneself with the waxing tide—growth, expansion, and creativity. To walk against the sun, to contradict its passage, is to ally oneself with the waning tide—decline, contraction, and destruction. Both are necessary for the shamanic Witch. To walk with the sun is to walk into light; to walk against the sun is to walk into shadow and darkness. We disappear beyond the veil (the shadow) that is caused by the tree obstructing the continuum of light. This, by pure will, is attested by the ways of nature. One must decide whether walking into the east (or any direction) is the initiation of a cycle or whether it is a journey of intent, focus, and investment in one direction for a time and its associated magicks and mysteries.

If we also associate the directions with elements, which for the purposes of this book we will, then each direction beholds certain powers and providence. If I choose to walk down the road to the west (often aligned with water), then I may either work some deep, oceanic love spell or begin a cycle of banishing an element in my life associated with water (if I were to walk against the sun) or draw in an element of water (if I moved deosil). Of course, there is vastly more to it than this.

I spoke before of the pathways of gnosis and manifestation in relation to the directions and the tree. It would be the general assumption that for these pathways to be the case, one would have to move to the direction associated with air and then travel to fire, water, and earth (manifestation) or to move from the direction of earth to water, fire, and then air (gnosis)—remembering, of course, that these formulae only exist because spirit (the predecessor and the "product"—the fifth that makes the four one) underlies these processes. However, we can also effectively place spirit in the centre, at the position of the world tree itself; the great above and the great below are extensions of this quintessence held from different perspectives. To effectively craft these pathways while moving between the worlds is not necessarily about placement or correspondence; it is, however, about orientation and attitude.

Orientation from the holy centre (spirit), acknowledging the great above and the great below (which hold me), and then moving to the east, I witness the rising of the sun and open to the element of air for clarity of intent and distillation of thought. I bow, give my thanks, and gracefully move deosil to the north (fire—impassioned intent and activation of energy). Witnessing the peak of the light, I give thanks and move again with the sun to the west (water—channelled intent and flowing energy). Giving thanks, I dance with the sun beyond what appears to be his final resting place for the tide of light and come to the south (earth—grounding of intent and planting of energetic seeds), and again give thanks. However, the cycle is not complete. I must, in fact, walk full circuit, return to the eastern point and then the holy centre, acknowledge above and below (as above, so below), and give and receive of the magickal charge that has been clarified, impassioned, channelled, and grounded by the elements. By spirit—the fifth element, the quintessence—we come to truly honour and realise (in the literal sense) our intent and accept it for ourselves; owning the charge and becoming actively responsible for our magick.

To walk the pathway of gnosis would be to again begin in the holy centre and walk outward to the south (earth—physicality), then to the west (water—emotional landscape held by the senses), to the north (astral—the star-fire of the spirit), and to the east (air—the mental sphere and conceptualisation and inspiration). To complete this pathway, one would walk the complete circuit, returning to south and then to the centre, acknowledge above and below (this time with the emphasis of *as without, so within*). One has ignited the spark of the Spirit, of Own Holy Self, and accepted and embraced it. Thus it is possible not only to activate either pathway within the external world but also when one is moving between the worlds and what some may view as the "internal planes."

Here I will briefly speak of the powers and providence of each direction, or "road."

The Road to the East

Walk this road to soar with the element of air and its associated qualities of thought, clarity, communication, resonance, intellect, and music.

The Road to the North

Walk this road to dance with the element of fire and its associated qualities of light, passion, courage, sexuality, and transformation.

The Road to the West

Walk this road to flow with the element of water and its associated qualities of love, cleansing, depth, intuition, and death.

The Road to the South

Walk this road to delve into the element of earth and its associated qualities of grounding, prosperity, sensuality, fecundity, and rest and renewal.

The Road to Sky

The realm of sky and thus the road to it is one of expansion, knowledge brought to wisdom, visions, deity, and freedom. We may scale the tree with hand and foot; however, it is far simpler to call upon the emissary of the heavens—the great bird.

chapter five

Upon the Great Bird:
The Mount of the Gods[67]

Before embarking on this journey, it is important to first place oneself at the world tree and come to the holy centre. Go through the world tree pathworking (see page 127).

> *Look up and witness the celestial interplay of light and darkness. Perceive the star-fire just as you feel the coolness of the breath of deep space. As you wonder at the possibilities, you hear the faint echo of a bird's call. You glance up and see this great bird tracing infinity patterns across the arc of the sky. The mount of the gods continues to echo its call out through the three worlds, and this call quickens your heartbeat. Your throbbing heart yearns to ascend, climb higher—fly! You feel ancient wings unfurl and unfold from the beating crest of your crimson heart, and at this the great bird looks down upon you; though the bird is high and far above you, you notice the graceful crane of its head and the startling clarity of its eyes. A soundless, wordless call emanates from deep within you, and the great bird hearkens and spirals downward to land directly before you. Extend your arms in a gesture of reverence and embrace. Remember to breathe...*

Counsel/Council with the Starry Ones

To ascend into the sky opens one to the possibility of counsel and communication with the gods. I have often pondered why the deities or gods are said to reside in the sky. My feeling is that, again, this is not a geographical (or hierarchical) inclination so much as a cosmological and mythic one. The sky is not simply the atmospheric layers

---

[67] The great bird of the sky can be the Muan bird of the Mayans, the Garuda of the Hindu traditions, the Eagle of many Native American tribes, and perhaps even the Phoenix of Regeneration. The great bird is your great bird.

of gas and light that encircle our planet, but simply the outward and upward (from our landlocked point of reference) expansion of reality. The sky is essentially the symbolic manifestation of what we nominally call space (both literally and symbolically). To say the gods dwell in the heavens or in the sky is not to negate chthonic or oceanic spirits and deities (or earth and forest spirits either) but to acknowledge the higher energetic vibration through which the gods express themselves. To travel to the sky is to raise one's vibration to meet with the vibration of the gods, and this therefore enables one to share counsel/council with the starry ones. This does not mean that the gods do not "descend" to share their counsel with us (hence, drawing *down*).

> *... The great bird bows to you in response to your gesture of reverence and embrace, and you bow to seal the exchange of honour. Cast your senses out to surround both you and the great bird. What is the feeling? Ask silently, "Are you to be my mount?" How does the great bird respond to this energetically or apparently? If you can determine the response as positive, then walk towards the bird and mount it.*
>
> *The bird unfolds its gracious, expansive wings, and a swift, clean draught of wind moves through the manifold celestial feathers. The great bird takes flight, and your body leans forward as your hands and forearms fold around the bird's neck. You notice as the wind rushes past and you climb in altitude that there seems to be one star brighter than the rest at the apex of the heavens, crowning the world tree. As you soar higher and higher upon the mount of the gods, the azure-blue sky melts and melds into the dark chasm of space filled with the campfires of heaven. It is here where that bright star seems to eclipse the swollen darkness with its diamond-white light. You draw nearer and nearer and find that the white light of the star unfolds, becoming a shimmering white plain.*

Then you land and dismount the great bird, turning to give thanks and staring directly into the jet-black eyes of your sky ally. You turn to face what seems to be an altar rising from the shifting diamond-white light; it swirls like mist and coalesces to form columns of light in a circle surrounding the altar. You enter the temple and make a silent prayer to the starry ones, the hidden potencies, the gods and goddesses, and you listen, wait, and watch …

When you have finished your counsel with the gods, you give deep thanks and reverence and turn to walk back to your mount, the great bird. You do not look back at the temple or the altar and simply settle onto your ally and lean in with a firm grasp as you are transported safely and swiftly back down to land beside the towering world tree. You give thanks and reverence to the great bird and watch as it returns home, skybound.

The Road to the Underworld

The road to the underworld can take us on one of two major highways—literally downward to visit the sisters of Wyrd or Fate who guard the Well of Memory, or across the sunless sea to the Isle of Apples. Of course, there are multiple byways and paths off the beaten track.

Within the Celtic cosmology of land, sky, and sea, it is sea that is parallel with or synonymous to the underworld. Briefly, again, the reasoning is that in the Celtic cultures, to the west was the great Atlantic Ocean, and as the sun set over the immortal horizon, it disappeared (across the sunless sea) through the mist and claimed the throne of the underworld. We often expect the underworld to be dark, obscure, and gloomy, but it may be our current paradigm of the Christian Hell that shapes this perception for us. We must remember that to many ancient and mystical cultures and societies, it was believed that there were stars or fields of light under the soil, and this is the power that the seeds drew their great strength and potency from to bring forth crops and abundance (fertility). The underworld/sea is, in fact, a place of prosperity, riches, renewal, rest, and revivification. Its companion is shadow self (or fetch), and thus we are also moving through the "subconscious"—the bridge between the conscious talking self and the unconsciousness of the star self—the realm of dreams. We walk upon the heaving, white waves of the cresting sea and find ourselves dancing through dream-swollen mists. The Other is all around. Here it is the true space in between (land and sky); we meet the past, present, and future and the infinite possibilities that swirl endlessly around our Wyrd.

The Well of Memory and the Sisters of Wyrd

The Well of Memory was discussed in *BLSS,* and I relayed the powerful, transformational story of a dear friend of mine and his journey through and with Death to re-membering. Memory is not simply a recollection of past events; it is, in fact, the reflection of the Weaver/God Herself within the vibration of the Web; within the unfolding of her holy being. Memory is the divine mirror to the thoughts, actions, and weavings of Own Holy Self. Memory is neither etheric nor entirely substantial; it is the breath in between and as such is a gift of the sea, of the underworld. It is upon reflection and in hindsight that we begin to perceive the "bigger picture."

This pathworking intends for an encounter with the sisters of Wyrd or the Keepers of Fate. Whatever names or faces they show to you are the right ones, and you will derive the insight and wisdom needed.

chapter five

Before embarking on this journey, it is important to first place oneself at the world tree and come to the holy centre. Go through the world tree pathworking (see page 127).

You stand before the world tree and listen to the deep, chthonic pulse of water against stone. You yearn to travel the road to the underworld. Nostalgia overwhelms your being, and you glide towards the great tree. In your mind an image forms—one of a perfect door—and as you near the tree you find that this exact image becomes the portal through which you must enter the tree. When you reach the door in the tree, you find that a key is required to unlock the door. Your hands come to your throat, and you find a key on a thread around your neck. This key is yours and yours alone, and it slides neatly into the keyhole, turns, and the door yields.

Before you twists and turns an ancient and shadow-swept spiral staircase. The stairs disappear around a corner, and your first foot forward is followed swiftly by your second. As each step down becomes broader and lower, you find that it becomes a gradual meditation of deepening. You sink more deeply into the rhythm and repetition of the descent. You are so involved and enraptured by this process that you are almost shocked when you see a warm, flickering light in the distance. It grows brighter and becomes more filled with a radiant warmth, and soon you find yourself at the edge of a wide and open cavern.

As you step inward into what feels like a warm, wet womb, you notice a cauldron in the centre of the cavern; the cauldron's base disappears straight into the soft earth beneath it—it seems to become a well. Three figures surround the cauldron-well. They are draped in robes of grey, and they emanate a feeling of timelessness. As you take a further step into the cavern, the sound piques their interest, and they glance up at you. Their faces are hidden by translucent veils, and yet you notice their bright, deep eyes, constantly watering at the edges as if tears of overwhelming memories are welling up inside. They open their arms collectively and call you into their embrace.

You drift over to the sisters as if wading through a dream, and you find that you are kneeling now, surrounded by the Wyrd Ones as they create a circle around you with their bodies and beings. Hands held, they begin to resonate a low chant, wordless yet ancient. You peer over the edge of the cauldron's lip. What do you see?

To the Isle of Apples Across the Sunless Sea

Continuing from the previous pathworking:

… You perceive a massing of shadow on the surface of the water, and you are drawn further in, your eyes coming to a clearer focus to behold the mystery of Shadow dancing with Water. The low chant becomes a high, vibrating shriek, almost bloodcurdling, and you hear the massing and writhing voices of beloved dead and ancestors from long ago. A desirous force moves you to lean farther into the cauldron until your nose and lips touch the velvet tension of the water's surface… you fall—you fall!

There is no splash or cold-wrapped shivering body, for you are in a boat, and you are sailing across a silver, shining sea. You are sailing upon calm waters and are weaving through wave after wave of blessed serenity.

Suddenly the scent of fresh-blooming apples washes over you, overwhelming and intoxicating your senses. Faintly, in the distance, you perceive a mass of land rising from the cresting waves. As a strong current of wind fills the sails above you, you glide swiftly to the shores of this soulful island. In your mind you name this place the Isle of Apples for the strong scent of this fruit.

Above you, a silver sun and a golden moon dance together and kiss sweetly. You walk across diamond-white sand and move to higher ground and into a thickly treed forest: a WildWood—twisted trees and tangled flowers, stones dreaming in the emerald hue of the sacred place, and herbs slithering like cunning serpents through the enraptured undergrowth. Tree-boughs heavily laden with apples appear at every bend, and you find yourself standing at the entrance to a perfect apple grove.

Your heart seems to grow silent, reverent of the stillness and solitude of this place. There is a cauldron in the centre of this grove too, and an old woman guards the liquid-flaming crucible. She gestures to you with one finger, and her dark, intense stare transfixes your spirit. You move, as if in a trance, to the cauldron in the centre of the apple grove. The nearer you come to the cauldron, the younger the woman becomes, until she appears as a playful, mischievous nymph. She is holding a wooden ladle and offers you a drink from the steaming broth she is stirring and keeping. You lean into drink, but she pulls the ladle away from you and laughs. The nine apple trees surrounding you begin to vibrate and shake, and seem to laugh in return. An apple drops from one of the branches and rolls to your feet. The young girl giggles and stares down towards the apple, and you hear and know her thoughts.

You pick up the bright, red apple, knowing that this is a gift, a blessing, from this otherworldly place across the sunless sea. You look up once more and smile at the golden moon and silver sun. You look back across the cauldron, and in the nymph's place is a full-breasted and bellied woman—a mother...a matrix. She holds the ladle out to you again, and as you lean in to drink, holding the apple in your left hand and channelling blazing intent from your right, a veil of black space folds around you. There is no looking—there is nowhere to look—until you seem to be floating in the cool breath of the primordial seas, and you gaze up at what seems to be three moons high in the heavens. These three moons bear timeless faces, and fluttering breezes shift the silken robes they wear... robes? Faces? The three sisters of Wyrd, of Fate, living and knowing itself, peer down upon you; you are kneeling in the waters of the cauldron.

You stand and step out of the cauldron, and the sisters hold out a white robe for you. You dress and breathe in the sweetness of the cavern—herbs have been burning. Sage, rosemary, peppermint, mugwort, and thyme, their smell strong to the senses. You look down at your left hand and see that you are still firmly grasping the apple the woman gifted you. You hold it up to the flickering flame of the cauldron, and the sisters kneel and bow their heads to the Mighty One— to the secret within. You know what you must do. The robe that you are wearing is fitted with a cord-belt, and hanging in a pouch is a blade. You unsheathe it, and it glimmers in the firelight—with your right hand and blade, you slice the apple in half, crosswise. The star!

chapter five

You find yourself at the topmost of the world tree, hands free and open to the winds of change—to the changing course of Fate. Your star shines radiant above you, resting upon your crown. You whisper this holy prayer as you look down upon the patterns of the undulating land: "Who is this flower above me?"

You sing this holy prayer as you cradle the bright star upon your crown: "And what is the work of this god?"

You chant this holy prayer as your hands fold upon the secret of your heart and the red-fleshed apple that reminded you: "I would know myself in all my parts."

chapter six

ecstatic spellcraft

"You must envision it to experience it. Summon it with every dancing molecule of your body, with every vesper, every wish and prayer, every uttered breath. Do not believe—know!"
    Phyllis Curott, *The Love Spell* (Nonna's words)

Those who have read *Spirited* will be familiar with what I call "successful spellcraft," which is tried and true methods and metaphysical laws that govern the energetic realms and ensure the Witch success in his or her magickal endeavours. In this chapter I will be introducing a technique of shamanic spellcraft (ecstatic spellcraft) that awakens the primal senses and inspires the spirit to embrace the destiny to manifest.

As Witches, our spells do not define who we are, but it is important to understand our spells as psychic imprints that can be effectively traced back to their point of origin (the caster/the dreamer/we who desire). When we cast a spell, we are making affirmed choices and devoting ourselves to seeing out the course until direct manifestation. At times this may be as straightforward as requiring extra cash and obtaining it through spellcraft within a matter of days or casting out energetic nets to draw in love or a well-suited lover and waiting a full solar cycle until the fulfilment of the charge. During that year, the spell will teach the Witch about the true nature of self-love and how when we stop looking, love finds us. Spellcraft is much more than it seems and is hardly a superficial or selfish act, unless it is approached in that manner. For instance, most of the spells I cast are for others' benefit. They range from selling property to evoking happiness and strength. I have also found that a spell is no discrete thing, and, in retrospect, once the "flood gates" are opened, they can rarely, if ever, be closed and will continue to take effect and express in a variety of ways.

Ecstatic spellcraft utilises trance states in order to propel the Witch's innate life force into an intensified spiral of power. This kind of spellcraft is generally performed on one's own; however, the presence of others will not necessarily detract from the raw energy being raised. Dance, songs and chants, columns of incense smoke, and the rhythmic pulse underlying effective ritual will aid in the efficacy of such workings. Here I will examine different aspects of ecstatic spellcraft and provide an effective method through which to implement the sacred practice.

Spellcraft as Empowerment and Liberation

"She who fain/Would learn all sorcery yet has not won/Its deepest secrets, them my mother will/Teach her, in truth all things as yet unknown./And ye shall all be freed from slavery,/And so ye shall be free in everything…"

Aradia: Gospel of the Witches
(Diana's Charge to Aradia)

In early 2010 I ran a series of workshops entitled *The Spirited Life: Walking the Talk of the Witch*. One part of the workshop involved the discussion of magick as psychology, magick as philosophy, magick as art and science, and magick as life force. After the preliminary discussion, I would then lead the group in a psyball creation exercise, in which we created energetic vessels for needs, desires, or wishes and, at the intuited time, we each released them into the cosmos (or ourselves or another physical container) so that they would come to manifestation in the natural order of things. Afterwards, during the debrief, I would ask everyone how they felt about being able to successfully create change with the power innate within and bring renewal or end to various aspects within their lives. The answers generally could be typified as the following—"I feel empowered, natural, alive, a part of all existence and inextricably connected. I feel that it is my destiny to manifest."

When we can truly embrace the destiny within all of us to cocreate with the cosmic forces (that also flow through us), we awaken to the deep source of primal power that reminds us constantly that we are divine and walk as gods amongst gods.

The practice of spellcraft is not merely for the attainment of "things," it is also medicine in the Native sense—we are able to definitively choose our own paths and therefore be an active and conscious part of the All of creativity. When I hear that spellcraft is akin to prayer I tend to shudder inwardly; this is simply not my experience and therefore not my belief. Spellcraft and its associated magickal methodologies are concerned with affirming a choice and willfully manifesting to attain a desire, fulfil necessity, and effect change. Spellcraft is acknowledging, accepting, and affirming the sacred principle or charge of the Witches: magick.

During Christopher Penczak's 2010 Australian tour, a few things that were discussed during the workshops enlightened me to how Maslow's hierarchy of needs can actually inform our magickal Craft and evolutionary pursuits. According to the hierarchy of needs, the reasoning behind casting spells at an early age (or at the beginning of one's Craft "career") aimed at financial prosperity, securing a job, invoking love/r/s and seeking popularity, confidence, etc., is because, realistically speaking, we require all of these physically or emotionally nourishing things before we can begin to holistically weave in spiritual and psychological well-being. However, I do not believe spellcraft is limited to the acquisition or attainment of only "physical" ends. Spellcraft is a method of throwing oneself into the current of life and successfully flowing in accord with one's pure will (in the Crowleyan sense).

Spellcraft provides a context for our empowerment and liberation as human beings. It does so because it is a sorcerous pathway.

Sorcery

The idea of "sorcery" in contemporary Craft traditions is often one met with derision or scepticism. Sorcery seems to negate the idea that Witchcraft is a religious tradition. Raven Grimassi often speaks of a distinction between Stregheria (the Old Religion of the Witches) and Stregoneria (sorcery). Grimassi places an emphasis on Aradia, her mother, Diana, and the horned consort. While magick and spellcraft is integral (or part and parcel) to the Witches' religion, the emphasis seems to be on the Mystery Tradition as interwoven into the theology.

My Feri teacher, Storm Faerywolf (founder of the BlueRose line of Feri), feels it is not the fault of the Traditional Craft that it has become associated with religion and Mystery Traditions, and that the entwined strands of spirituality and sorcery can be called the "crooked path," or what I call the wild way. I would also add to this that all things are Spirit, therefore all is implicitly spiritual. Storm also has this to say on the topic of sorcery:

> In some ways the popular portrayal of sorcery isn't too far off. The sorcerer, Witch, or wizard is someone who wields powers that are unknown or even frightening to most. They alone know the uses of special stones, of herbs or bones to heal the sick and to charm the Fates. They preserve the knowledge of arcane words and how to chant them until trance is achieved. They might speak with spirits and divine the future. Perhaps they burn candles dressed with oils or make charms of roots and wax or draw circles

with salt. Maybe they sing to the spirits, or dance 'round a fire, or drum up ancient powers from the earth. Whatever methods they might employ on the surface, the underlying commonality in these practices remains: the harnessing of metaphysical powers, otherworldly spirits, or occult forces in order to direct the alteration of circumstances and occurrences in the mundane world. While some forms of magic cast practical concerns aside and are concerned purely with spiritual development, sorcery deals with the real needs of real people, such as healing, protection, love, or money. To put it simply, sorcery is magic for the real world.

In my mind, this reiterates the applicability of Maslow's hierarchy of needs when studying the motivations behind magickal intent. To be sorcerous, then, is to be grounded in the here and now and to endeavour to enhance the fullness of one's quality of life. The road would then diverge, and this is where the analogy of the crooked path or wild way comes into play. We can continue on the path of focussing only (or largely) on the mundane, physical, and directly immediate plane, or we could also delve into the centre of the here and now and come to find the intense power of divinity that resonates within it and align or devote to it. Truly, however, if one cannot or does not respect this divinity (however we choose to relate to it), the power will not work for us. Therefore, there is great merit in both religion and what we normally class as "magick" but what I would call sorcery, as magick, in my path, is the name I apply to the vital life force that animates all things.

To be sorcerous is to endeavour to be of aid, not only to oneself but to one's human and nonhuman community (though one or the other may be specialised in) and eventually to the greater cosmos. These gradients have names in the ancient Greek traditions: thaumaturgy (sorcery and practical magick) and theurgy (magick and ritual for communion with the gods and with the Immanent Divine).

This all resonates with the original Charge of the Goddess—or, rather, the Aradian charge from Diana (queen of the Witches) to her divine daughter, Aradia. In this text first published in the late nineteenth century, we discover that in adhering to *la Vecchia Religione* (literally, the Old Religion), a Witch attains certain gifts, or powers. The following is a slightly modernised version:[68]

> *To bring success in love*
>
> *To bless and consecrate (and to banish and curse)*
>
> *To speak with spirits*
>
> *To know of hidden things*
>
> *To call forth spirits*
>
> *To know the voice of the wind*
>
> *To possess the knowledge of transformation*
>
> *To possess the knowledge of divination*
>
> *To know and understand secret signs*
>
> *To cure disease*
>
> *To bring forth beauty*
>
> *To have influence over wild beasts*

Spellcraft as Determination to Manifest Through the Elements

I have mentioned the elemental pathways of both manifestation and gnosis throughout this book, and in this section I will readdress how and why they are connected to the concept of and execution of spellcraft.

If spellcraft is underlined by the determination to manifest, then the pathway of manifestation is the obvious formula to achieve this. Beginning with air…

---

[68] The original terminology extracted directly from *Aradia* is as follows: "To bring success in love. To bless or curse with power friends or enemies (to do good or evil). To converse with spirits. To find hidden treasures in ancient ruins. To conjure the spirits of priests who died leaving treasures. To understand the voice of the wind. To change water into wine. To divine with cards. To know the secrets of the hand (palmistry). To cure diseases. To make those who are ugly beautiful. To tame wild beasts."

Air: Clarity of Intent and Distillation of Thought (To Know)

Ask yourself:

What is my intent? Why is this my intent? How will I specify my intent? Is my intent relevant to my context or circumstance? How will my intent help to empower and liberate my pure will? How will my intent help to enhance and deepen my living myth?

Fire: Impassioned Intent and Activation of Energy (To Dare)

Do:

Excite your senses; titillate your visual, olfactory, aural, oral, and tactile senses! Raise the body (and therefore spirit) to a state of arousal, provocation, and ecstasy—move into or through extremities, e.g., if you begin to tire of the rhythm or repetition of your method of raising power, ensure that you break through this barrier. Also ensure, however, that you tread the fine line between compulsion and exertion safely.

Water: Channelled Intent and Flowing Energy (To Will)

Feel:

The tide of magickal power (vital life force) heaving and sighing; know the breaking point, and open your consciousness to intuit the moment of climax and thus release. Feel absolute conviction towards your goal, and flow in that pure stream of ecstasy that has lifted your own vibration!

Earth: Grounding of Intent and Planting of Energetic Seeds (To Be Silent)

Know:

The intent has travelled towards its completion and has become a seed of itself to be nourished within the cauldron of spirit (the dark cauldron of nature). The seeds have been planted, and the Magician's Pyramid[69] advises that privacy, mystery, and reverence be held for the energetic seed as it begins to grow, imbued by a greatly focused power.

A Note on "Order"

During a workshop I held in Canberra (Australian Capital Territory), I presented this concept of what I have sometimes referred to as the "alchemical" formulae hidden within the elemental pathways. A friend of mine added that to effectively cast a spell or work towards the fulfilment of an end, one might not necessarily start with air and the clarification of intent; rather, one might be impassioned (fire) by a cause first and then seek to work magically, which I completely agree with. However, perhaps I am referring more to a mechanism than the unfolding dynamic of how one journeys towards casting a spell, or how motivation, or impetus, develops and arises. However, I maintain that in order to cast a successful spell, one must centre into clarity of intent and then move from that point into impassioning it, channelling it, and grounding it. However, to reiterate, one can be motivated and inspired by any part of this elemental equation to create change in the first place.

Elemental Pathway of Manifestation: A Spell

You need absolutely nothing external for this working.

Breathe into your centre.

As you breathe deeply and rhythmically, begin to draw down cosmic light, and let it pool at your crown. It amplifies as the vibration intensifies, and you feel the word *spirit* resonate through your being. You begin to feel heightened and truly connected to the All—to infinite possibility.

---

69 The Magician's Pyramid is sometimes referred to as the Hermetic Quadrant or the Witch's Pyramid: *To Know, to Dare, to Will, and to Keep Silent*. I find that the progression of the pyramid in linear order reflects quite well the air-fire-water-earth (respectively) formula.

As you breathe deeply and rhythmically and you draw this cosmic light of Spirit down through your crown, your head, it condenses into a seed of pulsing light. It hovers at the gateway of your lips, and as your breath cycles it begins to glow and radiate, and you clarify your intention. You create a visualisation—an image to target, to build upon—the outcome as you desire it and not the process of how it will develop. The word *air* vibrates through your being, and as it does it draws this visualisation into your chest, in which your primal heart is pounding ceaselessly and creating a meter for the power that is raising to a point and about to dance in the fire.

As you breathe deeply and rhythmically and you draw this spirit seed into your sex, the fire of generation glows brightly, and the flames in this ancient crucible dance with the vigour of passion and the courage of daring! The visualisation no longer needs to be held by the head or mind. It is now taken into the flame and is transformed into a thriving, lived experience—you feel it in every piece of you, and the word *fire* races through your being.

As you breathe deeply and rhythmically, this power becomes channelled to a point and swoops through your being, bringing you to your knees (perhaps physically, but definitely symbolically). The word *water* wells up inside of your swollen soul; pieces and pieces of desire, longing, ferocious need, and yearning to change and transform (yourself or a situation) begin to weave together and melt into a river that rushes towards a sea.

As you breathe deeply and rhythmically, this holy river of power comes to a broad delta and empties into a sea that becomes a cauldron—the dark cauldron of nature. The spirit seed that has been carried by this momentum of energy—this force; this writhing, excited power—is now dropped into the moist darkness of this cauldron, and the word *earth* moans from its belly (the centre and circumference). You remember now your feet and how they are rooted upon the ground and drawn down irrevocably by the force of gravity—calling all things to become fixed. And so shall your spell be fixed!

This technique is anchored by the same points that the fivefold blessing works with. In its reverse order it becomes the pathway of manifestation, as discussed (from least dense to most dense). The spirit seed (or seed of light) has come from Spirit—has been clarified and distilled by air in the chest, impassioned and activated by fire in the sex, channelled by water at the knees, and grounded and planted by earth in the feet. What is subtly implied, of course, is that the dark cauldron of nature that the seed has been planted within is, in fact, the cosmic matrix—and therefore we return to Spirit. This continuous cycle will actually affect the ether and impregnate it with the "thought-form" expressed by the seed; it will arrange itself to reflect it. This action triggers the process whereby the essential creation becomes embodied within the immediacy of the flesh and the direct here and now. So is the spell cast, and so is the outcome necessitated.

The Law of Three, Karma, and Spellcraft

"I am the owner of my karma.
I inherit my karma.
I am born of my karma.
I am related to my karma.
I live supported by my karma.
Whatever karma I create, whether good or evil, that I shall inherit."
The Buddha, *Anguttara Nikaya V. 57,*
Upajjhatthana Sutta

The capacity of spellcraft to instruct in the ways of the Witch is infinite. The Witch is forever learning the cosmic laws (the ways of nature) through the true Law of Three—a law that, in my mind at least, does not represent any kind of ancient Pagan morality or ethical code of conduct. The Law of Three has been explained by Rev. Shé D'Montford as the following, and it certainly rings true to me: "The Law of Three is action, reaction, and consequence."

In this way, certainly the Law of Three is the Witch's equivalent to the Eastern doctrine of karma.

We often speak of the Threefold Law in terms of aversion. Most beginner's texts on modern-day Witchcraft explain that our "ethics" stem from a desire to avert the wrath of the Threefold Law. Conversely, many authors seem to suggest that the only reason to do good is because according to the Law of Three we will incur three times the good we originally sent out. This, as Phyllis Curott so astutely points out, is not ethics. In many ways, however, it is certainly morality—or rather "do *not* do this" because you will suffer if you do. In this way, karma is not the Law of Three.

Karma translates literally as "action." Action implies reaction, and all reactions bear consequence. As Witches we are taught to be masters of our own destinies and therefore to accept the consequences of our every action—to fully accept and embrace our karma. To reject one's karma is to run from one's shadow, and this we know to be utterly foolish. The way of the shadow is the way of the Witch and certainly of the shaman (and thus the shamanic Witch, especially so!). If we reject or repress our karma, we negate the consequences (though we can never escape them), and we never learn. An instance of the rejection of karma and negation of consequences would be a malicious murderer who deludes himself by confessing his sins to a Catholic priest and then continuing to inflict harm. If we never learn, we never grow, and we can therefore never deepen, never evolve, and never transform. Or, when such transitions do take place, it happens to us and not with our agency; therefore, we are unconscious of the power presented to us, and thus we are truly dead. Or, if the power takes us anyway, we see only evil and turn from the wisdom that could be ours if only we understood the ways of nature and of the cosmos. This is the true message of the Tower card in the traditional tarot. Thus, the Tower represents the true shamanic initiation, regardless of whether it is consciously cultivated or shockingly revealed.

chapter six

We weave with karma at all times; karma, when understood in the pure sense, is almost synonymous with the Germanic concept of Wyrd. Wyrd refers to one's fate sown by one's intent, tempered by the path of the mystery. In many ways, karma refers to the mechanism; the Wyrd is the organic material karma seeds itself within. Thus we reach the point of truly blending the wisdom of the East and the West.

When we cast a spell, we are decisively and definitively aligning to a certain choice. Spells are always cast at the crossroads (either literally or metaphorically), and so we decide the path we will take thereon; the spell reveals the choice we must make in order to invoke, banish, or empower whatever it is we are working for. Allow me to illustrate this concept.

I decide to cast a money spell. I need and want a steadier flow of financial income in my life. I am working diligently in all aspects of my life to open as many doors to such a possibility as I can, and now, as a Witch, I make the affirmed choice to energetically and powerfully restore or peak prosperity to and in my life. The spell I cast effectively opens the floodgate to what it is I desire. It is backed by a powerful need and a powerful wanting (therefore a lack—a void that needs to and will be filled). I align myself with the powers of prosperity; I potentise the spellcasting through the technique of ritual and call upon various spirits to aid in aspect (e.g., Zeus for success and restoration to sovereignty, Hermes for commercial instinct and flow). I vow to myself that I am worthy of success and thus exhibit all outward and inward signs that I am the right candidate for financial prosperity from this moment on. I unleash the power. The gate opens. I receive. I am grateful and give thanks. I have made the choice. The ritual of the spellcasting gave that choice impetus and integrity in all the worlds (if I understand the dynamics of energetics correctly and align to all the worlds), and thus the spell will work; there is no way it cannot. I have simply given my spirit lease to venture down the path that will allow both energies (my own and that of my prosperity) to meet in the middle. I have called to myself a particular destiny and mirrored it within my being. The spell has revealed the aspect of fate that could have been, and now, because I decided it to be so, is.

Thus spells instruct us in the ways of the Witch both philosophically and energetically. I learn the reality that all things are connected because the self that is me (bound by the ego that declares "I am I") was able to create discrete certainty out of infinite possibility. I learn that choice is the determining factor and that the Craft teaches us that total freedom equals total responsibility. Thus, ethically I learn to revere the Law of Three because my actions will bear reactions, and those reactions give birth to consequences I am responsible for. I cultivate the quality of my life out of desire, yearning, and need.

The Goddess Who Is All Guides Our Magick

The Goddess who is All, who birthed Self from Self, came into being (into what was, is, and always will be) because of desire! She yearned to feel, to know, to touch, to be…she needed this, for whatever reason, and thus the eye of the Goddess opened, and forever there has been intelligence and consciousness in the worlds. That thing we call God, the awareness that life has for itself, is birthed itself because of choice: affirmation of self beyond ego!

"I am," she said; and all other I's were born within that one I. Thus all spells that are cast give birth to new "I's" (or eyes). However, because they come from original intent stemming from "you," the effects—the karma that ensues—will be your karma, and thus the true nature of sorcery, magick, and spellcasting becomes realised within the Witch.

We are able to steer our personal course through the rivers of the blood in the body of God. These rivers are infinite, the current is ever-changing, the tides accustomed to inner rhythms. We may choose to follow whatever river, row into new territory, alight on land

and nourish ourselves for a spell (literally), or continue to the ocean and subsume consciousness in the holy milk of All. Thus spellcraft is more than a basic methodology which allows us to secure what it is we desire or need; it is also a way to become truly real in a world of superficiality. We take it upon ourselves to truly create destiny and walk with fate (not against or away from); we restore self-sovereignty and regain the wholeness that is the agency of Spirit. We effectively become the gods we are. In that moment of spellcasting, we are utilising the basic elements of life to forge new realities from an ocean of infinite chance and possibility. We are saying "this shall be" and ordaining it so, thus establishing concrete foundations for change, growth, transformation, and rebirth; therefore this is both a powerful and a dangerous art. As with all things worthwhile, there is ever an element of risk.

What Spells Reveal about the Nature of Things

Spells also teach us about the nature of things, of the aspects—of what it means to love; to be prosperous; to feel protected, safe, and secure; to glow with beauty and attract wonder!

Let me speak of love…

In late 2008 I journeyed for nine weeks through the UK, Ireland, and Greece with two wonderful Pagan friends. We came together one afternoon in a small forested area in an Oxfordshire village and with three apples cast our destinies; we called for love. We envisioned what we desired personally, and we raised the mighty power and released it, allowing it freedom to manifest our wills. We each felt the pull in the next few months of what was to come, as all Witches do once they have affirmed decisions and chosen to work towards them with magickal impetus. When I returned to Australia, it was a week before our festival of Beltaine (October 31 or thereabouts in the Southern Hemisphere). I felt my wonder-voyage was punctuated by this holy day. Then my ex happened to be visiting from Japan, where he had moved after we broke up in early 2007. We decided to see each other in absolutely platonic circumstances—it had been the first time in nearly two years. A few weeks later I met and started dating a very attractive dancer. That was short-lived, and yet every card pulled, every song sang, and every wind blown spoke of love coming for me.

I cried out to Aphrodite, and both she and Freya came. They taught me that before I could truly draw true and powerful love into my life, I needed to claim the sovereignty of my Self—I needed to fall in love with me; to pluck the apple that was mine, and mine alone, to eat. Over the next few months I worked with the Grail—the receptivity and deep poetry of my own being—my own capacity to accept, receive, and be open to the mystery. One balmy January evening as I walked home from a friend's house, Aphrodite appeared before me; in my Book of Shadows I wrote that she "came with a sword and told me I was ready, and I know I am...but either way it's my journey. She poured the blessed waters of her/my grail over me, and then I prayed for blessings."

The Golden Goddess smiled as she held the cup above my head. I could hear the divine water inside of it—the water of my self-love—splashing around, brimming and ready to overflow. Her eyes shone with clear and ethereal radiance—her laughter echoing through my soul. She upturned the holy cup and down flowed the water of my love, and into the depth of me did it run. There was a secret in her smile as she shimmered into the air.

The new moon came in the month of April. We (the inner court of the Coven of the WildWood) meditated in each direction and with each element, and we banished and/or resolved those things which we felt hindered or blocked our soul growth. In my Book of Shadows, I wrote:

chapter six

We passed negative feelings concerning ourselves/lives into elemental objects aligned with these emotions, and released and accepted empowerment instead. With each one we only glowed more as we went around the circle…Air was my inspiration/growth/words/writing; Fire was my lack of embracing my sensual/sexual nature; Water was my sense of flow and sacrifice; and Earth was my criticisms of others' health choices. I watched my fire candle burn down and become two flames as the wick had split in two, and then the chalice tipped and the water spilt onto me. Love is coming…

At a healing weekend a week and a half later, my dear friend Becky read my cards. She saw that a particular individual would be coming into my life—a dark-haired foreigner. Indeed, two weeks later, while out dancing spontaneously, my eyes locked on a dark-haired, handsome face. He watched me from across the room as I danced happily and without a care. I waited, leaving it to fate and his own choice—if he wanted to talk to me, he would. It all flowed. Then, from behind, I felt his hand brush against me, and his fingers wrapped around mine. We danced. We also ended up falling in love and being handfasted.

Through one spell, one affirmed choice, one empowered intention, I shifted the course of my fate—or enhanced and deepened it. Not only does a spell have the propensity to manifest our desires and needs and effect change, spells cast successfully also, by their very nature, create karmic situations by way of Wyrd. This karma, this woven-weaving Wyrd, becomes us, and we become it. Through sovereignty of Self, we have aligned Own Holy Self, and we potentise the hidden potency—we are innately gifted with divine creativity. It is our birthright.

ecstatic spellcraft

The Greater Good

"Do good because it is good to do so."
Unknown

What is goodness? I must first make it obvious that I am not speaking necessarily of good versus evil—at least not in the dualistic, Zoroastrian way. I am speaking of "the Good" that Plato touched on and Plotinus affirmed. Most simply, goodness, or the Good, is the grace of the Divine manifest in the world. It is the flow that derives from the realised pure will as it journeys through life. Sometimes "bad" things will happen as part of this flow; however, they are not "evil"—they offer us opportunity to strengthen, deepen, renew, and learn. Often they are mirror reflections, or alternate, converse reactions to an overall trend or cause. The "good" things also do this in different ways.

We define good and bad in rather absolute ways in modern Western society. In the shamanic Craft, and in most Paganisms, the black-and-white philosophy holds no water; however, this tends to be the paradigm of the overculture. Often, a Pagan might cite the rainbow analogy (and I have done this in the past) to broaden the perspective beyond simply "black and white." Again, this might be too simple an explanation. Yes, there is indeed an entire spectrum of colour that could codify or represent a variety of "ethical" shades of moral fibre; but, in all truth, what is moral and ethical about nature? Ethics seem to be a distinctly human trait. What is "moral" or "ethical" about a hawk sinking its piercingly sharp talons into an unsuspecting field mouse? What is ethical about a tsunami that destroys a coastal village or annual floods that spread disease and kill thousands of the defenceless poor? However, ethics are decidedly present whenever humans are involved.

chapter six

When a hawk kills a field mouse, it is because the hawk has stalked, hunted, and skilfully manoeuvred a descent and swoop which successfully targeted and obtained the field mouse—we would call this survival of the fittest in Darwin's terminology, although this may be an outdated simplification. Nature holds a sacred balance, and ecosystems have evolved to thrive on an integrated and holistic pattern involving several hundred or thousand species that all rely upon another in an interlinked chain. It is not nature, however, which created the hundreds upon thousands of poor that swarm the regions vulnerable to monsoonal flooding in Bangladesh. It was and is human interference—economic manipulation, colonial imposition and dispossession, cultural caste attitudes (directing stratified human value), overpopulation, ignorance due to poor education (again resting upon society, government, and economy), and environmental degradation influenced by all of these factors and their side effects. When humans decided to shift from nomadic, tribal lifestyles and situate themselves permanently, farm and irrigate the land, and impact it directly and continuously, the natural balance began to suffer. It would be extremely difficult to turn back the clock on this; we must now innovate and invite new ways of living and sustaining our human cultures within the broader matrix of natural balance.

Ancient Australian indigenous cultures instituted clan laws and legends that directed the people on how to live with the land and have minimal impact. Laws governed how many eggs one could take from a bird's nest, how many fish one could spear from a river, and prohibitions on travelling into certain areas. Many of their actions, such as fire farming, also drastically altered the landscape over thousands of years; however, the intention of techniques like fire farming was both to flush out game (for food and survival) and to preserve and sustain the integrity of the bushland—many of the plant species benefit greatly from the heat and flame. Fire farming allowed for thick and old growth to die and for the germination of particular seeds in the now rich, active soil. Today, we ignore the ancient Aboriginal knowledge. We ignore the nomad instinct (that birthed the spirituality of the shaman) and understanding of the land as living, vital, and necessary—it is not real to us; it is an idea, nothing more. How do we resurrect the ethical systems that aid humanity to add to the balance of nature?

How does any of the above affect a Witch's ethics when it comes to the empowered choices we propel into momentum by casting a spell or committing to sorcerous intent? It does because we come to realise that, essentially, ethics is only applicable to the bigger picture (from the human perspective) when we align with the balance of nature—its equilibrium. We are not divorced from nature and neither are our lives and all that involves (prosperity, love, security, hearth and home, family, work, etc.). What we are actually asking when we state "for the greater good" is "how will this choice or action add to my life's balance, fullness, and equilibrium? How will I (as person and associated circumstance, such as quality of life) be enhanced, deepened, realised, and defined by this?"

I maintain that the only ultimate ethic a Witch (or anyone) can live by is that total freedom equals total responsibility. There are no specific moral imperatives (to be ever-loving, compassionate, peaceful, unaffected, unattached, etc.), there is only the understanding that to activate true sovereignty of Self (and that is all we can ever hope to be sovereign "over"), we must make ourselves worthy of that deep potentiality—we must be entirely accountable and responsible. The only way to achieve this is to work for ignited awareness and to reinforce this every day of our lives. This is the journey of the Witch and indeed of any aware being.

chapter six

The Shamanic Spellcasting

The spellcasting ritual below provides a framework for ecstatic spellcraft. This particular method, like much of what I am offering within this book, organically evolved through my cultivated practice and interaction with the spirits. Hekate particularly aided in my reception of this technique; the Great Goddess hinted to me that the four directions also have another function within sorcerous arts. Not only do they provide us with powerful and resonant orientation to sacred cosmology, they are gateways to the potencies that are magick that is life force. When we unlock the gates and open to the flow of magickal power, we become imbued with the holy spark of creativity, which meets with our own hidden potency and is ignited thereby.

Ecstatic spellcraft is just that, and it requires indulgence. I am not hinting at external substances or agencies, I am speaking of the attitude one brings to the process: one of treating the experience of the spell as one to be entirely present within. When I cast spells, I become them—I become the realised potentiality of what I am seeking to draw in, banish, or transform. Whether I am working for myself or another, ultimately I am working for the greater good and not in the moralistic sense.

The Technique

Meditate upon the elemental pathway of manifestation; reflect and ask yourself the questions posed, and become grounded in your intent.

This spellcasting requires one spirit ally who can act as a gatekeeper. In my case, this is Hekate—but for others it may be Hermes, Papa Legba, Ganesha, etc. This may also be mutable within your own practice—for instance, if Hekate does not stand at the gates for me, then I would most likely ask Hermes or Dian y Glas, the Feri Blue God. However, it is to Hekate that I go to first in this endeavour, especially as related to spellcraft and sorcery.

This technique does not require specific items and provides an open framework for the individual to personalise, adapt, and fill out. I personally work with minimal materials (sometimes none) when casting spells; however, depending on the circumstance, I might employ the agency of plant or stone allies, candles, pouches and bags, etc. Due to my cunning charge I leave the mode of the spell up to the individual's preferences, e.g., if something tactile is desired or needed, then I will create a necklace, bracelet, charm bag, etc. However, in many cases I will be working for someone physically distanced from me who is unable to physically retrieve anything from me in the timeframe. While these physical items can indeed help the process, either psychologically or metaphysically (and often both simultaneously), a spell that is cast effectively with power does not have to rely on a tactile reminder to manifest, unless of course the power is released into one. This then becomes the link of the spell and therefore must be burnt (e.g., a candle), kept on the person (e.g., a charm, amulet, or talisman), or released to the elements (into a waterway, the wind, burnt, or buried in the earth) in some form, and often only after the spell has worked and results have been seen.

The Meaning of the Words

I unlock the gates of magick
I untie the ties of time
I surrender to all space
Invoking power with this rhyme!

The initiating incantation for the shamanic spellcasting illustrates how one should approach the act and with what emphases in mind.

I Unlock the Gates of Magick: The gates of magick can be visualised or anchored at the directions (whether you focus on the four cardinal directions or the six/seven spoken of in Feri). They are the swirling vortices of ancient, ever-renewing power (mana, qi, prana, magick) that surge from the "corners" of the cosmos when we come to our holy centre. This power makes all things possible.

In the technique offered here, the directions would have already been acknowledged and honoured before this incantation or prayer is made. Therefore we are reiterating, reaffirming, but also placing our trust in one of our invoked allies—the gatekeeper. The gatekeeper fulfils the role of standing guard at these open portals and watching over the merging of worlds—facilitating the flow. As the Other realms become one with our own and infinite possibility is ignited, we are able to truly plant our energetic seeds in the Aether, in the Spirit, in the realm of the highest vibration. This will enact the metaphysical laws of manifestation, as has been discussed.

The gates also represent what we are barred from—the barriers to seizing power and making change. Thus, unlocking and opening the gates of magick is the beginning and stirring of power within the Witch.

I Untie the Ties of Time: Another reiteration of what the circle-casting has established both energetically and cosmologically for the working. To ensure that the linear A-B movement of time or illusion thereof is superseded and that in touching the flow of All, we effectively become the flow of All and thus the active agency of the will of fate.

I Surrender to All Space: As with untying the ties of time, this phrase reaffirms the sacred orientation to "space outside of space and time outside of time." To "surrender" to this is to allow oneself to be saturated by the very nature of all space, which equals spacelessness; therefore, it would be just as accurate to say "I surrender to all spacelessness." By doing this we come to the here and now, the tween, the All-in-One/One-in-All, and cultivate the poetic, philosophical, and fundamental truths of the circle.

Invoking Power with This Rhyme

This is perhaps one of the most important points. Rhyme comes from the Greek *rhei*, meaning "to flow." Rhei also gives us *rhythm*, and rhythm (which can be channelled by rhyme) allows for the powerful flow of magick to be raised, directed, amplified, and released. On a practical note, rhythm provides a framework through which we may enter a trance state safely and therefore lay aside the calculations of talking self (whom we already engaged through the elemental reflections) to delve into the indulgences of shadow self and thereby connect and commune with star self, who will aid us in planting the seed of our intent in the vibrating ether.

When I cast a spell, it is ecstatic because I do, in fact, become entirely entranced by the process. I revel and riot between the worlds where the power surges and flows free because I can be the totality of my being and step into my Own Holy Self—I activate my hidden potency and it becomes a living potency (I self-actualise; I become God/dess). I often ask to be left alone when I undergo a working because I am aware of how I transform and at times this can frighten others. It is akin to a kind of possession, and yet what I am filled with is myself in condensed and concentrated form. I have not only opened the gates of magick at the corners of the cosmos, but I have opened gateways within myself to enormous potential; I have dissolved into time and surrendered to space, and therefore I have placed myself firmly in the here and now, touching all. I invoke the power with rhyme and rhythm and draw the power to a point. I am Witch!

The Ritual

Breathe. Align both the three realms and the three souls (or reverse order, depending on your feeling). Cast the circle and honour the directions. Make your prayer or invocation to your gatekeeper, and then incant the following aloud, making the appropriate offerings or gestures:

> *I unlock the gates of magick*
> *I untie the ties of time*
> *I surrender to all space*
> *Invoking power with this rhyme!*

State the purpose—the intent—clearly, perhaps using the following formula as you instigate the visualisation and allow it to subsume your consciousness:

> *By air my intent (state intention aloud) is clarified*
> *By fire my intent (state intention aloud) is impassioned*
> *By water my intent (state intention aloud) is channelled*
> *By earth my intent (state intention aloud) is grounded*
> *In the name of Spirit, my intent is given to magick!*

Begin to raise the power in whichever way you wish or feel is appropriate for the particular endeavour. I will generally clap, stamp my feet rhythmically, or dance freeform within the circle. Rocking, sexual intercourse, masturbation, drumming, etc., are also options. I will also chant the following:

> *I raise the power, I raise the power*
> *I raise it well, I raise it well*
> *In this hour, in this hour*
> *For this spell, for this spell!*

Continue rhythmically until the energy begins to crescendo and then climax, and you intuit the moment to release (releasing not only the energy but the visualisation, the attachment, etc.). At this point it is important to be swollen with the knowing that the spell will and has worked, and for the greater good—it is complete, it is done. Fall to the ground; collapse in a heap and, depending on how overwhelmed you feel, one or both of the following can be done to ensure psychic equilibrium is restored:

1. If saliva has built up in your mouth, spit it onto the ground. Wet the forefinger of your power hand with the spittle and anoint your forehead with it and say: *"Power in me, with me, for me."*

2. Resonate the phrase "stone of the earth" through your body and being. This effectively restores balance to the body, equilibrium to the spirit, and sanity to the mind. I say sanity because in true shamanic spellcraft, one becomes frenzied with the power.

Post-Spell

In the Craft, the first thing we often learn with spellcasting is that we must never think upon our spells in the aftermath. I disagree. I believe we should not dwell upon them or become anxious about when and how the outcome will manifest. The best analogy I have ever heard was that casting a spell is like planting a seed; if you continuously dig up the seed to see if it is growing, chances are it will not grow. However, if you do think upon your spell, consider your thoughts to be like the water and sunlight a seed requires to germinate and grow. Ensure that your thoughts add to and enhance the possibilities of manifestation, rather than bar, hinder, or debilitate. Another important consideration is what I call the spell's seal.

In many mystical and magickal cultures, divination occurs to ensure that offerings and sacrifices have been well received by the gods or spirits. In ten years of casting spells (for both myself and others) I have noticed that in the following few hours (and sometimes instantly) a synchronous seal will present itself as to whether the spell was effective or not. Examples I have experienced include the opening of Aphrodite's legs after a love spell for a friend, a police car driving past the moment I exited a business that I helped to bless and protect, and receiving too much change back after a prosperity spell. These were obvious signs (or seals) to me that the spell had been successful, and therefore any or all anxiety concerning the spell's forthcoming results were put to rest. Generally speaking, if the spell is ineffective, one will feel this very strongly during the working or immediately after. This is a feeling of incompletion, disappointment, or even illness, depending on the nature of the working. Either attempt the working again or meditate on or divine the reason as to why the spell may have failed.

The Success of Spellcraft

I am of the opinion and experience that spellcraft works 90 percent of the time. If a spell or working fails, there are generally only two reasons:

1. The will was not aligned with the working (or the spell failed because of lack of focus or diligence on the part of the caster).

2. A greater will opposed the will of the Witch (or another spirit or force denied you access to the desired outcome).

The remedy to the first point is to simply try again and ensure that one is completely present within the working and flowing with the magickal current. Purifications and alignment techniques such as further spiral soul and three realms workings will aid with this. If materials are used or allies invoked, then all must be vibrating together—the materials should be charged to the task and the allies awoken and enhanced to the charge. Also check cosmic or celestial conditions—these may apply (e.g., phase of the moon, day of the week, astrological sign, planetary hour, etc.)—however, I generally maintain that if the need or desire is strong, so shall be the working, no matter what day or phase of the moon.

The remedy for the second point is further meditation and divination. It could be that a deity or spirit you are allied with resents what you are working for, or it may be against a binding, geis, or vow you are circumstantially forgetting or attempting to circumnavigate. In this case, counsel with the spirit or spirits will either clear the problem or at least enlighten you to it. If the will that is stronger is another human being's (another magician, Witch, shaman, etc.), then if you believe strongly in the endeavour, you may perform a banishing on the influence and a protection from it, or enter into battle. An example of when *not* to enter battle would be the following:

One of my uncles in Bali once told my mother and me about an instance in which one *balian* (a type of Balinese shaman) was working against rain for the smooth running of a ceremony; simultaneously, another balian a few villages over was doing the same thing for another ceremony. The balian with the stronger will won out, and it rained in the other village. The rain clouds were present in the atmosphere, they weren't going to simply evanesce, and so they moved over a few villages and emptied their bounty on the other village.

A situation in which it might be appropriate to "enter into battle" would be if someone had a personal vendetta against you and was simply attempting to thwart your every action. If this was persistent and effective, one might strike back with a banishing and protection (as mentioned above) or a binding or curse. The latter should never be entered into lightly, but their use is contextual, and in remembering the ethic of total freedom equals total responsibility, we are charged to act upon our volition as we each personally determine appropriate.

For further information on spellcraft and the mechanics or dynamics thereof, please refer to my chapter on successful spellcraft in my book *Spirited: Taking Paganism Beyond the Circle*.

chapter seven

healing with the power

> "Healing rituals transform the inner world of participants, especially patients. Rituals change experience and expectations, nourish a sense of relationship and support, and encourage reconciliation with the spirits and the sacred. These subjective experiences mediate and evoke objective effects on the body and its disease."
> Roger Walsh, *The World of Shamanism*

The healing art that has been passed to me through my Balinese family[70] has, for the most part, been a subtle one, though hugely important in our family's tradition. My late grandmother was a well-known healer in her community, and my late grandfather had a powerful gift with massage—he could almost instantly entrance those he massaged, or else they would fall into a deep sleep. My father has often asked for me to heal him but has himself offered healing informally to friends and family as "passing or giving power." *Sakti* is the Balinese word for "power"; it derives from the Sanskrit *shakti* for the wellspring

---

[70] Not to negate my mother's family, which has a strong and long history of healing. In fact, my mother's sisters all are/were either nurses or teachers. I have also mentioned my great-great-aunt Sister Elizabeth Kenny in my previous books.

of vitality that we identify as feminine and as the originator and the holder of all things—the partner to Shiva.

The healing I personally practise would be considered "pranic"—however, just like my gift of palmistry, I have never had formal training in any particular modality, nor do I wish to at this stage, though it has been offered to me freely several times. I find my methods are both potent and successful. I have healed headaches, migraines, cramps, stopped the flow of blood, and have generally restored the vital force on many occasions. This I do by simply grounding and centring, building up my auric field, accessing a flow of power from heaven through earth, and wilfully directing and channelling this force into the individual. As I do this, I simply let the light do its work naturally, or I facilitate the healing outcome through visualisation and energetic sensing.

I also employ shamanic ritual and spirit possession as techniques of healing, and these are the arts I will outline within this chapter.

The Laying-On of Hands

The title to this section might be misleading; however, it embodies the broader concept. To become a conduit for healing power or light and to let it flow through you and from you, directed perhaps by your hands, is an age-old technique; it is also effective. Just as in the art of Reiki (to which I have never been attuned), the hands may either be placed directly on the physical body of the patient or placed on or in the aura.

The laying-on of hands is an art that knows no religious bounds and is apparent within many traditions. I already mentioned that my father passes power, or sakti, through his hands (as did his father); in *BLSS* I speak about "pressure touch," a simple variant of this kind of energetic healing work. Depending on the situation and the individual, physical touch may actually be more beneficial; in other cases, *no* touch is desirable or necessary (e.g., for those who have been raped or physically assaulted). What pressure touch enables is the stimulation of the senses and thus the vital flow of life force, which restores the energetic integrity on every level and reconnects self to Self.

The Energetic Bodies and Centres

The Aura

The aura is seen to be the energetic field of vital force that emanates from the spirit core of our being and body. It is that part of us which can be seen to be the "Shining One" (T. Thorn Coyle), which equates to our talking self, as its golden hue surrounds us with a protective layer that also provides us with a telepathic modality of interface. However, the aura is not just the talking self, as the etheric skin that many seers will perceive (which is also often called the aura) parallels with the "Sticky One" (also a term of T. Thorn Coyle's Morningstar Tradition), which is our shadow self. Shadow self is also called Sticky One because the energy of this soul sticks—it is the etheric or psychic mark that we leave on everything we come in contact with. Therefore, for this reason, the healer must shield and protect before attempting to heal another; one must be able to enter into the patient's auric field and remain unaffected by the energetic manifestations of the illness. Even if the illness is "purely" physical, there will be energetic symptoms or ramifications and vice versa.

If we are visually oriented and can see the colour or colours of the aura, then we will be able to translate directly what emotional or psychic state the body (and bodies) is in. However, if one does not see in the psychic way, then it is still possible to interpret the aura through other senses (e.g., one might simply feel the aura and its colours and know the state). A general correspondence chart of colours in the aura might read as follows:

Light Blue: Calm, peaceful, healthy, and balanced

Dark Blue: Serene, tranquil, deep peace, and spiritually rich (or issues relating to sleep and dreams)

Purple or Violet: Psychic, attuned, and open

Orange: Magnetised, vibrant, vital, and attractive (in the dynamic sense)

Yellow: Clear thought and swift intellect

Gold: Spiritually charged and blessed

Silver: Lunar influence, dreams, and mentality (issues relating to mental health)

Pink: Loving and loved, emotionally supported and healing

Red: Impassioned and sexually charged (issues relating to the blood and stress)

Green: Healing and health, growth, grounding, and connection (issues relating to convalescence)

Black: Blockage and disease (or serious illness or imbalance in the body)

Grey: Weakness and ambiguity (may become illness soon if not addressed)

Brown: Grounded in body

Of course, it must be understood that the colours are relative and that they may change meaning if found in particular regions around the body. For instance, if I saw someone whose belly area was saturated by brown and black, I might ask if they were suffering from constipation because of the combined notion of brown being body-related (or body-static/grounded) and black implying disruption or blockage. If I saw pink surrounded by red around the heart centre with black spikes interspersed, and green and silver haloing the head, I might suggest that this individual is healing from a broken relationship and that while the thoughts are clearing and the dreamscape is providing relief, the emotional realm is still suffering from momentary lapses (which is of course entirely natural after a breakup).

The aura can give us a variety of clues and hints on exactly what parts of the self (both physically and spiritually) we need to address in a healing session. During a psychic whole-health consultation, the aura is the first thing I check, even before the patient openly discusses his or her problems; both to demonstrate the authenticity of my skills (and to test myself) and to therefore earn trust from the patient and also to energetically orient myself. Often the healing begins before the hands are laid, so to speak.

The aura flush exercise given on page 62 in *BLSS* is a highly effective technique for self-work on the aura.

The Chakras

It might not make immediate sense as to why I am referring to the chakras in this book, considering we are working with the three realms energetically and the three cauldrons and three souls. Why, then, would I challenge the triplicity by introducing a seven-fold energetic system? I have already spoken on congruence and contradiction, and this is one of the reasons I am speaking on the chakras now, but that is a peripheral reason. Truly, I am including a section on the chakras here because they are essential knowledge to a healer. I am aware that I might be skirting on the edges of cultural misappropriation by not referring to other Hindu or Indian traditions within this work, and there is always the risk I might decontextualise the system from its origin. However, I have worked with the chakra system for almost ten years now, and I was also born into the Hindu religion, though I do not believe this validates my use of the system over anyone else. Frankly, the chakra system belongs to each of us because it is not merely a spiritual metaphor, it is a profound energetic reality; we each possess the seven chakras. For the sake of parallels, one can associate the seven chakras with the three cauldrons:

Cauldron of the Belly: Root, sacral, and solar plexus chakras

Cauldron of the Head: Crown, third eye, and throat chakras

Cauldron of the Heart: Heart chakra

The Difference Between Aligning the Chakras and the Three Realms/Cauldrons/Souls

The three realms are broad, cosmic concepts or realities, and we align to them within our own energetic sphere; we actualise the holy centre. The three souls are private and personal to each individual; we all have three of our own souls each, and these are as unique as we are. When we align the spiral soul, we connect and commune with Own Holy Self. When we cleanse, balance, and align the seven major chakras (in the order of root, sacral, solar plexus, heart, throat, third eye, and crown), we are literally doing just that and connecting with what I like to call the rainbow ladder (or in Sanskrit *sushumna*) that ascends and descends through the body and allows the vital life force to flow steadily through us. The seven chakras, which are physically anchored in locations of the body that contain the prime endocrine glands, represent the places in which the life force naturally concentrates. These chakras must be cleansed and balanced within themselves so that neither extremity nor dullness is retained within them—the middle path is health.

When we open each chakra (Sanskrit for "wheel"), or energy centre, we open not a part of our soul/s but one of our psychic organs, and we direct cleansing and balancing power in hopes that the natural response will be to align with the rainbow ladder and to therefore open the physical body (that is the direct expression of the Spirit indwelling) to health.

Each chakra is also connected with different aspects of our humanity. Briefly:

Root (Red): Security, foundation, and survival

Sacral (Orange): Sexuality, sensuality, and intimacy

Solar Plexus (Yellow): Self-esteem, self-honour, and power

Heart (Green): Compassion, understanding, and love; the central chakra, the transmuter of life force

Throat (Azure Blue): Communication and expression

Third Eye (Indigo): Insight, knowledge, and thought

Crown (Violet/White): Connection, wisdom, and opening

Therefore, if particular magick aligning with any of the energies of the chakras is needed, one could work with that centre in meditation or trance and direct power from that place for spellwork. For example, to heighten one's psychic senses, it is a great idea to concentrate one's awareness at the third eye and to cleanse, balance, and align it within itself, then become open to receive universal information.

For an effective and empowering method of cleansing, balancing, and aligning the chakras, refer to page 73 of *BLSS*.

Working with the Spirits: Techniques for Deity or Ally Aid

When conducting a healing in the shamanic Craft, it is often the case that a deity or other spirit being will be called for assistance or even as the prime catalyst of the working. For instance, I will sometimes call to Brighid for aid in healing, or my ancestors (particularly my father's mother, although she has very much passed her power on to me). Other times I will simply "plug in," so to speak, to bring forth the healing light and provide the channel for it to flow into the recipient.

chapter seven

When working with an ally, however, the effects of the healing are often more immediate, tangible, and potent.

To call upon a spirit ally to aid in healing is a simple thing—simply call out, either aloud or within, to the spirits and make it known why you are asking for their presence and aid. When I call to Brighid, I might say:

> *O holy Brighid—triple goddess of healing, poetry, and blacksmiths—I call to you as healer now. I call to the gentle white cow and the green vital land; I call to the healing flame and the deep well. Céad míle fáilte!* [71]

When Brighid comes, I feel her overshadow me from behind and her hands will merge with mine. In this way, together we channel the flow of the vital force synergistically, and we benefit from the goddess's vast experience. I can simply let go, surrender, and let Goddess. Of course, my physical presence and conscious facilitation provide the framework of intent for the healing and thus lend to the overall efficacy.

In working with spirits, the boundary between possession and less intense forms of aid can often be blurry. Often I will feel as if the deity is half-sitting in me, and while I do not necessarily forget any details of the event, I will definitely feel altered and held in liminal space. This may happen spontaneously during a working (healing or not), in which case the spirit will most likely be one of my allies, or it will occur during a very strong working in which I have consciously called for the presence or influence of a spirit. This may be because I am a natural vessel (or "horse," as the Voudoun tradition might say). I also believe that this state should not be attempted in the context of a working that is not actively possessory; it is not a desirable or necessary state to achieve success in magickal workings. Therefore, unless

---

71 This is an Irish Gaelic phrase that means "a hundred thousand welcomes" and is pronounced *cay-d meel-ah fuhl-cha*.

it is something that happens naturally to you and it does not produce negative side effects, I would warn against it.

As mentioned above, your familiar spirits or totems may also aid in the work of healing by performing a number of "house-cleaning" tasks:

- Ensuring that you are kept energetically equalised and psychically protected
- Brushing off psychic debris or any attachments from the etheric contact
- Guarding against malevolent spirits who may be involved in the cause of illness
- Adding to and enhancing the power you are channelling for the healing

If you are conscious of and acknowledge your familiar and totemic spirits, it is quite possible that their aid will be automatic; however, it does not hurt to invite aid openly. In the case of familiar spirits (as they work in the periphery), as with any ward you may set up, assign and delegate specific tasks. Make sure that your tone is not commanding or oppressive but kind and conciliatory. This is manners, plain and simple. Emphasise the working together as cells within a body contributing to a wholeness greater than the sum of the parts. This is the aim of true, deep magick.

The Restoration of Wholeness

One of the powerful implications of the art of healing is that health is obtainable—in fact, it is around the corner; we must simply take the brave step into the darkness and seize it of our own volition. When I studied Western herbal medicine at college, we were often told by our naturopathic lecturers that the patients we might see in any natural health clinic would be expected to take the healing into their own hands. It would be our job as natural health therapists to facilitate and aid in the opening to healing and health rather than disempower or disengage an individual from the organic process. In contrast, many people find it preferable to lay the healing in the hands of doctors, who will (generally) hand over a drug to mask the symptoms; veiled medical terms will be used, and there is rarely a sense of equality or dialogue. The healing process is not facilitated so much as it is held in total by the doctor; in some circumstances, this is both necessary and desirable, but in many situations it is disempowering, weakening, and ultimately very dangerous.

To emphasise the art of healing as the restoration of wholeness (remembering the word is directly parallel to holiness) is to give credence to our deepest natures. We are always whole, all of the time; however, we often forget and therefore need to re-member. In other circumstances we become so off-centre, off-balance, that the wholeness blurs, and we lose our foundation and footing (the prime cause of so much dis-ease). We fall and we begin to fear; this erodes our self-esteem, self-honour, and power from within, and we begin to become deceived by the illusion that all is lost. Nothing can be truly lost that is truly yours. We are born from wholeness, with wholeness, and to wholeness we shall go. Our journey is to ride the shifting tides of this current and make ourselves worthy of this most excellent gift—the gift Self gives to Self.

In our individuation we are innately connected, and in our connection we have sprung from the body of being, and in being we are alive, and in living we are present: the constant and ever-present gift! These affirmations are eternal truths that are with us continuously—borrow from them, make them your own, sing them aloud and proudly, and we will each ignite the wholeness that we are. In knowing this, we learn to nourish it; and in nourishing, we deepen; and in deepening, we embrace the dark cauldron of nature.

Whole Self—Whole Earth

In December 2009 the esteemed Parliament of the World's Religions was held for a week in Melbourne, Australia. I was blessed to be a speaker and presenter at the POWR and presented a spiritual observance entitled "Whole Self—Whole Earth." The premise of this observance was to highlight the basic theology or cosmology of contemporary Paganism in its broadest sense—that the earth is holy, that the cosmos is alive, and that we are reflections of this truth. Thus, if we are whole within Self, then the earth too can become whole. This is akin to the principle of peace that the current Dalai Lama of Tibetan Buddhism engenders—that inner peace begets world peace.

From my Book of Shadows:

> We grounded and centred in a prolonged fashion, focussing especially on the groundedness and connection with earth and cosmos. Whole in ourselves—in our place. I spoke about interconnection—of cosmic/internal reflection; as above, so below; as within, so without. We cast circle: "From hand to hand…" Greeted elements through song: "Earth my body…" And the great mystery.
>
> We raised that power and asserted our inner wholeness as we each came forth from the chasm and claimed the rite/right to be! We turned to our neighbours and affirmed "You are whole"…taking that into our hearts, we then channelled and directed the power into the tween place. We spiralled, singing—"Mother, I feel you under my feet…" We raised, released, and grounded. We let that healing wholeness be absorbed by our Holy Living Mother. We unravelled the space and returned.

To cultivate living relationship with the earth and cosmos is to have this reflected in Self. This is part of the restoration of wholeness, because it is not a wholeness that is discretely yours and apart from others—the wholeness is an organic, unfolding web of interconnection that is not only a boundless circle to an ever-deepening centre but also an infinite spiral.

chapter seven

The Rite of Self-Blessing

The following self-blessing can be used as an affirmation, prayer, or ritual in order to instill this sacred awareness of wholeness/holiness in Self.

This ritual can be performed daily or absorbed into your discipline or rhythm however you see fit. It can also be called upon as a preparatory technique for intense energetic or trance work, e.g., drawing down. It may also be used at the culmination of rituals as another way to represent the Great Rite (hieros gamos or sacred marriage) without emphasising external or gendered polarities—the third, or middle way, of the shaman. For deepest effect, perform the three realms alignment (page 35) and/or the spiral soul alignment (page 38) before this blessing.

You may choose to use the following or to simply gesture them:

- A chalice filled with water
- An athame or sword

Breathe into your centre. Ground. Cast the circle, if you like (it's not necessary).

As you breathe deeply and rhythmically (kneeling, sitting, or standing), gaze at the chalice filled with liquid and say: "I am the cup; I am the wine of life."

Visualise and feel cleansing light moving from your heart centre (Own Holy Self—the place that is between and reconciles opposition and duality—the meeting place of the three souls) and into the chalice.

Stand and take the athame or sword (draw it from the earth as Arthur drew Excalibur from the stone), and draw a circle around the chalice and yourself in the air, saying: "I am the sword; I am the circle."

Bring the athame or sword down into the chalice and feel the charge of union—the underlying wholeness is re-membered.

Pick up the cup and say:

> *I drink deeply of the wellspring of my mystery*
> *From the earth I draw my life force*
> *Water is life, unbound and free*
> *Water—this water—will cleanse and bless me!*

Drink all of the liquid. Feel as if you are being washed clean and pure as the liquid moves through you.

Seal the rite by intoning:

> *I am the beloved of the Goddess, the gods, and my Own Holy Self. My divine mystery is revealed and beheld. I am my own blessing. So mote it be.*

A Shamanic Craft Healing

In the shamanic Craft, a "healing" speaks of consciously created sacred time and space in which the facilitation of the restoration of innate wholeness occurs, directed by the healer. Shamans and Witches have always been healers, and we are empowered to heal because we embrace the sanctity of the life force, and by our most sacred principle of magick we are able to harness the vital flow for benevolence and well-being. When we speak of healing, we imply the desire for health on all levels; on what is casually (if not erroneously) thought of as physical, mental, and spiritual. To borrow a definition from Rob, a WildWood Witch: "Health is the optimum state of being." I would qualify this by adding "for the autonomy and thus sovereignty of the individual within the interconnectivity of the web."

Health is a deeply penetrating radiance that creates equilibrium within the bodies. It also ensures that we are honouring our implicit connections and interdependence with all things in life. When I heal, I sometimes weave in the Feri Star Goddess prayer,[72] as it reinforces, to

---

[72] The "standard" Anderson Feri Star Goddess prayer is: "Holy Mother, in you we live, move, and have our being. From you all things emerge, and unto you all things return."

me, the reality of sacred exchange and purity of flow—that all things by their very nature are born to die and be reborn. This is the truth of immortality, and so to heal is to also bring awareness to the forces of being that hold the limitlessness of life.

The following sections form the foundation and (dare I say it) steps for my usual way of conducting a healing:

- Ground and centre (three realms alignment, spiral soul alignment, etc.)
- Work through/with the aura
- Open, cleanse, balance, and align the chakras
- Call upon the aid of allies
- Channel the light of healing
- Restore and re-member wholeness
- Water blessing (rite of self-blessing, or *kala*)

These steps unfold to encompass a space of relaxation, re-membering, and revivification for the client/patient. As I outline each of the steps, I will also add finer details and deconstruct the inherent meaning or purpose behind the act.

Ground and Centre

This step is quite self-explanatory: both the healer and the patient ground and centre. This can be done as a facilitated exercise simultaneously, or, depending on the personal inclinations of the patient, the patient can simply lie down (or sit comfortably within a chair) and breathe deeply (cycling their breath) as the healer centres privately.

This step is, of course, essential. At this point, you might also wish to set up a temporary shield against psychic debris or attachment. This can be done quite simply through either calling upon one's familiar spirits to draw in light and cocoon it around the body or setting specific wards (of flame, light, web, etc.) at particular locations around the body.[73]

---

73 For more information on shielding, refer to pages 55–58 of my book *Spirited*.

Work Through/With the Aura

At this point, the auric field is "lifted" to a higher vibration in order to open the patient to the light of healing (which is both cosmic and earthly—consider it as starlight, knowing also that there is a star within the earth). The way in which I approach this is to quickly clear the aura of any peripheral energetic distractions by sweeping my hands with intent across the surface of the body (a few inches above the physical boundaries) and flicking the debris off to be absorbed into the ground, with a prayer to the Earth Mother for recycling. I then hold my hands at the centre point (either around the solar plexus or belly region) of the body, and with simple will (applied) heighten the auric vibration. The sensation that settles within me as I do this is of a blooming flower. This could be visualised as the auric energies elevate and open.

Open, Cleanse, Balance, and Align the Chakras

To do this, begin at the base chakra (the red root) and make direct and empowered conjurations to the chakras as you continue up the rainbow ladder. Hold your power hand over the area of the body (in the case of the root chakra, if the patient is lying face-up, the region would be location at the genitalia), and begin to make sunwise (deosil) circles as you visualise the sphere of light opening like a flower and spinning like the sun. As you do this, begin to connect with the light and channel it through to aid in the cleansing and balancing of each chakra. The conjuration I make is the same for every chakra, and I simply replace the name and colour:

> *Red wheel of light—root chakra—open like a flower and spin the sun! Cleanse, balance, and align within yourself!*

However, for each chakra upwards, I will add:

> *...Connect and align with the lower [however many chakras] of orange and red [if it was the solar plexus chakra].*

Therefore, as I facilitate a gradual progression upwards through the system, the patient is aware that we are not just working with the chakras in isolation but as organs within the energy bodies that connect and work as a whole greater than the sum of the parts.

As I work to open, cleanse, balance, and align, I also visualise that each chakra becomes brighter and more vivid and visceral as I channel light. I make a special point of also connecting the root chakra through a red cord of light to the very centre of the earth. When I reach the crown chakra, I tap the head very lightly and quickly with the first two fingers of my power hand and perceive a great rushing of light from the heavens into the patient. This establishes a direct and empowered link to the light for the patient and consolidates the connection to that power within the healer. I will then move my hands over the patient's body downwards to distribute the light throughout. I also ask the patient at this point to take that light where they feel, either intuitively or logically, it is most needed.

Call Upon the Aid of Allies

As I have explained briefly, a healing (or any working) can become much more powerful and successful if one is working in concert with an ally, or two or more. The connection between the healer and the ally should be a firm one, and the invitation or acknowledgement (of presence and power) of the ally can be either an inward or verbal declaration (depending on the nature of the healing and the patient). An example has already been provided with Brighid; see page 176.

Channel the Light of Healing

The light I am speaking of (almost vaguely so) is not of any particular current as far as I can tell. I am not attuned to Reiki in any form but have been told that what I am working with is very similar. Although I am by no means an expert on Reiki, it has been mentioned to me that we are all innately and intrinsically connected to this force anyway because Reiki means and is universal life force. Therefore, I find the point moot. We all partake in this force because it is universal, and therefore we all have personal access to it at all times. Those who are attuned in the specific energetic disciplines of healing are endowed with particular lineages[74] and esoteric technique, lore, and knowledge that create a particular shape or form within the healer, thus the power/light/energy moulds to that vessel and a particular shared experience may unfold. This could all be conjecture as well, but this is my understanding.

The light I work with is something I also think of as universal but particularly aligned with the stars—or, rather, that convalescing liquid, diamond-like flame that emerges from the campfires of the angels. It is alive, potent, and serpentine—like water and fire married.

To channel this light after having opened the patient to the current is to breathe with the intent of drawing down the light and bringing it up from the earth. Feel how it meets, mixes, mingles, and marries together in the heart centre and then flows down your arms and out your hands like rivers returning to the sea. This light is intelligent and is deeply aware of where it is needed, and so as you breathe, affirm yourself as a vessel for its force and simply go with the flow of light. You may psychically become aware of regions in the body that require the light, too, and direct it that way; in my experience, this is quite organic. The light penetrates to the very subatomic dark-space within the cells, and there it pools, saturates, and vibrates.

Restore and Re-Member Wholeness

After the channelling of the light, the way in which I aid in the restoration of wholeness is to brush away any remaining debris or attachments, flick them to the ground, and ensure that they are banished and recycled by drawing banishing (earth) pentagrams over the ground and invoking the aid of the Mother:

---

74 Lineages build up psychic momentum and thus become currents or connect us with currents.

> *Great Mother, I pray that this energy will be recycled by you and cleansed, balanced, and aligned within itself.*

I then move my hands very swiftly from crown to foot over the patient's body through the charged aura and gently bring down the aura to almost skin-level so that from there it will become its natural shape and fullness again. Also, to bring the aura to the skin is to reconnect the patient with physicality and to reaffirm that the body is spirit and the spirit is body.

To affirm and seal this, I will draw a pentagram of light, tracing it from head to right foot, from right foot to left shoulder/hand, from left to right shoulder/hand, and from there to the left foot and back to the head. I make a sixth stroke by drawing a line of light from the head straight down over the body, over the feet, and then I swiftly and surely touch the earth. This grounds the patient. By invoking the pentagram over the body I call upon the knowledge that we are each a star and thus cosmically oriented and whole from self to Self.

When the patient is ready, I ask them to reacquaint with the surroundings—perhaps vibrate their name clearly within the mind three times to reconnect with identity and to gently but firmly pat down their own body. I also ask the patient to seal each chakra from crown down to root by tapping the associated physical point three times with the intent to seal. This is a further grounding to ensure that the chakras will not leak psychic "fluid" and therefore weaken the recharged being. I have been doing this for years and had never really seen or read about it anywhere else until my first Reclaiming WitchCamp experience, in which it is a point of order before all leave the camp to "dial down" the chakras. This ensures not only the psychic integrity and therefore safety of each individual, but also emotional and mental balance and equilibrium and a smoother transition from highly charged magickal and mystical experiences to the "mundane" world.

Water Blessing: A Simple Rite of Kala

A water blessing in the form of the rite of self-blessing on page 180 works to reinforce the wholeness of self after the event of healing. It is also an exercise or technique that the patient can take away and return to when needed through the process of convalescence. Physically drinking fluid will also activate the bodily processes once more and therefore serve to further ground, which is so important. Kala, a Hawaiian/Feri technique, is another form of water blessing that, in its simplest form, would also serve the purpose of this closing step beautifully.

You will need a glass of fresh water.

Align the spiral soul and hold the glass of water at the belly, the place of shadow self. Consume yourself with all of the emotions, paradigms, memories, and attachments that hinder your flow and block you from being present and being able to engage with the here and now. Indulge in the actual feeling of these things as they move through your being like wild animals—thirsty, hungry, and wanting. Take a deep breath, and pull as much of this "stuff" as possible up through your throat and then out of your mouth and into the water as you breathe the vibration *ha* (preferably elongated). Do this twice more until all of it is within the water. See the water become murky, dull, and obscured.

Hold the water before you at heart level and simply connect with the power that sits in Own Holy Self; radiate this outward to encompass the water. Watch as the water loses its obscuration, its dullness; watch as it begins to shine with light. Say with conviction:

> *Water is life, unbound and free*
> *Water—this water—will cleanse and clean me.*

Gradually draw the glass of water closer to your heart, and feel how the heartbeat travels into the water and ripples it. As you draw it closer and it nears your chest, you are welcoming in—from poison to power—threads of your original and pure essence. Light shines from within the water radiantly and powerfully.

Drink all of the water there and then, as in the rite of self-blessing, and feel as it cleanses every piece of you, allowing you to vibrate with that same radiance the water possessed. It is done.

Shamanic Soul Retrieval

In *BLSS* there is a short section on soul retrieval. I relayed the story of one of my spiritual brothers and his revivification through the interface of the goddesses. I did not, in fact, refer to any particular technique for shamanic soul retrieval; however, I will offer my suggestions, frameworking, and personal understandings below.

In the aforementioned section, I refer to the power of memory and the act of remembrance, citing the Well of Memory and the world tree, Yggdrasil—how these things renew our underlying wholeness, allowing us to reclaim the sovereignty of Self and become self-possessed. This is the aim of shamanic soul retrieval—to aid another in recalling what seems lost (but isn't) and empowering them to accept the right/rite to wholeness/holiness.

The theory of shamanic soul retrieval involves the idea that the soul complex (its underlying wholeness) can become splintered or fractured by both external and internal trauma. The psyche (soul) of the individual may break or snap forcibly and be lost to consciousness in a car accident, medical operation, physical/sexual assault, or something of that nature—sudden, abrupt, physically abrasive. The psyche may lose its integrity in less overt or instantaneous ways as well and be seen to be seeking refuge in the darkest recesses of our own Self (hidden away).[75] This may happen due to enduring psycho-emotional belittling or bullying, child molestation (which of course fits into the above category as well), substance or chemical addictions, and men-

---

75 This is synonymous with the idea of the underworld as a realm. The internal/external dichotomy is an unhelpful illusion, like most dualities.

tal pathologies or disorders such as anorexia (these pathologies/disorders are also products of soul loss). There are actually many instances within Western societies in which shamanic soul loss or fragmentation can be seen to be the cause of several states of mind and being. Therefore, shamanic soul retrieval would be a useful remedy alongside other forms of psychotherapeutic modalities. Remember, all things are connected; what we might consider depression caused by a simple chemical imbalance (though it is never that simple) will generally have deeper roots, as even the chemistry of our bodies is a signature of the Divine and thus is open to healing of and from the Divine.

When all is said and done, it can actually be quite difficult approaching an individual whom we believe suffers from soul loss; not only is the condition rarely heard of, it generally sounds truly out of this world and thus not applicable. Many medical associations or professionals would either laugh at or condemn the notion as being supercilious and ultimately dangerous to the patient's care and health. However, shamanic soul retrieval in its varied original forms is actually an age-old, well-respected, traditional technique of healing that has enormous potential and implications.

To effectively perform a shamanic soul retrieval, the malady must be identified correctly. This can be diagnosed through communication with the spirits, guides, and totems of the patient or through divination (see next chapter). Another way to diagnose would be to perceive the energetic bodies or psychic signatures of the individual, either through auric analysis or the Sight in general. You may also simply know. Either and every which way, make sure that in a soul-loss circumstance you approach the patient carefully and considerately; especially if you have seen the soul fragmentation initially and are wishing to communicate. Again, the notion may be completely rejected, in which case it is not up to you to convince them of it—the individual chooses the pathway with the information known. If someone approaches you and reports most (if not all) of the following, there is a high probability of soul loss or fragmentation:[76]

- Disconnected
- Ungrounded
- Unfocussed
- Lost and uncertain
- Psychically disparate and splintered
- Energetically drained
- Irrationally frightened or terrified
- An unmistakeable yet ambiguous feeling of not being whole

The concept of soul loss, while it may not appeal to the broader community, will definitely be contextual to those who either include themselves under the umbrella of Paganism or who are mystically and magically oriented. Therefore, for those who approach you from these backgrounds, it will be a much more straightforward discussion. Once the soul-loss phenomenon has been accepted as a viable explanation for the underlying condition, then the actual methodology (which is decidedly trance-based) can be implemented.

The Technique

To renew an underlying wholeness, the spiritual pragmatism that "you are always whole; you simply need to renew and reclaim your sovereignty of Self" should be postulated and passed as a form of mantra or affirmation. Pass on the rite of divine fire (page 15), spiral soul alignment (page 38), and the three realms alignment (page 35) as a worthy integration of discipline for at least one week leading up to the soul retrieval itself. A form of water blessing (the rite of self-blessing

---

[76] I must remind the reader that many of these traits are symptoms of various mental illnesses. If you suspect mental illness, consult a doctor, psychotherapist, or suitable health care professional.

on page 180 or kala on page 187) should also be suggested and taught to the patient. The rite of divine fire will wrap the patient in enduring and all-encompassing love; this will create a strong foundation to carry him or her through the pain of soul loss. The practice of both the spiral soul alignment and the three realms alignment will centre, align, cleanse, and balance the individual and create a point of continuum and connection between what is normally perceived as external and what is felt to be internal; again, a dichotomous illusion that ecstasy dissolves. Water blessing helps to provide a source of further energetic cleansing and also of spiritual sustenance, which enriches and nourishes the patient.

The technique itself is one in which (most obviously) both the healer and the patient should be physically present. The patient needs to be as comfortable and warm as possible, appropriate according to the existing climate. For psychological reasons, it is best to keep the space dark (also to mimic the chthonic realms—the underworld/sea—which is where the soul pieces are apt to travel and hide) and then to create a lightness in the room (either through sunlight or candlelight) at the culmination of the rite (reborn to light). The patient should also be in a rested state so that when breathing and becoming entranced, sleep is avoided. The nature of the rite should generally keep the patient alert enough.

Breathe. Perform the spiral soul and three realms alignments. Cast the circle and honour the directions and sacred elements of life. Call upon any allies that may be required for assistance or that the patient has asked be called. Psychopomp deities and spirits are perfect for soul-retrieval work, as are the chthonic deities, although they are rarely mutually exclusive. In the space you will require a rhythm keeper (a drum or rattle is best) and one tall white candle and black stone (obsidian, jet, onyx, etc.).

When you are aligned and prepared and you have directed the patient into a cycle of conscious, deep breathing, call openly for the light of the cosmos to dwell within the light of the candle. A prayer like the following will suffice:

> *Holy light of the cosmos, spinning and spiralling into eternity*
> *I call upon thee to settle in the hearth flame here*
> *which is also the flame of the heart.*
> *Let there be peace and stillness in this place*
> *and presiding over this time outside of time.*
> *Let there be peace.*

Light the candle and bow to the light of the cosmos. Begin to drum or rattle and chant:

> *Call Wild to Wild*
> *Call Self to Self*
> *In the circle that lies*
> *Between the worlds.*[77]

As you drum, allow your trance to deepen until you feel the ripple of the veil. At this moment, slip between the worlds and follow the thread of light that you will see—it calls you to the lost soul piece.

Race upon the wind or dive through the water or dance through the fire. There may be many challenges to endure and realms to surpass as you follow this thread of light; however, with your allies you are strong. You will be able to accomplish this journey and undergo this feat of magickal strength. At last, when you come to the end of the thread of light, you will have found the refuge place of the lost soul piece, and it is not important as to whether this is considered to be a realm outside or broader than the autonomy of your single human patient or whether it dwells within the patient's psyche. At this point, call to the black stone as an ally by name and attributes (for the stone will be the storehouse of the soul piece) and, when the spirit of

---

77 I recorded this chant and uploaded it onto YouTube with several others—the URL is http://www.youtube.com/watch?v=9JBpyKKclE0.

healing with the power

the stone arrives, charge the stone to accept the soul piece, and then take the stone in your power hand and ride the rhythm through the worlds back to your body. Ground and centre.

Tell your patient that you have retrieved the lost soul piece and that it is contained within the black stone (refer to the stone by its name and its attributes), and ask the patient where on the body he or she feels the stone must be placed. The patient will know. Ask the patient to physically show you the place. When the patient has done so, place the black stone there, and charge it by name and attribute to return the soul piece to the wholeness of the patient by name (whatever name they have previously told you is preferred at this point). The black stone ally will transfer the soul piece, and the wholeness will be naturally affected.

To affirm and seal the renewal, instruct the patient in the rite of self-blessing. After this has been completed, direct attention to the light of the cosmos and recite the following prayer (or something like it):

> *Holy light of the cosmos, spinning and spiralling into eternity.*
> *Thy presence has been felt and adored!*
> *Let there be peace and stillness in all places, in all times.*
> *Let there be peace.*

Note: A soul retrieval is not a bandage and neither is it necessarily going to succeed. It really depends on several factors, not least of which is the skill of the shaman or Witch undertaking the retrieval. Often a human helper who journeys with the retriever simultaneously or simply acts as an anchor or watcher allows for energetic support and safety and is therefore recommended. The journeyer/retriever may also be tricked by stray or chaotic spirits in the search for the lost soul piece/s. Remember: intuition and instinct! Know the arts of shielding, and keep in contact with your allies.

One of the keys to truly engage the patient in the process is to speak aloud the experience being undergone as the retriever/

journeyer travels through the worlds. For me, because I am in trance, I am quite breathless as I communicate what I can, and it is often hard to divorce the speaking of the words from the exact terrain that is unfolding almost as the words fly from the lips. It is a very eerie and chilling experience, but one which evokes great response from all present; something deep and primal awakens.

All things said and done, the lost soul piece/s desire reunion with their origin, and though there may be some difficulty in coaxing the fragile, wounded, bruised/shocked, or abused pieces, it is with strength, determination, and compassion that we triumph. Once the soul pieces return, it will not always be an instantaneous restoration; it will be gradual and steady even when there are immediate triggers and renewal of lost memory or surging happiness and catharsis.

Self Soul-Retrieval

There are instances of soul retrieval that ultimately do not require a being external from us to facilitate the healing and re-membering process.

When we fall in love or create psycho-emotional bonds of any kind, we are often apt to give up what may be termed a "soul piece" to our beloved ones. When we share a loving connection, a psychic cord or attachment is formed (depending on the nature of these, I sometimes call the cords "ego attachments"), and while some of these are simple, pure, and flowing with "the good," some of them become channels through which poison pours and slowly destroys our integrity from the inside out. I experienced this in my first long-term relationship, which lasted for nearly two years.

My boyfriend and I lived together in a very small, confined apartment. We had been dating on and off throughout the last year of high school (both of us enduring year 12 in different cities but in the same state), and when the first year of post-graduation bliss arrived we found ourselves both moving to Brisbane and reforming our relation-

healing with the power

ship. At first, this was a joyous and exhilarating thing; then it gradually became, on both our parts, a very poisonous, codependent relationship. Towards the end of our relationship I remember looking across the living room at my boyfriend and thinking to myself, "Who are you?" and then, more startlingly, "Who am I?" I had completely lost myself, and our relationship had become one of those senseless entities in which we were absorbed in only one another (or the sum of one another) that I shudder at the thought of it. I had truly lost myself, or at least pieces of myself.

A month after our official breakup, I was at my altar having my devotion when a presence filled the space. I was not familiar with this being, and yet there she was in her golden majesty, stalking the bounds of my circle and staring through me, daring me to surrender. She was a lioness, so I took her to be Sekhmet, lioness-headed Egyptian goddess of rage, retribution, and cleansing. This was confirmed by the feeling of affirmation as the thought arose. I welcomed the Goddess in my circle, and then, just as suddenly, she began to swipe and claw at me, scratching and severing the tension of my skin. I felt every blow, and at first my reaction was shock and fear; however, I realised that Sekhmet was extracting the poison of my newly ended relationship and letting me bleed until I was clean of it. The psychic pus and fluid that poured out of me was not attractive and resembled a befouled green, oozy substance. This was one of those timeless experiences in which the process endured for a natural cycle until I awoke to myself, and somehow the job of the restoration of my wholeness was mine to take on—of course! Ever since that day over four years ago, Sekhmet has been in my life, ever on the periphery, watching and waiting, guarding and protecting.

Sekhmet taught me a valuable lesson, which is echoed by a powerful Feri maxim postulated by the late Grandmaster Victor Anderson: *never submit your life force!* Never. We may share it, and this may form cords between us that, as I said, flow with the good, but if the connections are soured or unhealthy and imbalanced, we all suffer the consequences, and hence the popular aphorism "the ties need to be severed." Obviously, and more overtly, a toxic relationship of hate, jealousy, struggle, intimidation, or fear constitutes cords or ego attachments that will need to be either cleansed and released or completely severed. Ultimately it is up to personal volition as to how to confront the shadows amassing behind the cords, but the cords must be allowed to disperse first, before the work of confrontation can begin. In many ways the dispersal of the cords affects the confrontation of what is hidden behind them. These shadows are actually pieces of our soul that have mutated in being distanced from one's personal integrity. They need to be confronted face-on, challenged (this goes both ways), accepted, danced with, and integrated in a pure way.

Below is a technique which involves scanning the bodies for these cords or attachments and applying intuition in regard to what are healthy or unhealthy attachments. If these are healthy attachments, they still need to be cleansed (between partners, siblings, parents, children, etc.)—these attachments need to be watched, however, in case they take on the quality of codependence or toxicity in any form. If the cords are vampiric, oppressive, draining, or destructive, then they must be severed in such a way as to remove the core of connection from whichever "body" it is directly attached to.

The Technique

Perform the spiral soul and three realms alignments.

Breathe into your holy centre; find equilibrium. When you have reached the point of stillness, expand your consciousness to cocoon your body and being, and scan for any cords of attachments. These will generally appear as tendril-like channels—some will glow with light, others will appear dull or murky, others will appear as almost pulpy, blood-filled veins (and then some). Wherever you find a tendril, cleanse it by directing light through it; this is done by connecting to the wellsprings of power (the three realms, the world tree) and drawing upon the light that radiates from or is present within. This light will purify and cleanse the cords. During this process, some of the cords will naturally fall away and disappear or disintegrate. Let this be the case. Others will remain and continue to shine or glow or flail like enraged serpents. It is now time to follow each of the remaining attachments or cords to the points of connection or origin; remember that you may be responsible for the sending or forging of some of these cords—it is sometimes complicit. At the other "end" will be one of several "things"—a memory, a place, a being (human or nonhuman), or even a concept or belief. We share relationships with all and more of these things, and though we have already done the work of cleansing our connections, we now need to feel and intuit whether or not these are healthy and supportive connections or draining and compromising ones. Spend time working through these revelations and discoveries of what is on the other "side" and, once there is resolution (knowing that there is more work of confrontation and integration to be done), we must draw upon a sword of light.

Call for the sword of light from the swollen darkness. Draw it forth from chaos. Open your hands (physically, energetically, or both) and accept the sword as it is conjured; grasp it, wield it with force and intent. As you nurse the sword, open your awareness to its intelligence and listen to its wisdom. Take it and begin to sever the unhealthy, imbalanced, and poisonous cords and attachments. As you do this, banish the influence and let it be released. Wherever you sever a cord, ensure that you direct light to that place to remove the core of connection. Visualise the light amplifying in vivid brightness and see it coalescing in that place, cycling and spinning with a deep passion and ecstasy—it will disperse and disintegrate the core of connection and then heal the wound. Any psychic scars will be minimal, but if they do remain, the energetic imprint was so strong or enduring that the scar provides a reminder of the dangers of toxic connections. The sword of light does its work and moves around the bodies, severing attachments. While at first you will find that your entire concerted presence of will is required for facilitating this, gradually and earnestly the sword will take on a mind of its own and do the work for you. When all cords have been severed and all wounds have been cleaned out with light, the sword of light is reabsorbed from whence it came. Thank the sword, and be grateful. You will always be able to conjure it again for future work.

To seal this work, perform the rite of self-blessing. As you do so and the water rushes through your being, open to the lost soul pieces and gradually, one by one, they will return, and not always in drastic ways. Some of them may take longer and will be more difficult to merge, but they will do so in peace and balance. Light a candle and make the rite of divine fire.

chapter eight

oracular seership and divination

"Shamans were among our earliest diviners, and their many roles as diagnosticians, counsellors, and healers demanded many methods. Most often they rely on their spiritual helpers or spiritual vision."
Roger Walsh, *The World of Shamanism*

In *BLSS* I wrote two chapters that referenced what can be referred to as oracular seership—chapter 12, To Journey and Vision, and chapter 13, To Channel. There is a rationale to the linear order of these two chapters; channelling follows vision journeying because we must attain a vision before we can communicate it. Therein lies oracular seership. Neither the vision journey (which is not the same as a Native American vision quest) nor the channelling can be taken away from it. In this chapter I will deepen into the art of oracular seership and divination and provide several techniques for approaching both in the shamanic way. This chapter will therefore be broken into two overall sections dealing with both topics separately.

chapter eight

Seeking the Vision

How is the vision sought? How do we perceive the Other reality or attain what core shamanism refers to as nonordinary states of reality? To perceive the Other in life is to become intrinsically and instinctually aware of its indwelling presence. However, it must be said the Other is not necessarily better or more holy or sacrosanct than what we "ordinarily" perceive to be reality, and I am not simply referring to consensual reality either, which is a product of the overculture. The Other is simply that shade (and I use this word intentionally) of reality that we are not conditioned to, that we are often warned against, that may unsettle us regardless of any perceived or inherent moralistic value.

Humans are creatures of habit, goes the old saying. Largely this seems to apply to our species, and it may be a purely instinctual survival mechanism—routine creates confidence in certainty, certainty breeds a belief in security. However, while routine may have its practical aspects of structure and security, making it worth it in many regards, the element of risk needs to be balanced with a regard for routine. Routine and risk, when balanced, create a powerful synergy for a life lived courageously and with conviction. To peer through the "shades" (the veil, the shadow) and see into the Other, we are able to attain the visions that we have opened consciously to. Visions may also choose to reveal themselves to us either through patterns of synchronicity or through spontaneous ignition.

My first spontaneous vision that I can clearly remember came in 2001, when I was in my first year of high school. During the September holidays my mother, sister, and I usually travelled to Bali; this year was no different. The only difference was that I was now consciously practising Witchcraft, and I had just performed a ritual to make me more aware and sensitive.

One night in Bali I woke up sweating and with a pounding headache. I screamed for my mum. My body was physically repulsed at the strangeness of what I had been dreaming/seeing. I saw two buildings (nondescript, as if this detail was not the important one) come crashing down, and I saw George Bush, though at the time I was thirteen and did not know clearly who he was; I only recognised his face from somewhere. Bush was standing on what I realised later was the car Hitler would drive around in waving at the people; the American president stood on the bonnet, pointed at the rubble, and laughed in a maniacal, frightening way. All night I was tormented by this dream. My mother would try to get me to fall asleep again, and I would wake up either screaming or vomiting; several times during that night I curled up on the tiled floor like a dog because it was so cold and I was completely overheated.

The next day I awoke, still feeling absolutely sick. I rested and then I began to feel a part of the world again, and in the early afternoon my mother took my sister and I into Singaraja (a large city on Bali's northern coast, where I was born), to the markets. A man we talked to at the markets told us the news about an attack on the Pentagon. Later on we heard the rest and watched the unfolding news reports at my uncle's house. I sat there with a strange feeling watching this all play out, and I turned to my mother and said simply, "Remember my dream?"

This is an example of both seeking for (although unwittingly) a vision and having one spontaneously imparted. These experiences are shamanic initiations of sorts. While I often emphasise the self-determined nature of the Witch (and Own Holy Self—sovereignty of Self), self does not exclude the fullness of reality and the experiential nature thereof. There are many times in which it will not be the Witch who initiates the communication—it will be the spirits, the deities, and the powers that be. Therefore, think of the vision journey as you choosing to seek and the vision choosing to be found.

It is a very fine line indeed between unbidden and consciously called-for visions. The difference is qualified by the impetus of either. A spontaneous vision is inspired by connective (whole) impetus; sent from a deity or other spirit to the seer, or engendered by the vibrating of a particular strand of the Wyrd intersecting with one's own. A sought-for vision is inspired by personal (autonomous) impetus and the volition is decidedly self-determined. How these two things can truly be definitively separate is, however, beyond me.

The Technique

In *BLSS* I wrote a whole chapter on channelling, as mentioned above, and for it I channelled divine/universal information and received an epic message which, when analysed and deconstructed, embodied a methodology to become an open vessel and safely and successfully channel. It must be reiterated that all of these techniques are simply steppingstones for a personal path of evolution; they are mine (or have come through me), and I am making them accessible to all as springboards in their whole or partial forms to then inspire others to create and come upon their own ideas and ways of approaching the magickal arts. In this vein, I will not reproduce the technique for channelling discovered in *BLSS*; I will note, however, that the technique in my previous book is one that works effectively to condition individuals energetically to receive information and then communicate and express it. I have taught the method openly for three years now, and it has always been of aid. What I will offer here is a three-soul specific way to translate what I call "universal information" and spin golden threads of wisdom from it for those who seek.

Align the Spiral or Triple Soul

Focus on the person before you. Concentrate your awareness at your brow, the third eye, and open this chakra. From this point, send a soft, tubular tendril of light to the very edges of the person's aura and ask that they begin to project any questions (or aspects or areas of life they feel need clarification or direction) to you and that they consciously cause the edges of their aura to "ripple" like the surface of water. When the aura ripples, it becomes as the ripple of the veil

oracular seership and divination

between the worlds and we are oriented once more in sacred cosmology. As you receive them through the tendril or tube, this will be transferred into talking self, then down through shadow self, and then be taken directly to star self.

Invest your presence and attention within your star self and open to the divine wisdom/universal information that is coursing through the cosmos. Do this by knowing the ancient truth that you are profoundly All That Is (the centre to the circumference). Allow the circumference of the cosmos to zero in to the point that is you, and open your star self to channelling that light.

Move the light through the body down into the belly, in which shadow self is anchored. Feel the tension that emotion produces by its very nature, but allow this to be naturally facilitated and transmuted by the "bridge" of the three souls. Through the emotional lens of the dreamscape, the information is then channelled upward again into the talking self—the soul that will communicate the information/vision. Remember and bless your open third eye.

Speak with ease; allow yourself to be free of judgement, criticism, analysis, and evaluation (for now)—leave this until after the experience. Indulge in the flow of information and in the expression thereof. Either describe what you are seeing and feeling or simply speak to the person before you.

Previous to the vision seeking and then the channelling, you should encourage your partner (at the point of communication flow) to simply remain in a receptive state without judgement, criticism, analysis, or evaluation. Their job is simply to allow the information to enter through the filter of the talking self, and then transmute to shadow self, then be absorbed by star self and have it returned in the opposite order. The reasoning for this is that talking self will understand the words and so welcome them freely. What must happen, however, is that the portals from each soul should be wide open to ensure that the information is not stuck in any one soul but experiences the lens and quality of each. As the information flows through shadow self, it will arouse certain emotions that are certainly associated with the pieces of wisdom. That the information will return to star self provides a polishing of the "gems," so to speak, so that when they rain down upon you again and filter back through shadow self to talking self, they will shine in truth and find the doorways to ignite your awareness.

In having taught channelling to many people now, it seems the first and foremost problem arises when actually speaking or conveying the information received—which is a confidence issue. No one ever has trouble receiving a vision or feeling an intuition; however, many people stumble when they feel forced to express this in a way that will sound cohesive and coherent to their partners. The best way to ensure freedom of flow here is to not judge yourself as you convey. Simply go with the flow of whatever is received and understand that you do not have to sound like some archaic prophetess or Renaissance magician to be an effective vessel or channel thereof. Be aligned within your spiral soul, know that you are the holy centre, and claim your worthiness to the innate title of seer and Witch; you will begin to touch on the ancient and forever-renewing quality of our wild magick. Unbidden, it will change our lives; bidden, it will shake and remake them.

The Rite of Cleansing and Opening the Eye

This succinct ritual is intended for the opening up of the psychic senses and faculties. The ideal timing for this ritual would be the full moon. For this rite, you should either be skyclad or wearing clothes you are not afraid to get wet.

You will need:

- A ceramic or glass bowl of warm spring or rain water (you may need to heat the water on the stove slowly)
- Mugwort (a teaspoon of dried herb)
- Rosemary (a teaspoon of dried herb)
- Amethyst (a medium-sized gem)

Place the bowl directly in front of where you will be positioned. Place the rosemary on the left hand of the bowl and the mugwort on the right. The amethyst gem can be placed between you and the bowl. Breathe into the holy centre and align the three souls.

Gaze peacefully at the items gathered before you, and then bring your awareness to the water. Charge it with the light of the heavens and the earth as you draw it through your being and down through your hands held open over the water. Chant:

> *Water flowing*
> *Water knowing*
> *I am flowing*
> *With the water.*
> *Water shine*
> *Open mine*
> *Eye is open*
> *Water flowing.*

Once you feel the water is charged and blessed, take up the rosemary in your left hand and speak with the spirit of the plant. The following formula is useful:

> *Rosemary, cleansing herb of the sea, awaken thy spirit and enhance thy potency. Grant me your gifts, I pray. Blessed be.*

To name the herb and then address the quality or aspect you wish to draw upon within the working specifically is to respect the ally and its gifts, not to mention good Witchcraft. It is simply polite to speak directly to the spirit and ask for its aid rather than assume authority over it.

chapter eight

You should feel the response of the rosemary spirit. Assuming this is positive and you are continuing with the rite,[78] sprinkle the rosemary into the water and wash your hands and then your face with the potion. This is to cleanse your senses.

Now take the mugwort into your left hand and recite a similar formula over this plant ally to invoke the gifts of the Sight. When you feel a positive response, take the mugwort between the fingers of your power hand and push it against your third eye as you chant:

> *Witch's Sight, Second Sight,*
> *Enchant herein the powers raised!*
> *Witch's knowing, magick flowing,*
> *Ignite in me the seer's gaze!*

Repeat this as many times as needed to arouse the power to a surging peak, which at the point of release you should direct immediately into your newly cleansed and newly opened third eye. This will feel quite intense, but ride the tide and surrender to embrace the magick. When you have taken in the power, sprinkle the mugwort into the water.

Now address the piece of amethyst in the same way you have done with the herbs. You may even like to tap the gem gently three times to wake up the spirit within. Again, assuming the amethyst spirit wishes to cooperate, pick up the gem and drop it reverently through the water and into the centre of the bowl. Incant the following again aloud three times:

> *Water flowing*
> *Water knowing*

---

[78] Generally speaking, if the spirits are approached with respect, the response will be open and clear. If the response for some reason is negative, then it is wise to not continue with the rite, spell, or working. Enter into a meditative or trance state to perhaps engage the spirit/s and enquire as to the deeper meaning behind the negative response, unless simply ending there and then is intuitively more aligned.

I am flowing
With the water.
Water shine
Open mine
Eye is open
Water flowing.

At the culmination of the third recitation, end with: "Friend Amethyst, now heed my call!"

Quickly lift up the bowl and upturn it over your head, letting the contents spill onto you. The rite is done, and the eye has been cleansed and opened.

The Mythic Reality

When we vision and ignite the Sight to perceive and receive, we open ourselves to the underlying forces that inform the manifest world. I would call this the mythic reality; I also tend to see no particular difference between the two (the underlying forces and the manifest world); perhaps it is merely a functional differentiation. However, it is all the mythic reality. The dynamic is evident within the apparent.

It would be far too cliché of me to claim this rested on the web of Wyrd—on the vibrating, spiralling interconnections of the flesh of spirit and the spirit of flesh—but it is absolutely the truth as I know it. What does this mean for us, incarnate beings participating within something firmly identified as consensual reality? Does the fact that I am a Witch imply that I am absolutely Other at all times and in every circumstance and especially in contrast to the majority of human beings populating our planet? Should I allow the archetype of the crazed shaman or the Witch on the edge of the village to justify a martyrlike inclination to loneliness and emotional estrangement? How does one walk the fine line, straddling "both" the worlds but able to exist fully in each, whilst in fact inhabiting that nebulous space in between and requiring it? This is the source of panic most of the world feels towards the Other—a difference of context which discomforts our previously accepted notions and ideologies of reality.

As a Witch I am fully submerged in the mythic reality, engaged with my own soul story woven of my living myth. I am not enabled to see visions, I simply see them. I am observing, witnessing, waiting, watching, learning, listening, and growing with it all. The currents that move, shape, and break the worlds are the currents that I ride; therefore, I am wild. I am strange to those who would cast me as delusional, sick, evil, or fanciful.

I was once at a youth interfaith training gathering in which a fellow participant of the Baha'i faith expressed to me that Witches didn't exist. She completely accepted that I was Pagan and understood the basics of what that meant for me, but Witches, to her, were fantasy figures from childhood tales and nothing more. I could have responded with anthropology, sociology, history, poetry, etymology, art, or simply religion and metaphysics to assert the valid and continued existence of Witches in the world, but I simply said "I am a Witch." Therefore, Witches exist. It is no more delusional to state that about myself than for a Muslim accountant to refer to himself as such, or for an androgyne to embrace one's genderlessness. I am not speaking to the postmodern ambiguity of constructed and thus empowered identity; I am speaking of the mythic reality that is alive and not separate from anything.

I mention this here within this section on oracular seership because without understanding this earnest truth, a vision is both baseless and useless. To vision-journey and then to obtain a vision is an unfolding process that occurs in synchrony with reading or writing a book, getting dressed, having a shower, or brushing my teeth. There is nothing that upholds its inherent worth above or out from the rest. A vision is as relevant as I make all of my life.

A shaman may dance around a campfire and drum and rattle all he likes; a Witch may peer into a dark pool of water and scry until her eyes bleed—the vision is not found unless we can see the forest for the trees. We behold the detail and simultaneously and without pause for thought apply it into not just a broader matrix but an infinite boundlessness—the mythic reality.

Last night the Feri guardian of the east gave me an answer I asked him for that, of course, led to a new search for a new detail within an overall journey engendered not by him but my own yearnings as given up to Aphrodite, inspired within me because of my love for another. It doesn't stop there, however. I look for the detail because I know it swims within the wellspring I am diving into. Aphrodite, Persephone, my mother, the world tree, the *Way of Wyrd* by Brian Bates, the ice cream I ate and felt awful about—all dwell together in the same house, the same forest, the same living cosmos that my unfolding soul story inhabits. I search for details and seek visions not for the sake of solving anything but to create an enhanced awareness of my own being, and therefore to embrace the gnosis that is innate within me, which will constantly reveal the depth of my divinity.

These are the secrets that are immortal and yet indefinable. Remember that the vision is a proffered piece; our job, once gifted with the piece, is to return it to the whole.

What Is Divination?

Divination is the art whereby a skilled individual interprets symbols, signs, patterns, and/or omens in an attempt to read the processes and dynamics of Divinity as it expresses itself throughout eternity. A diviner (one who participates in divination) may also target a particular expression or manifestation of Divinity (e.g., a human being) and interpret their particular pure will and the orbit or current thereof. At least, this is how I define divination most broadly.

To divine is to "plug in" to the current of the Divine and to assess the quality of its presence at any given time, or, as Persephone once said, "Wherever time has placed thee and space has prevailed over thee."

Divination is almost an essential component of any shamanic Craft or vocation, and this definitely echoes the charges of the cunning folk in the British Isles as well. To think upon the old Witch at the edge of the village or the hedge is to think of a wise woman or cunning man who not only casts spells and speaks with spirits but reads the signs of nature to portend the future, understand the past, and provide wisdom for the present.

In contemporary Witchcraft, it is a staple of many traditions to suggest to its aspirants or students that they learn at least one form or medium of divination. For many of us this will be the tarot, for others the runes, and for some astrology or palmistry (chiromancy). Ultimately, however, the technique and theory is similar or the same, though the attitude may differ, and sometimes this makes all the difference.

The Technique of Shamanic Divination

Shamanic divination—what might that be? Initially it is simply the concept of divination qualified by the shamanic paradigm we have discussed. Shamanic divination honours the depth (infinite possibility) of any particular individual, treasures the mythic life and soul story of all beings, and therefore understands divination to be a methodology through which we are blessed enough to witness for a brief moment an aspect of that unfolding legacy and mark it on the Wyrd.

The technique of shamanic divination, therefore, is not necessarily a discrete thing; the secret is in the attitude that manifests in how the reading (divination) is conveyed.

My preferred form of divination is the tarot. I have been working with a particular deck for several years now, and it has passed through many hands. It has been a part of my cunning charge that divination is a skill of mine, especially as it relates to tarot and the signs of the palm. The last few times I have visited my birthplace of Bali, I have been inundated with requests for divination, as it is an art that is highly respected in the Balinese culture, and though the Balinese have not necessarily seen divination with tarot or even cards before, they are familiar with the concept and therefore do not even falter at the appearance of the tarot. It is the indwelling concept, technique, and attitude orienting the experience that is familiar.

When I read the cards for another person, I will breathe into my centre and firstly cleanse the cards (even if I had cleansed them after the last reading). I will do this to ensure that the energy (mana, axe, life force, etc.) of the previous querent (person being read for) is dispersed and gone so that the energy of the new querent is not confused or "impure." I never perform a reading unless I know my cards are cleansed and blessed. I will shuffle my cards to do this, while focussing on channelling light into and through them and chanting, "I bless, I cleanse, I consecrate, I purify, I charge!"

I then hold my cards up, blow on them, and draw a pentagram over and around them to seal the cleansing. If you are reading with the runes, then you might simply shake the pouch that holds them until it feels right. With dice you might hold them in your hands, breathe over them several times, and then shake them to roll. With palmistry, the medium belongs physically to the person being read for, so it would be almost rude to cleanse; simply centre yourself.

If you feel the need to create or affirm a space for reading sessions, the following is a very succinct but potent way in which to do that:

1. Breathe. Align the spiral soul.
2. Gesture to the ground and say: "By the land…"
   Gesture to the sky and say: "By the sky…"
   Cup your hands together at your heart and say:
   "By the sea…"
   Seal this three realms blessing with: "By the
   ancient trinity, so mote it be!"

3. Touch the ground once more and focus on the spirits of place. Say with conviction: "O holy spirits of place, I honour your providence and presence. I work with you and not against you. May you welcome me as I welcome you." Hit the ground with your hands three times as if to vibrate the blessing into the earth.
4. Stand and turn to the east and give peace to each direction (east, north, west, south, above, below, and centre).
5. Return to the east and draw a circle while chanting: "I cast this circle to cleanse and banish all that hinders my limitless flow." Repeat this until you feel the area is cleansed of any vibrations that may have limited your work.
6. Recite the final prayer: "May my ancestors (and any other specific allies) bless me in this holy work of the seer and guide and guard me in the fulfilment thereof. May there be truth, power, wisdom, insight, and clarity for all who come to share in story here."

Once the space has been created and affirmed, the reading may begin. When reading, open to the flow of the Divine and do not attempt to interpret the signs of the medium (cards, runes, lines on the palm, etc.) independently of one another (if you have laid down a spread or group of signs). Read each sign within the context of an overarching theme, pattern, and story that will become apparent. Once the signs are revealed, do not simply confine your glance to the first sign "in order" and read each in isolated progression. Look at the totality and study the themes and patterns that emerge. For example, if reading tarot, this may be how many cards of which suit or suits appear, how many major arcana as opposed to minor arcana, etc. For the runes it might be significant if a disproportionate amount of a certain *aett* (eight) appear (if using the Elder Futhark) over other signs.

oracular seership and divination

These constitute certain patterns, but when divining one is also looking past the superficial and delving into the unfolding soul story or mythic life as conveyed through the agency of the medium. This is where one must work with intuition and instinct rather than the simple mechanics or constituents of the divinatory medium. An example might be the following spread[79] of tarot cards:

- The Magician
- Two of Cups
- Three of Swords
- The Empress
- The Hierophant
- The Devil

Firstly, assuming the "order" of these cards wish to be read in that particular direction of progression, I would simply open my awareness (and not just physical sight) to the spread of cards. I would mentally follow the intuitive flow and prepare to receive specific knowings—"facts and figures" which generally either appear spontaneously in my mind or I will hear them told to me or see them. I will then generally begin with the card I laid down first, as this initiates the unfolding.

In this case, I would speak to the querent about the power of manifesting will through determination, conviction, and a quiet or innate understanding of the "fusion of factors" that enables such potent wielding of the force for and of change (the Magician). Then the story flows from there.

I might mention the cards by title or name and contextualise its presence or placement; however, generally I am still attempting to remain fluid. To continue on, I would caution the querent to be wary

---

[79] I actually don't use traditional spreads, although I find them helpful guides for beginners. I lay the cards down as they require or as I feel and generally refer to the first one laid down as the "pinnacle" of my "spread." I start from that point and move organically through the whole.

of using this Magician's gift to draw in passionate, soul-entwining love (at the present time), as the Three of Swords qualifies that if this is to be the case, it will be underscored by emotional torment, manipulation, and entanglement. However, this also feels to me as if the love is already opening, and therefore the cards that follow create a resolution within themselves.

The Empress and the Hierophant speak of abundance and the structure to contain and secure it. At this point, I would encourage the querent to understand that abundance, prosperity, and fecundity are all in store and in overflowing dimensions; however, to respect and nurture this divine blessing, one must ensure that balance and organic structure and disciplines are put in place (which reflect one's core values) to reinforce the blessings. Ultimately, it seems that the focus on creating a life that reflects one's values and honouring it by living in congruence with one's Self and pure will is the way to the light at the end of the tunnel and out of the implied emotional tumult. The Devil's message is that any binding we perceive or feel in our lives is actually illusory, and any limitation or emotional shackles we might feel locked into or cornered by because of the Three of Swords has a simple resolution: walk away and let it go. Focus on the cultivation of abundance and all will fall into place.

In reflecting on this process, I might also add that there are four major arcana cards to two minor arcana, and therefore I would mention the "fated" implications of these events as a domino effect, or chain reaction. These events might also have the capacity to shift one's attitude to life and all relationships thereof. The story as a whole is the significant thing, although attention to the detail is also important. To balance both and convey a fully fleshed account, with considerate and deliberate effort underpinned by intuitive flow, is to provide a shamanic reading in the truest sense. Remember that the majority of querents seek out diviners for clarity and direction, in that order.

oracular seership and divination

Just Knowing and the Deep Well

Every now and then I reflect on the process of divination and perhaps the last tarot session I was involved in. In retrospect, I realise that at least half of the information I expressed to the querent did not derive at all from the cards themselves and not even necessarily from the qualifying cards in relationship or the pattern in wholeness. Sometimes I just know. Some might call this claircognisance (clear knowing); however, I feel that it derives from a strong connection with the deep well.

The deep well is sister to the world tree, and though we could easily relegate the well to the guardianship of the Wyrd sisters (and therefore to the province of the underworld), it is something more than that. Cosmologically speaking, the well sustains the strength, vitality, and growth of the world tree. Without these nourishing, sweet waters of life, the tree could not and would not exist. In many creation stories, the primordial waters of life are preexisting. When Eurynome dances with the north wind, Ophion (the serpent), and mates with him to bring forth the cosmic egg from which all come, she dances upon the waves of the sea. In Genesis Yahweh hovers over the waters of deep seas before the god even creates the heavens and the earth. It is by splitting the seas vertically that Yahweh creates the firmament, and by splitting them horizontally Yahweh creates dry land (earth).

The sea is the realm in between; it is the substance of chaos. The sea reconciles the implied duality of the sky and the land, opposites in everything—above/below, etheric/solid, masculine/feminine. This is also why the sea is considered a frightening and hellish place in many mythologies—a realm of death, uncertainty, and chaos in the most feared sense. The sea is bitter and deadly, and yet it is the womb from which we came. To many, the duality of binary opposites and polarities formulates a safe and generic container, whereas it is the shamanic prerogative to smash these illusions and remind everyone of the centre, which is everywhere—of the sea which, in fact, subsumes reality.

The well lies in the heart of the sea; the well of the underworld beneath the world tree and nourishing it is one and the same with that realm I have identified as sea. Sea is both the child (the third factor) of the alchemical love of the heavens and the earth, or sky and land, and also the predecessor and origin of them both. The waters, the seas, the deep well—these are the powers of chaos that brought forth creation. It makes a great deal of sense when we consider the role water has to play in the vast majority of the world's religious and spiritual traditions. Water is life!

I mention this because to simply know is to hover above the primordial waters and to behold the unfolding of creativity. It is to rest in the primal origin and flow from that place and to that place, over and over. When I am connected with the underworld, my ancestors, that vast and unravelling lineage of legacy, I am tasting the salt and the sweetness of the sea and drinking from the well; this is how I know.

A Prayer to the Deep Well

Deep well, well deep, though I rest, I do not sleep;
Thou art the mighty origin, of all without, of all within;
And so I call for every wave of knowledge pouring from your cave.
I see the holy majesty of the wholeness of infinity;
I dip my cup into your stream and behold the unseen;
Before time was, you were, and so I pray:
Deep well, well deep, I am awake, I do not sleep.

The Nature of Time

If divination is the art of interpreting the flow of the Divine (which is both immanent and sentient) and this can be accessed at any time, this implies that time is not so much a thing drawn out, differentiated, and named "time" (to be objectified as such). Time is not a law of the cosmos that must be obeyed; it is a quality of the living, limitless cosmos.

oracular seership and divination

It precedes the "creation of things" and therefore is sewn into the very fabric of being. The Orphic cosmology paints the picture beautifully:

> *First, there was the Aeon—Infinity—an ageless and undetermined presence of Time (Kronos). Kronos dwelt with Ananke (Necessity), two serpents breathing in the stillness of space. They came together, and from their sinuous union of undulating ripples came Bright-Shining Aether, Erebos (Darkness), and Kaos (Chaos)—the primordial spirit and matter; deep potentialities already dwelling within Time and Necessity. Time came together with Aether in raw and fruitful desire. Upon the dark chasm of Kaos, Aether spread open her wings, and from between her legs came forth the silver cosmic egg. When the cosmic egg cracked open, the top half became the heavens above the stars and the lower half, the earth, and Protogonos (First Born) stepped forth—androgynous and beyond gender. Protogonos is also Phanes—Light Bearer—with golden wings shining like the sun, four eyes, the voice of bull and lion, and many headed, invisible, yet radiating light!*

This myth continues on to explain the sovereignty of certain gods through whom the passage of time moves. However, it is Kronos (Time), who is Infinity (also called Aeon), who clarifies the forethought—the preclusion to the "creation." Time and Necessity and the dynamic tension they share together is the propulsion for the expression of desire and thus creativity.

We've all heard it said that time is an illusion, or that Pagans and Witches do not necessarily subscribe to time as a linear concept or even as a cyclical concept but more of a spiralling flow. Is this enough? Should we look more incisively into this "time" we speak of? Time is one of the Orphic serpents who dwelt in the "time before time" and is also seen to be Kronos, who manifests later as the same-named son of Ouranos, who castrates the Old King and then attempts to devour all of his children, and passes through Zeus and then to Dionysos almost as progressive incarnations of the same spirit. How, then, do we relate to this force or idea? There seems to be one spirit swimming through this majestic river and manifesting as diverse expressions in apostolic succession—what spirit passes? It is the spirit of time—Kronos the Serpent. So time is a "thing," a presence, a quality of the cosmos that we do not abide by but partake of.

If time is ever-present and is a being, an idea, and a presence and quality of the cosmos within itself, then all of time is accessible at any "point." To see into any phase or part of time is to recognise this principle and to cultivate such an attitude towards time. In so doing are we opened to the first time—Aeon—infinity.

chapter nine

the soul story/the mythic life

"Guard the Mysteries; constantly reveal them!"
Lew Welsh

"I am that which is attained at the end of Desire."
Charge of the Goddess (Doreen Valiente)

The material within this book has laid down a framework for Witches to establish a shamanic Craft practice held and nourished by an open and simultaneously deep cosmology and philosophy. The art of altering consciousness is just as much about shifting paradigms as it is about inducing psychic trance. The shamanic Witch ignites awareness and thereby fulfils the pure conscious state that is the gift of life in mystery—in its fullness. The All-Self is not merely a model or metaphor for the limitless Divine, it is the sacred reality and truth enlivening all to be as it will be. To initiate and receive initiation is to dive into the cosmic current and embrace the infinite depths—the potential you, the hidden potency. This is the distinct expression that creates identity and sings the song that blurs and breaks the barrier between so that all may be all-together. The web and its vibrating Wyrd are the mother and child of this communion.

chapter nine

This chapter is a conclusion exploring the notion of the soul story and the mythic life. It embodies the distillation of the lessons of the whole and aims to offer delight, hope, presence, meaning, power, and magick to any individual who would aim to align the spiral soul and become the world tree. There are no techniques or methods to be found within this chapter; only simple poetry, which will be as a goodnight kiss. When you rise to claim the new day, seize it with vigour and with endless joy, and you will have found the fruition of desire, which seeds itself.

Be free and ever hold your flame as the sacred illumination that shines forth from the stars in darkness before you as you journey. The depth of darkness breeds the bright light, and we will soon find that they ever court, ever dance, and ever spiral together.

The well reflects you, and all spirals join together the continuum. We are initiates because we are humbled by witnessing wonder,[80] and we have become worthy of the deepest of things. Ignite consciousness like fire in the head, but remember to quell the flame and bring it to your heart and belly so that the three are one. You are aligned to fully accept the essential—we are each an essence of the essential. Embrace the uniqueness of yours.

I always say that once one is initiated, every day, every moment, becomes an initiation—constant and changing reinforcement and actualisation of that primal communion with the source. To touch that source and to hold living relationship with the mystery is to flow with the rhythms and tides of what is, was, and will be in the eternity of space and time, unbound and free.

If the Mysteries are mysterious, then they are of the original meaning intended behind the usage of the word *mystery*. In ancient Greek culture, "mystes" referred to the initiates themselves—those to whom the great and potent truths of the worlds were revealed in splendour,

---

80 A saying of Jarrah Staggard (Awen).

the soul story/the mythic life

and those who had received gnosis and chosen for themselves to seek, wander/wonder, and discover.

To know the Mysteries is to surrender to the ever secret. We are the holy ones—the children of earth and starry heaven. We are not only houses of Spirit but expressions of Spirit, and thus we are all sons and daughters of God/dess. We are gifted with love, truth, and wisdom (the gifts of initiation) so that we may live, thrive, and flourish.

The Deep Well

The world tree has a sister—the deep well. And though the three worlds are joined by the majesty of the oak, ash, and mountain, it is the deep well that feeds and sustains the world tree. We are therefore urged to look down and deeper than we could dare to conceive.

The well says drink deep of me, but first you must make yourself worthy, and that only you can do. You are sovereign over nothing and no one but your sacred self—know the truth that self is Self, and hold the grail, the fulfilment of mystery, which is engendered by yearning, and you will have come home to the wandering centre (the initiate who lives in the holy centre) which dwells in all things. Jesus Christ, one of the greatest shamans the world knows today, once said, "Split a piece of wood, and I am there."

To truly understand what is meant by "soul story" and "mythic life," we must reflect on She in whom we live, move, and have our being; from whom all things emerge, and to whom we shall return. I will refer to this Mighty One, this Holy One, by the title I first knew her by—the Weaver.

Quite recently, I knelt in fellowship with other WildWood Witches to be present with a dear friend with whom I have shared both laughter and wisdom. There is a ceremony within our tradition that is conducted with the aspirant who has been accepted for dedication into the Inner Court of Mysteries, whether this is into a coven or more broadly into the fellowship of the WildWood. As I watched this rite unfold, I realised that it embodied the true nature of our tradition. It is not a rite that we have received from the ancient past in a linear, historical fashion. It is not a rite that we wrote or devised in any intelligible sense. Like many things that are part and parcel of WildWood Witchcraft (which at its core is deeply shamanic), it is a rite that simply formed itself through a coalescing of Spirit that came forth in communion and celebration. It is a rite that self-sprouted and organically enmeshed into our lore and mythos. It is a rite that typifies the quintessence of who we are as wild Witches and what it is we connect and commune with.

As the aspirant merges with the WildWood itself (the realm) and perhaps explores it for the very first time (in this incarnation and recollection), he or she touches the very core of our spirituality and the profound implications thereof. In literally moving between the worlds (the preeminent shamanic technique of ecstasy), we remind ourselves that we are bound by nothing and challenged by everything. The worlds form around an infinity that expresses its consciousness as Self. This All-Self, this Great Cosmic Goddess, star-born and unfolding into the limitless creation, is my Grandmother Weaver.

As I witnessed the unfolding of this WildWood rite for this WildWood Witch, I felt both strangely distanced and wholly present. I believe that this strange paradoxical emotion was kindled because not only have I been involved since the "beginning" of the makings (weaving) of our tradition, but I have felt every shift and change so viscerally that it is as if I have breathed through a greater being and lived by the will of it. Is this a state that is spiritually and philosophically desirable? Is it enlightenment—absorption into the wholeness of reality—or am I sacrificing my autonomous nature and thus sovereignty of Self? Am I losing myself to the Self? I listen to the words of the shamans, and I remember that I am a wild Witch and I walk the middle way of balance—straddling the worlds and moving into and moving through.

the soul story/the mythic life

As I walked home from that park, from that tree that has been imprinted into my memory, I beheld the Weaver's voice, and she spoke to me:

> *In the belly of the ocean is the well of creation—*
> *All rivers flow from the well of creation...*
> *All rivers return to the well of creation...*

I realised then that if I call her limitless being "Zero" to ensure that I do not refer to any numerical value (and therefore draw it out, objectify it, and confuse it for infinity), I am surrendering to her circumference. If I surrender with consciousness, then I am aware of the deep love that saturates every piece of the body of God. If I ignite my awareness and look out upon the pregnant, swollen darkness and see myself in All, I become the holy centre that is ever-wandering and ever-wondering. I introduce myself for the first time to the living myth, or my own soul story. For if I can truly look out and, in doing so, pierce the depth of my mystery, I have seen that every single part of life is joined in the wholeness that surrenders to itself in infinite potential and infinite possibility.

If I choose to view the world through this paradigm-shattering paradigm and renew my sovereignty of Self from the place I call Own Holy Self, then I am capable of both writing and reading the story that is encoded in my breath, beat, blood, and body.[81] I become cognizant of my pure will and reflect that while all flow with the pure will, to embrace and re-sacralise our own pure wills is to wilfully, and with desire, step into the momentum and moving current of Will. To do this and invest every piece of awareness in the mythos (story reality) that lives in the nature of meaning is to make the pure, pure. I possess my Self through mastery of choice, and I determine to become the centre of the circumference and the circumference of the centre. All pure will is the Pure Will. All rivers, though they flow through

---

81 Thank you, Dylan!

different lands, are home to different creatures, experience different climates and seasons, and represent the embodiment of different ecosystems, return to the ocean from whence they came. These are the primordial waters of life upon which the breath of the infinite ripples the surface of the deep well.

My Soul Story

It is past midnight as I write this, and I am keenly aware of a shifting and changing inside of my being, catapulting me into the momentum of my pure will. I have struggled for so long in truly accepting this charge as priest and Witch as my vocation in this life, and I will continue to struggle as well as rejoice, but not without meaning. Yet it seems the spirits, as my equals and friends, would encourage nothing else. For if I am to truly stand as I kneel and become both the world tree and the deep well, I will surrender to the All-Self that is within me, that gave birth to me.

I am my own divine origin—I am my own seed and outcome. How do I choose to join the past to the future? What is the present but a fleeting moment that engenders itself continuously? Time is a serpent, a spiral, a river through which life flows and shines its splendour upon us. When I say, "I was asked to take the sword (and I have) and crowned by the Mother of Angels (and I was)," am I speaking literally or metaphorically? For me, this dichotomy is a deeply misleading one, and I wish not to be trapped by its limits. My living myth has been shown to me at every point, with every breath and every time I have forgotten and forgiven. In embracing my living myth, I begin to understand my soul story and see it not as a preordained destiny or fate handed down from "up above," but a song of connection that pierces the very heart of me and opens me to the holy truth that everything that is possible is so because of my presence and participation.

T. Thorn Coyle asserts, "God Herself is the fabric of All. Change can occur in conformity with love and will. Our presence is required."

the soul story/the mythic life

What does this mean? For me, it means that I am God Herself unfolding into the holy centre that by my ignited awareness has become illumined as the investment of my presence in the here and now. The realisation of the pure will as "stepping into the current and momentum" reflects to me that it is with love and will together that I open to the great mystery as All-Self and as my mirror. Without love my will is void of meaning and spirit, and without will my love is irrelevant and useless.

My prayer to Self is this: "May my pure will be empowered and liberated; as I wander/wonder through the landscape of my living myth, may it be deepened and enhanced to my Own Holy Self." As a Witch who is a shaman, I am a walker between the worlds and a healer, knower, wise one, singer, dancer, and vessel. I speak to the spirits, gather up power to make change, transform the essence of my soul to take on other guises, and open to receive the powers and forces of potent beings. To what end?

To and of myself, I am capable of infinite potential. By becoming the sovereign of my Self and igniting my awareness to cultivate initiation in each conscious moment, I share the power that is kindled within me with the All. I activate my hidden potency and engender the living potency. I truly become a god, and the spirit within me rejoices in the process, in the dynamic and in the dancing of it. I am remembered, married to Memory, and reborn through the dark cauldron of nature into the Spirit which is my birthright/rite. I am truly the holy child.

Living Myth/Mythic Life

"Not all those who wander are lost."
J. R. R. Tolkein

Life is neither literal nor metaphorical. It is neither a symbol of itself or is itself a direct embodiment of an answer. Life is myth, and recognising this fact enables us to become the true heroes and heroines.

chapter nine

We become enlivened to the charge of existence and stand to wander through the shifting paradigms, endlessly causing change to occur in conformity with the pure will of God Herself. This pure will is seamless, and yet this mighty fabric, this woven tapestry, is eternal and undying. Our threads as woven into this grand design are the details that meet with the infinity and make the darkness light and the light revealing.

In the centre of each of us is an unwavering mythic life that yearns for expression. I am not referring to any one archetype that may seem to reflect our life experience or embody our cause or principles. I am speaking of one simple and profound truth that the shamanic Witch may embrace: nature is our sacred foundation. Magick is the essence of nature. Magick is our sacred charge. To translate—I am nature. Magick is my life-blood. I am magick. If we are to be literal, now is the time. Literally, I am the magick that the eons have spoken of and shuddered and delighted at! Literally, I am the soul-spun story of the shimmering height and the darkest depth! Literally, I am whatever I behold and whomever I choose to be. My purpose, my woven soul story and my humming living myth, is to take what is literal and transform it through the poetry of the soul into the wisdom and grace of the Divine. If I am able to surrender without losing my centre and to glimpse the eternal within the sentient and the sentient within the eternal, then my pure will is flowing, and the mark of the spirits has ignited upon my brow.

If you have read this book and your soul has stirred in response to the poetry of the tripartite cosmos, or your senses have been aroused by the ecstatic techniques and rituals, and you long for initiation into the shamanic Craft, these are my hard-won pieces of insight and wisdom.

Humble yourself by doing the Great Work of knowing yourself, and in knowing yourself become potent. In becoming potent, reveal the holiness of Self; in revealing the holiness of Self, revel in it. In revelling in it, claim and possess it; in claiming and possessing it, allow for freedom. In freedom there is eternal responsibility, and so you must do the Great Work of knowing yourself and making balance with the Wyrd and web. If you receive initiation in this way, then it is right, and you may celebrate this threshold moment (and they are countless—mark them all) by singing to the corners of the cosmos, "As I stand, so do I kneel."

appendix

shamanic craft terminology

All-Self: The totality of self-aware being. In the Upanishads this may be referred to as the atman/Brahman, which the atman (soul) reflects—the universal soul.

Being: All that is because it is.

Dark Cauldron of Nature: The dark, fecund void that nourishes being and recycles and renews all life. It is the womb of the Goddess and represents Spirit as predecessor, child, and alchemical elemental fusion.

Great Mystery: A term used by some Native American traditions to refer to the ultimately unknowable essence of life. This term has been absorbed into contemporary Paganism as a poetic reference to the Divine Origin (to God Herself of the Feri Tradition; to the Goddess of Reclaiming and similarly inspired traditions; to the Weaver of the WildWood).

Here and Now: The eternal present as a concept stripped of any time-ordered meaning. The place one finds oneself is the immediate outcome of investing presence in one's consciousness—igniting it.

Hidden Potency: For the many forms of life to be expressed as beings, we must all be endowed with hidden potency. To live in alignment with one's pure will, from Own Holy Self, is to cultivate sovereignty of Self, which activates the hidden potency whereby we become living gods.

Holy Centre: The place within that is beheld consciously as the centre to the circumference of the limitless, unfolding cosmos. As there is no end to the universe, there are no "physical" co-ordinates to arrive at a specific placed centre; this poetically and fundamentally enables us to affirm that the centre is in all places. When we consciously embrace ourselves as a "centre," we become/arrive at the holy centre.

Living Cosmos: The worlds in their infinity.

Living Myth (Mythic Life): The idea or truth that our lives are not linear, void of meaning, or obsolete—that our lives are spiralling and therefore deepening into continued synchronicity, revelation, and liberation. Each of us is a hero or heroine dreaming our existence into being, expressing the wonder-voyage of Own Holy Self.

Overculture: A term popular in the Reclaiming Tradition of Witchcraft. It refers to the monolithic societal paradigms that rule the consumerist, industrial, and heavily fragmented and compartmentalised human culture.

Own Holy Self: The embodiment of the totality of being within the Self. When we are at our pure state—with talking self, shadow self, and star self aligned and unified—we are greater than the sum of our parts, and we come to our Own Holy Self. When we live from Own Holy Self, we cultivate sovereignty of Self and self-possession.

Pure Will: The flow of the Good, which each individual is charged to actualise. We all flow with Pure Will, but determining one's life path through its unfolding is to consciously enter its current and momentum; to stand proudly in the river of will, remembering that all rivers flow to the sea.

Sovereignty of Self: The life-work of realising one's inherent divinity and claiming it as a sovereign right; that we are all kings and queens and therefore autonomous rulers of our unfolding fates. Sovereignty of Self is to be in accord with Own Holy Self and enhance and attune it to the pure will of the living cosmos while maintaining an equal balance of individuality as unique expression thereof. T. Thorn Coyle calls this self-possession.

Wild Way: Another way to say "the crooked path." The wild way is the path that the wild Witch walks; it is seemingly the middle way between God and Oblivion (the Faerie Way) and yet, ultimately by its own twisting and turning, it becomes all paths as woven into one. The wild way is ever-changing; it is the innate primal root of all things in existence.

Wild Witch: A Witch who pursues the shamanic path.

Shamanic Craft Principles

- Magickal worldview of infinite possibility
- Nature is our sacred foundation: magick is the essence of nature: magick is our sacred charge
- Principle of sacred equality
- Total freedom equals total responsibility

bibliography

Adler, M. *Drawing Down the Moon* (updated resource guide). Penguin Group/Compass, 1997.

Anderson, C. *Fifty Years in the Feri Tradition*. Self-published, 1994.

Aswynn, F. *Northern Mysteries & Magick*. Llewellyn, 1998.

Bates, B. *The Way of Wyrd*. Hay House, 2005.

Coyle, T. Thorn. *Evolutionary Witchcraft*. Tarcher, 2004.

———. *Kissing the Limitless*. Red Wheel/Weiser, 2009.

Cummer, V., editor. *To Fly By Night: The Craft of the Hedgewitch*. Pendraig, 2010.

Curott, P. *Book of Shadows*. Broadway, 1999.

———. *The Love Spell*. Gotham Books, 2005.

Danielou, A. *Gods of Love and Ecstasy: The Traditions of Shiva and Dionysos*. Inner Traditions, 1992.

De Angeles, L. *Witchcraft: Theory and Practice*. Llewellyn, 2000.

d'Este, S., and D. Rankine. *Wicca: Magickal Beginnings*. Avalonia, 2008.

de Lint, C. *Spirits in the Wires*. Tor Books, 2004.

bibliography

Digitalis, R. *Shadow Magick Compendium*. Llewellyn, 2008.

Eliade, M. *Shamanism: Archaic Techniques of Ecstasy*. Bollingen Paperback Printing, 1972.

Farrar, J., and G. Bone. *Progressive Witchcraft*. New Page Books, 2004.

Filan, K., and R. Kaldera. *Drawing Down the Spirits: The Traditions and Techniques of Spirit Possession*. Destiny Books, 2009.

Gerber, R. *Vibrational Medicine: The #1 Handbook of Subtle-Energy Therapies*. Bear & Company, 2001.

Goodman, F. *Ecstatic Trance: New Ritual Body Postures*. Binkey Kok, 2003.

Grimassi, R. *Hereditary Witchcraft*. Llewellyn, 2007.

———. *Witchcraft: A Mystery Tradition*. Llewellyn, 2008.

———. *The Witches' Craft: The Roots of Witchcraft & Magical Transformation*. Llewellyn, 2002.

Heaven, R. *The Sin Eater's Last Confessions*. Llewellyn, 2008.

Hutton, R. *Shamans: Siberian Spirituality and the Western Imagination*. Hambledon Continuum, 2001.

Johnson, K. *Witchcraft and the Shamanic Journey*. Llewellyn, 1999.

Keeney, B. *Shaking Out the Spirits*. USA: Station Hill Press, 1994.

Leland, C. *Aradia, or the Gospel of the Witches*. Phoenix, 1990.

Mumford, J. *Ecstasy Through Tantra*. Llewellyn, 2002.

Mynne, H. *The Faerie Way: A Healing Journey to Other Worlds*. Llewellyn, 1998.

Parma, G. *By Land, Sky & Sea: Three Realms of Shamanic Witchcraft*. Llewellyn, 2010.

———, editor. *Crafting the Community*. Conjunction Press, 2009.

———. *Spirited: Taking Paganism Beyond the Circle*. Llewellyn, 2009.

bibliography

Penczak, C. *The Temple of Shamanic Witchcraft*. Llewellyn, 2006.

———. *The Three Rays of Witchcraft: Power, Love and Wisdom in the Garden of the Gods*. Copper Cauldron, 2010.

Polson, W. *The Veil's Edge: Exploring the Boundaries of Magic*. Citadel Press, 2003.

Roads, M. J. *Journey into Nature: A Spiritual Adventure*. H. J. Kramer, Inc., 1990.

Starhawk. *Dreaming the Dark* (fifteenth anniversary edition). Beacon Press, 1997.

———. *The Earth Path*. HarperCollins, 2004.

———. *The Fifth Sacred Thing*. Bantam, 1994.

———. *The Spiral Dance* (tenth anniversary edition). HarperCollins, 1989.

Stein, C. *Persephone Unveiled: Seeing the Goddess & Freeing Your Soul*. North Atlantic Books, 2006.

Walsh, R. *The World of Shamanism: New Views of an Ancient Tradition*. Llewellyn, 2007.

index

Aboriginal, 108, 159

Aegean, xviii, 23, 101

All-Self, xvii, 11–12, 25, 42, 78, 119–120, 127, 219, 222, 224–225, 229

allyship, xix, 1, 6, 55, 62–65, 67, 73, 76, 89–93, 100, 106–107
  defined, 55, 67

ancestors, 30, 56, 94–96, 98–99, 107–108, 137, 175, 212, 216

Anderson, Cora, 54

Anderson, Victor, 8, 30, 61, 116, 195

animism, animistic, 3, 5, 23, 53–55, 57, 67

Aradia, xvii, 142, 144, 146, 234

archetypes, 2, 24, 53, 59, 61, 207, 226

aspecting, 53, 65, 121

Aura, auric, 42, 79, 87, 108, 122, 147, 170–171, 173, 182–183, 186, 189, 202

axis mundi, 20, 116

Bali, Balinese, 16, 23, 32, 94, 113, 167, 169, 200–201, 211

beloved dead, 20, 55–56, 94–96, 137

body of God/dess, 12–13, 16, 23, 30–34, 44, 46, 58–59, 69, 71, 85, 153, 223, 234

breath, 14–15, 36–39, 44, 46, 63–64, 77, 97–99, 104, 106–108, 110, 114–115, 120–122, 125–127, 132, 135, 139, 141, 148–149, 163, 180, 182, 185, 187, 191, 194, 196, 205, 211, 217, 222–224

cauldron, 17–19, 31–33, 36–37, 136–139, 147–150, 174, 178, 225, 229, 235

index

Celts, Celtic, 5, 13, 24, 56, 100, 102, 134

centre, 18, 26, 29–30, 32–36, 38–39, 48, 50–51, 65, 75, 77–80, 91, 93, 95–98, 104–105, 107, 110, 113, 116–117, 122, 124–130, 132, 136, 138, 145, 148–149, 162, 170–172, 174–175, 179–180, 182–185, 191, 193, 196, 203–206, 211–212, 215, 221, 223, 225–226, 230

chakra, 75, 173–175, 182–184, 186, 202

Charge of the Goddess, 12, 70, 145, 180, 219

Christ, Christianity, xxii, 8, 12, 14, 31, 71, 110, 134, 143, 221

Church of All Worlds, 34–35

circle, xv–xvi, xx–xxi, 4–5, 8, 23, 41–51, 53, 64, 73, 75, 90–91, 95, 97, 111, 114, 119–120, 134, 137, 156, 162–164, 167, 179–180, 191–192, 195, 212, 234

Cosmic Goddess, 21, 45, 116, 222

cosmology, 5, 29–30, 34, 47, 116, 118, 121, 134, 160, 179, 203, 217, 219

covens, xix

crooked path, xxi, 144–145, 231

cunning, 2, 44, 124, 138, 161, 210

dark cauldron of nature, 33, 147, 149–150, 178, 225, 229

demons, 7, 16, 22–23, 30, 33, 42, 59, 100, 113, 173

Dionysos, 15–19, 22–28, 217, 233

Divine Fire, Rite of, 15, 45, 97, 104, 190–191, 198

drawing down, 5, 7, 32, 53–54, 61, 65–66, 68–76, 79, 81, 83–88, 90, 120–121, 133, 148–149, 180, 185–186, 205, 233–234

family tradition, xvii, xix–xx, 5, 23, 107, 169

Faerie, xx–xxii, 30, 89–90, 109, 125–126, 231, 234

familiar, xx, 3, 77, 100–101, 104, 107–109, 113, 116, 141, 177, 182, 195, 211

fate, xviii–xx, xxii, 35, 55, 70, 117, 134–135, 139–140, 152–154, 156, 162, 224

Feri, xv, xx, 5, 8, 21, 30–31, 33–35, 44, 54–55, 82, 109, 116, 124, 144, 160–161, 181, 187, 195, 209, 229, 233

Ganesha, 20, 24–27, 64, 160

Gardner, Gerald, xviii–xix, 8, 44, 54, 85–86, 112

index

Gardnerian, xviii–xix, 8, 44, 85–86

genius loci, 93, 109, 112

Gnosis, Gnostic, gnostic, xviii–xix, xxii, 5, 29–31, 34, 41, 44–45, 71, 116, 118, 128–130, 146, 209, 221

God Herself, 116

Godhood, 12, 45, 58

great mystery, 4, 8, 11–13, 41, 69–71, 78, 114, 123, 179–180, 220, 225, 229

Greek Mystery, 5, 11, 220

Hekate, 20, 60, 65, 73, 101, 160

hereditary, xx, 4, 102, 234

Hindu, Hinduism, 19–21, 23–25, 132, 173

holy centre, 28, 34, 36, 39, 79, 97–98, 105, 122, 124, 126–128, 130, 132, 135–136, 149, 162, 174, 179, 181, 196, 204–205, 212, 221, 223–225, 230

Holy Communion, 13, 34, 70–71, 79, 84, 221

immrama, 95, 98

Indigenous, 3, 32, 112, 158

initiation, xviii–xxii, 16–17, 19, 84–85, 91, 129, 151, 219–221, 225–227

Kala, 113, 182, 187, 191

Karma, 35, 70–71, 150–153, 156

land, sky, and sea, xv, xviii–xix, xxi, 1, 14, 17, 26–27, 31, 33, 35–40, 43, 77, 80, 93–94, 96–99, 102, 104–105, 109–112, 115, 117, 122, 127–128, 131–135, 137–140, 149, 153, 158–159, 176, 185, 191, 205, 211, 215–216, 231, 234

Law of Three, 150–151, 153

living myth, 59–60, 99, 109, 147, 208, 216, 223–226, 230

magician, 89, 103, 122, 148, 167, 204, 213–214

manifestation, 44–45, 58, 128–129, 133, 141, 143, 146, 148, 150, 160, 162, 165, 209

Mediterranean, xviii, 23, 101

middle way, xxi, 88, 180, 222, 231

middleworld, 31, 116–118

mythic life, xvii, 4, 6, 54, 208, 210, 213, 219–221, 225–226, 230

Neopagans, Neopaganism, 3, 18, 54, 63, 77

New Age, 13, 23, 107

Old Ways, 2, 14, 30, 144

Orphic, 5, 12, 15, 18, 27–28, 217

Own Holy Self, xxi, 34, 40, 69–70, 98–99, 119, 130, 135, 156, 163, 174, 178, 180–181, 187, 201, 223–225, 230–231

pantheism, pantheistic, 53, 55, 57

pentagram, 12, 32, 186, 211

Persephone, 17–18, 60, 65, 73, 112, 209, 235

polytheism, polytheistic, 5, 23, 53, 58

power animal, 6, 39, 64, 99, 107–108

power deity, 13, 20, 53, 64, 71, 79, 83, 90, 107, 124, 174–175

psychopomp, 102, 124, 191

pure will, xxi, 12–13, 27, 55, 71, 75, 78–80, 82, 129, 144, 147, 152, 157, 188, 194, 196, 209, 214, 219, 223–226, 230–231

rainbow ladder, 174, 183

Reclaiming Tradition, xviii, 43, 53, 65, 229–230

Reiki, 170, 184

reincarnation, xix

rite of divine fire, 15, 45, 97, 104, 190–191, 198

rite of self-blessing, 179–182, 187–188, 190, 193, 198

runes, 210–212

sabbats, 3, 18, 20, 43, 101

seership, xviii, 119, 199, 208

self-initiation, xix

shadow, the, xvii, xxi, 31–34, 39–41, 68, 117, 121–123, 127, 129, 135, 137, 151, 163, 171, 187, 200, 203–204, 230, 234

shadow self, xvii, xxi, 31–34, 39–41, 117, 127, 135, 163, 171, 187, 203–204, 230

Shamanic Craft Apprenticeship, xv, xvii, 3–4, 40

shielding, 171, 182, 193

Siwa/Shiva, 13, 15–16, 21, 24

sorcery, 102, 142, 144–145, 153, 160

soul story, 5–6, 47, 188, 208–211, 213, 219–221, 223–224, 226

spiral soul, xviii, xx–xxi, 5, 29, 31–32, 35, 38, 40–41, 49, 92, 95, 104, 126, 166, 174, 179–180, 182, 187, 190–191, 196, 202, 204, 211, 220, 224, 235

spiral soul alignment, 35, 38, 40–41, 104, 179–180, 182, 190–191

spirit beings, 1–3, 7, 22, 44, 46–47, 54–55, 62–63, 67, 87, 89–94, 206–207, 225, 229

index

Spirit-flight, 94

spirits of place, xx, 3, 28, 32, 49, 87, 93, 108–115, 118, 122, 191, 212

spirit worlds, xv, xix, 1, 6, 34, 58–59, 75, 89, 114–115, 119, 124, 129–130, 152, 192, 207, 221–222, 225, 229, 234

Starhawk, 43, 82, 92, 94, 235

star self, xxi, 31–33, 39–41, 70, 135, 163, 186, 203–204, 230

talking self, xxi, 31–33, 38–41, 135, 163, 171, 203–204, 230

tantra, 19, 21, 234

tarot, 151, 210–213, 215

three cauldrons, 31–36, 38–40, 173–174

Threefold Law, 150–151, 153

three realms alignment, 34–36, 38–41, 97, 104, 113, 180, 182, 190–191

Titans, titanic, xxii, 17–18, 101, 127

totem, xx, 3, 44, 55, 99–101, 104–109, 177, 189

trance possession, 53, 61, 65–69, 72, 74–76, 78, 82, 87, 120, 163

tree of life, xvi, 20, 34–35, 95, 112–113, 116–117, 119, 127–129, 209, 215–216, 221, 223

triple soul, xx, 5, 30–32, 35–36, 40, 75, 202

Tuatha de Danaan, 56–57

Tungus, 2, 14

underworld, 17–19, 31, 34, 38, 94, 101, 103, 116–118, 134–136, 188, 191, 215–216

upperworld, 31, 116, 118

veil, 45, 68, 94, 96, 105, 107, 115, 117, 119, 121–123, 127, 129, 137, 139, 178, 192, 200, 202, 235

Voudoun, xvii, 20, 55, 69, 116, 176

Well of Memory, 68, 117–118, 134–135, 188, 224

whole breath technique, 36

Wicca, Wiccan, xv–xvi, xviii, 3–4, 8, 12, 30, 48, 71, 81, 86, 110, 120, 233

wild way, xxi–xxii, 41, 71, 144–145, 222, 231

wild Witch, xviii–xix, xxi, 41, 144–145, 208, 222, 231

WildWood Tradition, xv–xvii, xxi, 4–5, 31, 33, 43, 66, 72, 92, 103, 221–222, 229

Witch hysteria, 2–3, 103

world tree, xvi, 20, 33–36, 38, 110, 116–119, 127–130, 132–134, 136, 140, 188, 196, 209, 215–216, 220–221, 224 world tree pathworking, 127, 132, 136

Wyrd, 35, 70, 92, 117, 134–135, 137, 139, 152, 156, 202, 207, 209–210, 215, 219, 227, 233

Yahweh, 215

Zagreos, 17–18